Praise for *The Public Relations Handbook*

"*The Public Relations Handbook* is a must-read for all communications professionals looking to navigate a complex, ever-changing digital media environment."
—Fabienne De-Brebisson, Valeo Group Communications Senior Vice President

"Bob Dilenschneider, the Dean of public relations professionals in this country, has created an updated volume of *The Public Relations Handbook* which, true to the first edition, is full of wonderful information from a star-studded cast but is now fiercely relevant to the times in which we find ourselves. This book is not just for public relations professionals, rather it is for all who find themselves in the public space."
—Dr. E. Gordon Gee, President, West Virginia University

"So often, a company, an institution, a family office, or even governments don't think about the value of real public relations until a crisis happens. Then it's all hands-on deck to get the right message(s) out to the community, media, employees, family members, or political partners. Wouldn't it be so helpful to have a handbook written by experienced professionals who have already dealt with so many issues over their careers? That is exactly what this handbook does, and I praise Robert Dilenschneider for putting this guide together. However, I don't recommend this handbook just for PR and Comms professionals, I recommend it for daily living. After all, aren't all successes built on relationships and communication."
—The Honorable Linda McMahon, 25th Administrator of the Small Business Administration and Chair of America First Policy Institute

"*The Public Relations Handbook* is an indispensable tool to understand how from a formal technique a few decades ago, PR has become a fundamental and strategic management asset to succeed in our enterprises, business or others."
—Patrick Thomas, Former CEO, Hermès

"A rare density of wisdom and practicality, uniquely possible through the lens and curation of a master of craft and culture. Once again, Bob Dilenschneider brings fresh perspective and strategic vision to the stewardship of reputation with integrity. The fundamentals are what have brought my organization from the founder's home more than 158 years ago to world leadership, with opportunities that have never been greater."
—Louis Shapiro, President and Chief Executive Officer, Hospital for Special Surgery

"Bob Dilenschneider and his fellow experts have outdone themselves with *The Public Relations Handbook*. Insightful, vibrant, and compelling—a must-read for anyone working in the ever-evolving world of public relations and crisis communications. This remarkable compendium covers all the fundamentals and is guaranteed to become the go-to resource for PR professionals across the world."
—Lou Nanni, Vice President of University Relations, University of Notre Dame

"As its title indicates, this is a handbook—not a philosophical treatise. It is a book for real leaders facing real problems with real consequences. Having worked for a Fortune 100 company that was the target of an (unsuccessful!) hostile takeover wherein we survived by purchasing the would-be acquirer; saw our established market decline by nearly 50% during one five-year period; and ultimately prospered by consolidating all or major parts of 17 different companies, I can attest to the importance of effective communications and marketing. In this book, Robert Dilenschneider has collected a hall-of-fame group of experts who not only tell it like it is, but also what to do about it!"
    —Norm Augustine, Retired Chairman & CEO, Lockheed Martin Corp.

"This book is essential for every provider of public relations and communications advice and every person or company that is dependent on the advice. The accumulated wisdom and experience discussed is not just of great value, it is frequently what makes the difference in a transaction or reputation. In advising our clients, we recommend that the team handling a significant matter include advisors like those described in this book."
    —Martin Lipton, Senior Partner, Wachtell, Lipton, Rosen & Katz

"Public relations is a profession that must always stay on the cutting edge of communications without ever losing sight of the basic principles of the craft. At a time when communications technology is constantly changing, that is an enormous challenge, and so this new edition of *The Public Relations Handbook* is a must-read for anyone in the profession, whether a seasoned pro or a hopeful newcomer. It's all there: winning clients, planning PR programs, mastering social media, handling crises—and everything in between."
    —The Honorable Georgette Mosbacher, Former
    Ambassador for the United States to Poland

"Effective communication is essential in today's ever-changing landscape, which makes *The Public Relations Handbook* a must-read not only for PR professionals but also for business leaders managing public corporations, private firms and not-for-profit institutions. Bob Dilenschneider, recognized as "the dean of American Public Relations Executives," has fully updated The handbook with chapters authored by the most experienced PR veterans and most forward-thinking PR professionals. These experts provide knowledge, insight and wisdom on a broad range of topics including government relations, strategic intelligence, and crisis communications. Comprehensive in scope and practical in focus, this handbook is an indispensable and unparalleled resource."
    —Robert H. Rock, Publisher, *Directors & Boards*
    magazine; and Chairman, MLR Media

"Congratulations, and thank you, to my friend Bob Dilenschneider and his outstanding group of collaborators on *The Public Relations Handbook*. This is an important reference volume that is full of real-life experiences from Bob and his colleagues, essential reading for CEOs and others that may be thrust into the spotlight, as well as public relations professionals."
    —John P. Surma, Retired Chairman and Chief Executive
    Officer, United States Steel Corporation

THE
PUBLIC
RELATIONS
HANDBOOK

ALSO BY ROBERT L. DILENSCHNEIDER

THE
PUBLIC
RELATIONS
HANDBOOK

EDITED BY
ROBERT L. DILENSCHNEIDER

Matt Holt Books
An Imprint of BenBella Books, Inc.
Dallas, TX

The Public Relations Handbook copyright © 2022 by Robert L. Dilenschneider

BenBella Books, Inc.
10440 N. Central Expressway
Suite 800
Dallas, TX 75231
benbellabooks.com
Send feedback to feedback@benbellabooks.com

BenBella is a federally registered trademark.
Matt Holt and logo are trademarks of BenBella Books.

Printed in the United States of America
10 9 8 7 6 5 4 3 2 1

Library of Congress Control Number: 2021039359
ISBN 9781637740613
eISBN 9781637740620

Copyediting by James Fraleigh
Proofreading by Michael Fedison and Lisa Story
Indexing by WordCo
Text design and composition by PerfecType, Nashville, TN
Cover design by Brigid Pearson
Printed by Lake Book Manufacturing

CONTENTS

Introduction: Why Public Relations Matters | 1

Robert L. Dilenschneider

1 **Engaging the Community: Public Relations Is All About People** | *Cristyne Nicholas and George Lence* | 5

2 **Gathering Information and Intelligence: How to Harness Intelligence for Your PR Advantage** | *Jack Devine and Amanda Mattingly* | 13

3 **Preparing Your Argument: The Medium Is Always the Message** | *Robert Laird* | 23

4 **Words That Work: The Role of Language and Polling in Public Relations and Policy** | *Frank Luntz* | 35

5 **Preparing the Communications Program: A New Way to Approach a Vital Task** | *Art Gormley* | 49

6 **Government Relations: Setting a Public Policy Agenda** | *Edward Rollins and Jonathan Dedmon* | 69

7 The "New" Investor Relations: Transformational Changes in a High-Profile Discipline | *Ned Raynolds and Art Gormley* | 85

8 Working with the Media: They Are Not the Enemy, but Care Is Required | *Jonathan Dedmon* | 97

9 Social Media: Evolving Best Practices for PR Practitioners | *Shel Holtz* | 113

10 Internal Communications: Enduring Themes Focusing on Company Priorities | *William Kemmis Adler* | 139

11 Crisis Communications: Not If, but When | *Jonathan Dedmon* | 157

12 Communications for Private Families: The Fundamentals of Public Relations Apply Here, Too | *Dr. Stephen M. Coan* | 173

13 Going Forward with China: A Guide to Success | *Virginia A. Kamsky and Michael N. Kamsky* | 185

14 Cracking the Code of Japan: Ancient and Modern Island Nation | *Dr. Joshua W. Walker* | 203

15 Communicating in Canada: Welcome to Canada— *Bienvenue au Canada* | *Sarah L. Manley Robertson* | 215

16 Public Relations in Higher Education | *Donna Caprari Heiser* | 233

17 Communicating in Europe | *Valerio De Molli* | 257

Acknowledgments | 267
Index | 268
About the Authors | 275

Why Public Relations Matters

ROBERT L. DILENSCHNEIDER

When this book was being written, at the start of the third decade of the twenty-first century, it was not an overstatement to say that unprecedented challenges were forcing change upon businesses, governments, and individuals.

The ongoing global coronavirus pandemic remains chief among the factors roiling human existence now, followed closely by intertwined financial, economic, political, societal, and other issues. Together, these challenges—and those yet to emerge, because change is constant—pose a unique opportunity for public relations to demonstrate its vitality. Yet COVID-19 has shown us that there is no such thing as life or business as usual—or public relations as usual. Even when the virus itself is defeated, by therapeutics and vaccines, the residue of the pandemic will persist, and many of its effects will be permanent. What had been normal is evolving into an as-yet unknown new normal.

The need for connections and understanding, at every level of society, has never been greater. Public relations is uniquely positioned to address that need. Using effective communications to forge, nurture, and sustain relationships between and among people and their organizations and institutions is the core of public relations.

This book is an indispensable resource for public relations practitioners who want to meet these challenges and changes. It will ensure that practitioners, at all levels of experience, in any organization, can navigate this new world effectively.

One of the most important trends in recent years has been the integration of public relations into virtually every phase of American and global life, from the political and nonprofit world to business, colleges and universities, and beyond. No longer is public relations viewed as a separate and narrow tactic isolated from other activities. Public relations professionals must be prepared to deal with a staggering variety of people, issues, and subjects. After all, "it takes a village"—public relations, as we know from its very name, is not done in isolation. It is a collegial endeavor.

Today it is a given that public relations must be linked with other activities and disciplines within any organization. It is also a given that planning and implementing a public relations program must harmonize with overall objectives, whether that means selling a product, raising money, or advancing a cause or a candidate.

Likewise, public relations is not a one-off, transactional type of business. It used to be enough for a public relations professional to be great at writing a press release or terrific at throwing a party; no longer. Certainly, short-term tactics are often employed, but only in the support of long-range objectives. Certainly, emergencies and crises require immediate responses, without the luxury of a long horizon. But public relations—good and effective public relations—entails time, development, relationships . . . leading to understanding. And that begins to show why public relations matters.

The seventeen chapters in this book will flesh out what the practice of public relations is. Think of it as a big tent or a giant umbrella, under which are gathered any number of focused and coordinated disciplines. Think of it as a global enterprise whose distinctions can change depending on conditions, but whose core principles of credibility and truth telling remain the same. Think of it as an essential component of life, because it relies on human connections.

TAKEAWAYS

1. Virtually every part of life has changed. And it will continue to change, affecting who we are and just about everything we do.

2. Our goal in this book, which is a 100 percent change from previous Handbooks, is to bring you the latest thinking on the many elements that govern how we live and what we do.

3. There are two overriding pieces of guidance in this book: (1) always continue to gather intelligence—assume everything around you is constantly changing—and (2) always recognize how life is being shaped differently, often by men and women whom you do not understand.

4. Content is key. Ways of delivering the content are important, but forming the message comes first. Always select and adapt your language and images to fit the situation at hand.

5. Recognize that throughout the world, those who have not had it well have recognized that the only way they can achieve even close parity to those who *are* doing well is to create havoc and change. It is happening every day. This is not going to change and in fact will accelerate, thanks to advances in technology that make us move faster these days. The stakes are huge as society changes, sometimes not for the good.

6. The writers and counselors in these pages have been very successful. They are involved in a 24/7 world where today is different from yesterday and tomorrow will differ even further.

7. Take seriously the ideas and lessons offered here. Understanding and following them, and adding the wisdom of your own experience, is crucial to being part of a civilized and organized world. And *that's* why public relations matters.

CHAPTER 1

Engaging the Community

Public Relations Is All About People

CRISTYNE NICHOLAS AND GEORGE LENCE
NICHOLAS & LENCE COMMUNICATIONS

At its core, public relations is about communities—communities of voters, buyers, neighbors, thought leaders, and potential partners. PR is the art and science of reaching and influencing those groups as efficiently and affordably as possible. The tools of the trade are constantly evolving.

Throughout history, likely back to the very first newspaper published in Boston in 1690, PR, or "earned media," has been considered a more affordable but also a more effective investment and means to reach an audience.

PR professionals largely knew what people read, watched, and listened to—their choices seem so limited today—and they worked with journalists on behalf of clients to shape the stories communities consumed. For firms such as ours that specialize in community and government relations, as well as traditional PR, this was the tried-and-true method for shaping public opinion.

Money aside, there was an additional advantage to PR over other forms of marketing: the public was more likely to believe information it got from the press. Paid advertisements arrived with a believability discount; information that came from newspaper, television, and radio outlets, on the other hand, was understood to have been put through a "truth filter" by reporters and editors. It was consumed accordingly. "I'm not making that up—I read it in *Life* magazine."

To some extent this is still the case, but in recent decades public trust in the media has plummeted as subjectivity among some news outlets increased and cries of "fake news" proliferated. In a 1976 Gallup poll, 72 percent of Americans reported trusting the US news media. By 1996, that percentage had fallen to 53 percent; by 2016, it dropped to 32 percent. In Gallup's 2020 survey, only 9 percent of Americans reported trusting the mass media "a great deal"; 31 percent trusted it "a fair amount," 27 percent had "not very much" trust, while 33 percent had "none at all."

Yet public relations has never been more important. What gives?

The digital communications era changed everything; at the same time, nothing has changed at all. Newsrooms may have dwindled in size, but companies, public affairs groups, and individuals still need to tell their stories to the communities they wish to influence. The biggest difference between today and yesteryear is the number of channels available to target and deliver one's messaging. And much of today's PR goes directly to the consumer, bypassing the news media entirely. But the craft of storytelling remains the same.

In crises, though, news consumers tend to return to the outlets they trust. At the time of this writing, for example, the US is in the midst of a terrifying pandemic. People want facts. Does my family need N95 masks or will three-plys suffice? Is it really safe for my child to go to school?

Social media sites and fly-by-night online publications can—and do—say virtually anything to attract eyeballs. Genuine news organizations sift rumor from the truth, so people go back to them when things hit the proverbial fan, even when they suspect them of bias.

Our firm has learned in times of crisis that working with the best-established news outlets is more essential to PR success than ever. Social media remains important, but mostly as a delivery mechanism for old-fashioned, earned-media stories. It's the embedded hard-news links in the messages that matter most—the rest is a teaser to get readers to click them.

BE NIMBLE, TRANSPARENT, AND OUTSIDE THE BOX

As COVID-19 took root, grim stories about the future of cities and their hotel and office spaces abounded. For PR firms with clients in real estate, tourism, and the hospitality industry, like us, it was bad news heaped upon more bad news. Thousands of businesses shut down.

A key to our success during COVID has been the transparency with which we communicated with clients who had everything at stake. It is tempting to shield clients from alarming bits of news one is receiving from reporters, government officials, and other reliable sources with their ears to the ground. But that doesn't serve the clients' interests. They need to know.

Our approach is to share with clients the worst eventualities we're aware of—sans any sugarcoating—so together, we can best prepare a plan to get through the slog ahead. It's how we've maintained our credibility and trust; it's how we've retained clients in the middle of a catastrophe. We've also made sure to think outside the traditional PR box more than ever before.

For example, we work on behalf of a major organization representing the interests of dozens of high-profile restaurants in and around New York City. That industry and its employees were flattened by COVID. Roughly 40 percent of the city's 325,000 restaurant workers found themselves instantly out of work. City Hall dithered. There was no time to throw up one's hands.

We immediately convinced our client to hire a well-known engineering and transportation firm to come up with a city-wide outdoor dining plan, complete with schematics and maps. No one else was going to do it, so we did. This took arm-twisting, and it wasn't cheap, but again, we had to improvise.

As the blueprint was being developed, we spoke with New York City Police Department leaders and other key city officials to advocate for temporarily restructured street-permitting rules, and to assure them that emergency vehicles could get past these structures under our plan and diners could be kept safe. We then gave the plan to the Gray Lady of legacy media, the *New York Times*. That got attention in all the right places. Before long, restaurant lights were flipped back on, stovetops were firing, and al fresco diners were appearing around New York—a small gift to a beleaguered city at a time of deep sadness.

Did our client's plan create all this? Of course not. But by creating a solution to a vexing government challenge, and by publicizing it in the exact right publication at the exact right moment, we drove a conversation that eventually helped put diners back in our client's establishments. It's a powerful example of how PR-plus can bind together a government, an industry, and the community at large for the betterment of all three.

During this current crisis, we have found other ways to get clients exposure. One client published an op-ed about the struggles faced by the often-overlooked events industry. Another wrote about how real estate transactions will change in a virtual world. He was subsequently quoted in the *Times* because his opinion had become valuable.

COVID-19 arrived with no training manual. Americans were instructed by government officials to lock down and keep away from one another in public, prohibited from communicating face-to-face and banned from addressing large audiences. Naturally, this created a significant challenge for PR pros, particularly those whose work involved direct contact with the public. Gone overnight was the news conference, the ballroom presentation with a row of media in the back, and the in-person editorial board meeting. In its place came platforms such as Zoom, Webex, YouTube Live, and Google Meet—services we already knew about but rarely had to rely upon.

These services quickly became the bully pulpits for elected leaders such as New York governor Andrew Cuomo (who won an Emmy Award for his televised COVID presentations), California governor Gavin Newsom, Michigan governor Gretchen Whitmer, and Florida governor Rick DeSantis, to name a few. It was not only how they reached reporters; for the first time ever, the public at large could follow along at news conferences in real time. Those who adapted fastest won the largest audiences—a lesson to remember.

BE PART OF THE BIG STORY

When the 2010 *Deepwater Horizon* spill leaked 4.9 million barrels of oil into the Gulf of Mexico, Gulf Coast communities were badly in need of federal attention. These areas relied heavily on beachfront tourism. In the blink of an eye, it all shut down—mile after mile of powdery white shoreline and the thousands of mom-and-pop businesses that had served visitors.

Our company was among several PR firms hired by fourteen beach communities spanning four states to get their stories out. Politics almost derailed the effort.

We recommended that local leaders invite then-president Barack Obama to come to their communities and see the damage himself. He needed to hear directly from those hurt, to see the effects of the spill on local economies, we explained. But there was a problem: most of the affected states along the I-10 Corridor were run by conservative Republicans, and many of their constituents weren't exactly fans of Mr. Obama. Appearing next to him in a photo could pose a reelection risk, they feared.

The PR team persisted. We argued that the president of the United States is the president of the United States, and his presence at the scene would be near universally appreciated. Besides, the president was coming anyway. (How could he not visit such a sensational disaster site?) Would local officials rather be in that historic picture, or be invisible at a time of such importance to their communities? Did they want to be part of the conversation with the president, or to hear what he had to say without their input on the nightly news?

The officials saw the light. An urgent invitation was sent and the president came. With him arrived major media attention for our clients, and even more importantly, the well-targeted Federal Emergency Management Agency dollars they needed.

National crises can be tricky for PR professionals, and it's important to know how to operate under them.

In May 2020, race relations in America exploded when video evidence revealed the unconscionable killing of George Floyd at the hands of Minneapolis police officers. The ensuing public outrage was broadcast live for weeks across the nation. And understandably, virtually no other news story could break through.

Floyd's murder, and other tragic national news stories like it, can pose personal and professional conundrums for communications professionals. Often, the stories affect us personally, and we ask ourselves, how can we be promoting clients at a time such as this? Timing is key to any PR messaging.

Even in the midst of national tragedies, books need to be promoted; CEOs need to report to investors; hotels need heads in beds; product information needs to be shared. While recommending pause and reflection, we also know, sadly, that the world stops for no one. At the same time, it can be incredibly difficult to get reporters to focus on anything other than the Big Story.

The question we immediately ask ourselves in these instances is, *how can my clients be of help?* How can they connect to the greater story in a positive way, and what can they say to their constituents or customers to show they care? Those words can be the glue that binds us more strongly to our communities. Choose them wisely because they matter.

Not every all-consuming news story is tragic. Many arrive perennially, such as Halloween, Thanksgiving, and Christmas, and every good PR firm is prepared beforehand to attach their clients to them in some way. At other times, big stories come unexpectedly.

Some years ago, the New York Jets made the playoffs—yes, it was a while back—and it was wall-to-wall Jets coverage in New York and New Jersey. Meanwhile, we had just begun representing the original black-and-white cookie manufacturer on Manhattan's East Side, and the company wanted its confectionery pedigree to be better known and its online sales to increase. Seemingly separate things.

We turned to sports to connect them. Black and white became Jets green-and-white cookies for the playoffs, and the local news media ate them alive. Sales and media attention grew so much that we began marketing the cookies to out-of-state sports fans: purple-and-whites for the Minnesota Vikings; bay-green-and-cheese-gold ones for the Green Bay Packers. It's amazing how much press (and sales) a little food dye can create when attached to a bigger story.

Another time, a major sports celebrity and product endorser got caught up in a sensational personal scandal. It was the talk of the town everywhere for days. We put on our thinking caps and quickly convinced an insurance client to create a reputational risk policy nicknamed after this sports figure. Boom!

A final example of making connections to move a client's needs forward: In 2008, Texas oil billionaire Boone Pickens unleashed a series of nationally televised advertisements promoting natural gas as a clean alternative to oil. Lots of people noticed. Meanwhile, we'd been asked to promote a new line of pizza trucks that just so happened to be using natural gas to power its truck engines and ovens. Environmentalist Michael R. Bloomberg was the mayor of New York City, and we often worked with his administration. After a flurry of phone calls and some persuasive emails, we put it all together. The resulting news conference outside of New York City Hall, featuring Pickens, Bloomberg, and our client, resulted in wall-to-wall coverage. Each of the participants got what they wanted out of the event, including some of the tastiest pizza in New York.

CRISIS LEADERSHIP

September 11, 2001, changed the world in two hours—and again demonstrated just how much of a difference effective leadership and communication can make in people's lives.

Portions of the city were covered in smoke, bridges and tunnels were closed to all but emergency vehicles, and thousands of people were missing. It was hard to imagine how New York could go on.

"America's Mayor," Rudy Giuliani—the old Rudy, the one New Yorkers remember—was at his finest, channeling Winston Churchill following the Blitz of London. "Never, never, never give up!" he told the public, and it was just what they needed to hear. Following Churchill's example further, the mayor directed his team to open the Broadway theaters, a symbol of New York's cultural vibrancy, as quickly as possible. Broadway reopened two days later, on September 13, 2001.

Eight million New Yorkers instantly got the message: if we abandon what we cherish, if we sink into despair, the terrorists will have won. It was a moment of supreme leadership, but it was up to public relations professionals to make it a reality, to execute the mayor's vision and spread his fierce resolve.

NYC & Company, the city's public-private tourism marketing organization that we then led, went all in. We got Broadway performers, stagehands, musicians, and directors into Manhattan any way possible, "lights and sirens" if necessary, so that the shows could go on. The city's preexisting tourism campaign became "Paint the Town Red, White and Blue." The theaters weren't crowded right away, but everyone knew their lights were back on. Those who saw shows those first few nights will never forget them. "God Bless America" was sung by casts and audiences alike following standing ovations; arms were linked, with people facing the future together. It was one of New York City's finest branding hours.

The patriotic spirit was everywhere, and the New York City economy, which relies heavily on tourism, needed it. There was deep concern that Americans would eschew air travel for months.

Days after 9/11, we got a call from Sho Donozo, a travel agent in Portland, Oregon. He explained that he usually brought thirty Oregonians to New York

City's Columbus Day Parade, but after seeing the 9/11 attacks he wanted to know if he could bring more. He had been getting calls from people who considered heading to New York their patriotic duty. In a discussion about the parade with City Hall, the mayor asked how many Oregonians might show up for the parade. Within a week, the travel agent called back. He said he had five hundred tourists ready to fly to New York, with or without the parade.

The October 8, 2001, Columbus Day Parade was New York City's first major event following 9/11, and the travel agent had underestimated. It turned out that nine hundred Oregonians sporting forest-green "Oregon Loves NY" T-shirts marched in that parade at the mayor's invitation. Those patriotic visitors were besieged by grateful local journalists, and word spread that traveling to New York City was a way to stick it to the terrorists. Jamaica, Canada, and Italy sent planeloads of tourists in the following weeks.

Professor Klaus Schwab, the founder of the World Economic Forum, also reached out. In February 2002, he hosted "Davos in New York," the first time the gathering of world business leaders had convened outside of Switzerland. More than 2,700 participants from 102 countries, and throngs of international news media members, safely met for a week at the Waldorf Astoria Hotel, sending the message to the world that New York was open for business again.

It all began with leadership.

TAKEAWAYS

1. Public relations is about people and the communities with which they associate.
2. It's the job of PR professionals to bond to those communities on behalf of clients.
3. Be nimble, creative, and transparent in everything you do.
4. When your client can't be the story, make it part of the broader conversation.
5. Life happens. Always be ready to adapt to changing circumstances.
6. Words make leaders, and leaders can change the world.

CHAPTER 2

Gathering Information and Intelligence

How to Harness Intelligence for Your PR Advantage

JACK DEVINE AND AMANDA MATTINGLY

THE ARKIN GROUP

When the coronavirus pandemic hit in early 2020, many companies were caught flat-footed. Companies scrambled to gather information about what the pandemic meant for their operations, employees, and share price. They needed real-time, on-the-ground intelligence about how COVID-19 was spreading, how governments were responding, and how it would impact their company and industry.

Companies also needed to make immediate business decisions, such as whether employees should go into the office, how they were going to provide personal protective equipment for their workers, and if they should halt operations altogether. And they had larger questions, too: Could they handle a surge in online sales, could they staunch losses from shutdown orders, and what could they do to help their community deal with the crisis? Around the globe, companies large and small faced a dizzying number of questions needing immediate answers.

To answer these questions and create a strategy, companies needed timely intelligence. To convey their decisions, they needed good public relations.

In the intelligence community, we talk about the "black swan" event that has the lowest probability but the highest potential negative impact. In other words, the black swan event lies beyond normal forecasting or reasonable expectations. The coronavirus pandemic of 2020–2021 is the black swan event of our time, causing major disruptions to the way we live and do business.

The companies that have handled the pandemic and accompanying global shutdowns the best have been those that gathered pertinent information quickly, made sound judgments using the intelligence gathered, and successfully conveyed their response strategies to their employees, customers, and shareholders. Setting industry specifics aside, companies that are best positioned to emerge stronger from the pandemic are those that can (1) access information from their existing intelligence networks to make critical business decisions, and (2) communicate their decisions with a savvy public relations strategy.

The most successful and reputable companies worldwide increasingly rely on sophisticated information-gathering programs—known as "business intelligence"—to assess developments in their industries and operating environments before making key decisions. These companies also use the information they gather to inform their public relations strategies. Whether those strategies involve responding to an emergency or touting a company's successes, the most successful ones are those backed by business intelligence and analysis.

Best-in-class companies develop intelligence-collection efforts in support of their business objectives. Working closely with senior decision makers, they build a tailored network of intelligence sources to deliver a proprietary stream of timely and actionable information—which they can then use for a public relations strategy.

In this chapter, we share our experiences working in private business intelligence to demonstrate how to harness intelligence for your public relations advantage. Case studies involve the following types of intelligence gathering programs: (1) "know your partner" due diligence; (2) strategic intelligence; (3) monitoring political, economic, and security risks; (4) intelligence-based media campaigns; (5) exposing wrongdoing; and (6) crisis management.

"KNOW YOUR PARTNER" DUE DILIGENCE

Reliable information about business partners is critical to sound business decisions in the United States and around the world. This requires due diligence designed to assess the risks associated with partnerships, mergers, and investment opportunities. Companies need targeted due diligence and background research that combines thorough public data and traditional investigative research with well-sourced, on-the-ground information. Individuals and companies need to know their partners and any potential "red flags." They need advance information and analysis of the individuals and entities critical to a transaction or investment.

The best-case scenario uses intelligence to prevent potential black eyes, rather than waiting until problems emerge and force the client into damage control mode. We often conduct such background due diligence investigations on companies and their principals as part of a transaction or acquisition in order to identify reputational issues, among others, that may not have cropped up as part of the client's financial analysis. While we often identify potentially problematic issues that can be thought through and managed, in some cases we uncover real deal breakers.

In the case of a recent acquisition of a major eastern European construction firm, we determined that one of its executives had consistently provided sizable financial incentives to state and municipal officials across the region to win contracts. While further investigations indicated that this was not a firm-wide practice, we did find, not surprisingly, that the compliance culture at the company was significantly underdeveloped.

In another case, a large multinational financial institution was preparing to buy a smaller bank in Central America and asked for a thorough review of the bank's senior management in the region before concluding the deal. The due diligence methodology included inquiries with corporate, regulatory, and industry sources to determine the senior managers' reputation. Through this process, the acquiring bank learned that a member of the target's senior management team had business ties to a known criminal in the region, and that the same individual had been investigated for alleged involvement in criminal activities. The due diligence process was critical for the larger institution's visibility and allowed it to take appropriate steps before concluding the deal. Had information about this individual come to light after the deal, it could have significantly harmed the entity's regulatory and reputational standing. The acquiring institution would have had to deal with the public relations fallout from its involvement with the individual as well. In the high-stakes world of global finance, a competitor could have seized on the association as a way to tarnish the reputation of the financial institution. Having information ahead of time made all the difference.

In a post-pandemic world, many emerging markets will see an increase in mergers and acquisitions, and a consolidation in some sectors where distressed assets are newly available. This makes it all the more important for companies entering the market to feel confident about taking advantage of these opportunities. They also need to feel confident about the partners they are going into business with, to mitigate any potential public relations fallout from those who may be trying to hide corrupt business practices, unsavory dealings, or questionable associates. This comes down to protecting a company's reputation.

STRATEGIC INTELLIGENCE

Because information is so important to mitigating risk, many companies operating and investing globally have come to rely on sophisticated, ongoing information-gathering programs. These are business-intelligence collection programs that are designed to provide strategic information to company decision makers. Many companies have developed internal processes to collect external information that could affect their bottom line and to assess critical developments in their industry and operating environments. Companies often work with outside providers to help build the internal intelligence systems and capabilities they need to use external business intelligence—all of which is designed to improve their decision making and overall public relations strategy.

For example, we worked with a multinational corporation with worldwide operations, including in Brazil and Colombia, to develop internal intelligence mechanisms to manage incoming competitive and security-related information that impacted their most important operations. The company developed the internal systems and protocols necessary to then analyze information coming from external networks. These external networks were able to provide real-time intelligence about ongoing and emerging threats to the company's operations.

In one of their country markets, the company was able to learn about a rival's potential interest in assets considered to be in competition with its own operations. Having advance intelligence about the competitor's interest in the market gave the company the time it needed to assess its own investment in that desirable market and to devise a public relations strategy to convey the company's strength there.

In another market, we were able to provide the company with intelligence about security risks emanating from violent street protests. Thus informed, the client was able to create and implement a risk-mitigation strategy and protect its valuable investment there. The work the company did to safeguard its assets also mitigated potential public relations blowback had the company been caught unprepared.

Another case involved sensitive strategic intelligence support for a commodities company with an extensive production operation in Asia. The client's concern was that it had made a significant infrastructure investment in an area that had become embroiled in civil unrest. Suddenly, the local plants had to deal with an unpredictable insurgency, labor strife, and a shifting government regulatory structure, all of which could imperil their staff and seriously affect the bottom line. One option was simply to relocate facilities, but that would mean jettisoning a major investment. Together with the client, we put in place a strategic intelligence program to help it stay in front of events and respond quickly to the unexpected. This required establishing a nimble network of people on the ground who could report on events in real time and, even more importantly, anticipate problems before they occurred so the client was not blindsided.

The first piece of an effective strategic intelligence program is to develop the intelligence, and the second is to ensure a communications structure is in place to securely convey the information. Our next step for this client was using operatives in Manila and London to ensure operational security. We then relied on a variety of advanced encrypted communications platforms to transmit intelligence. Last, we helped the client utilize the information to manage a local public relations campaign.

MONITORING POLITICAL, ECONOMIC, AND SECURITY RISKS

In addition to ongoing business intelligence collection and the internal protocols to receive and process it, companies operating in regions rife with political violence and criminality also need to monitor political, economic, and security risks. But they also need ongoing intelligence collection and surveillance of political and economic risks. Understanding the political, economic, and security environments in which business units, factories, retail stores, headquarters, partners, or acquisition targets operate is essential to a company's risk-mitigation strategy. The most successful companies develop an intelligence-based approach to making these risk assessments and ongoing monitoring that provides timely information from external networks of on-the-ground sources. Watching the headlines is not enough for many corporate executives. These companies and their C-suite executives need proprietary information relevant to their specific corporate business objectives.

For example, we worked with a nonprofit service organization seeking to expand to several different countries around the world, including Ukraine, South Korea, and Mexico. The organization required a series of reports analyzing each country's political, economic, and security situations, as well as the reception it would likely receive in each country. Part of what made the reporting successful was that the initial reports developed a list of key contacts for the organization, a road map of governmental bureaucracy, and real-time intelligence about the security environment to help make important expansion decisions. Ongoing intelligence monitoring has helped the organization mitigate significant risks to its mission and personnel posed by political violence and organized crime in these countries. Further, the ongoing stream of information about the political, economic, and security environment has enabled the organization to implement a robust public relations campaign designed to fortify its work in the eyes of the community and the governments of the countries where it operates. A strong, forward-leaning public relations campaign can help create necessary alliances between an organization and the community in the face of security concerns. Such relationships become invaluable in circumstances when assets or personnel come under attack.

In another case, we helped a company with operations in Egypt to navigate the changing political landscape during the period of the Arab Spring protests and the ousting of two consecutive governments between 2011 and 2013. The company's assets in the country were located in an area subject to protests, and the company itself came under assault for its association with the former government of Hosni Mubarak and his privatization program. Company executives needed to understand the immediate security risks as well as the longer-term political and economic consequences of regime change. Given the ongoing dynamics in the country, we worked with the client to develop a stream of political, economic, and security reporting based on intelligence gathered from key on-the-ground sources in Egypt. The long-term monitoring project continues today, even as the political situation in Egypt has stabilized, because the information provided to the client continues to inform operational and strategic business decisions in the country, as well as its public relations strategy there. Understanding the risks of the operating environment has also helped the client develop a positive posture in the community and with the government, which helps to insulate the company from potential future targeting.

INTELLIGENCE-BASED MEDIA CAMPAIGNS

Intelligence-collection programs help companies and organizations develop proactive media campaigns in an effort to influence their operating environments. Rather than just reacting to unfavorable conditions, these entities use information to create favorable conditions. Companies with robust intelligence networks develop ongoing streams of information to feed continuing media campaigns designed to benefit the entity.

Over the past years, we have worked with authoritative media outlets in Asia, the Middle East, and eastern Europe on behalf of clients for this purpose. After developing information specific to a client's interest, we move to the implementation stage, which entails strategically deploying the information collected in an effort to help the client influence events in a beneficial direction. Moreover, we have the capability to follow up traditional media with a second layer of supportive social media, providing clients with a ready platform for honing and implementing effective global messaging.

In one such case, our client was an opposition figure in a Middle Eastern country who was trying to repair relationships with key establishment leaders. The first step was to use knowledgeable sources close to the regime to determine likely opportunities for connection and what messages might be most effective. We were able to bring critical information to the attention of journalists who might be interested in covering the issue, ones with authoritative voices in the target market who were already covering the issue at hand. In this case, we worked with a respected international journalist who covered political factions in the country in question and who wrote a positive piece about our client's contributions to political stability in that country.

In such media campaigns, the goal is to work with journalists who can quickly learn about an issue, find the hook that makes it newsworthy for the general public, independently verify the information with their own network of sources, and then develop stories for publication. Such a concerted media campaign can yield significant benefits for a company or organization—but the key is to have solid, verifiable information developed via established intelligence methodologies to back up the narrative.

EXPOSING WRONGDOING

In the course of doing business around the globe, clients have found themselves faced with unscrupulous actors who might be impeding their business interests or actively working to sabotage their work in certain regions. Companies used to a level playing field of competition in areas where the rules and regulations are more transparent and better enforced may have difficulty operating in environments where competitors may take unlawful action to secure advantage. In some cases, clients may seek legal recourse. But in others, a savvy media campaign using sourced intelligence could be an effective way for companies to expose adversaries' wrongdoing or neutralize competitors seeking to undermine their business objectives.

For example, we worked with a client to develop information related to a financial institution's ongoing ties to an Iranian bank, which controverted international sanctions. The client believed that the financial institution was involved with the Iranians, so the first step was to verify its theory. We launched a discreet investigation into the financial institution using sources close to the entity, who confirmed the entity's continuing relationship with the Iranian bank. This type of intelligence-gathering effort must be carried out with operational security front and center, so we used a seasoned team of intelligence professionals to develop the information. With this information, we worked with a journalist to publish an article about the financial institution in a reputable publication in Europe. As noted, in such media campaigns, the goal is to work with journalists who are already working on and interested in the relevant issues, can independently verify the information provided with their own sources, and then develop a story for publication. After we exposed the financial institution's wrongdoing, the client then crafted its own public relations campaign designed to capitalize on the information conveyed in that initial article.

CRISIS MANAGEMENT

Often, a global crisis such as the coronavirus pandemic, a natural disaster, or domestic unrest provides a stress test of firms' crisis-management capabilities. Corporate entities need to develop security and crisis-management protocols when operating in unstable environments, including effective and sustainable security and safety programs, emergency-response systems, and disaster-recovery plans. These plans could be related to threats to a facility, employees, and information, or to unforeseen crises and location-specific concerns. As noted, companies that had existing crisis-management plans in place were much better equipped to handle the coronavirus lockdowns in 2020. They were able to enact existing safety protocols and plans for operating remotely, thus mitigating the health risks to their employees and financial harm to their bottom line, while promoting their strategies via an organized public relations campaign. Faced with uncertainty, steady public relations messaging backed by good intelligence and sound protocols can do a lot to build confidence in the ability of a company and its leadership to handle a crisis.

For example, when a small international law firm found itself flat-footed in response to civil unrest in Chile, it realized that its crisis-management function had to be expanded. While the law firm had well-developed internal communications surrounding its life safety function, its crisis-management team needed to include an external communications element and protocols to guide its communications with external clients and other stakeholders, as well as local authorities and its national embassy. At the same time, we decided that the life safety function could use further refinement to include a component responsive to a potential pandemic flu outbreak. This meant building in plans for when sick employees should stay at home and return to work, when to suspend travel, and—critically—what infrastructure key employees would need to work from home if needed. Although we did not foresee the coronavirus pandemic, the company's plans were readily adaptable.

In another case, we worked with a multinational conglomerate seeking to revamp the security protocols for its Latin American subsidiary in an area subject to paramilitary and insurgent activity. We conducted physical security assessments and recommended ongoing security protection for corporate facilities and management—including everything from armored cars to a vetted security detail, surveillance cameras, and safe rooms—to safeguard them from threats.

Using on-the-ground intelligence, we also developed and executed a strategy for continued production in the unstable area. It was important to identify and remediate weaknesses in its security posture and create a proactive and ongoing risk assessment capability for the company. With security protocols in place and public relations messaging at the ready, the company felt confident it could protect itself and its workers from a variety of potential threats.

Most recently, we worked with a multinational corporation with operations in the United States and Europe to help shore up its emergency management plan during the coronavirus pandemic. Fortunately, we had already established protocols with the client during the H1N1 outbreak in 2009, so its immediate response to COVID-19 was ahead of its competitors'. This was invaluable to the company and its employees from a health, financial, and public relations perspective. While its competitors were struggling to make crisis management decisions and figure out how to operate remotely, our client was already shifting gears to community outreach through a robust public relations campaign. The company was able to demonstrate stability and leadership in the communities where it is present and received much praise for its corporate social responsibility.

TAKEAWAYS

Top companies can and do utilize business intelligence for their public relations advantage in several ways:

1. Companies operating in the United States and around the world face a variety of challenges—from the everyday challenges of getting product to market to unforeseen black swan events such as the coronavirus pandemic. Best-in-class companies, however, are successful in navigating these challenges with the help of good intelligence and good public relations.

2. Companies cannot wait for a country's political, economic, or security environment to stabilize before continuing operations, just as they cannot count on a competitor to openly advertise its interest in entering a desirable market.

3. Companies need information and public relations to defend their positions and to advance their objectives. Intelligence can help companies avoid certain pitfalls before they become public relations disasters. Intelligence can also arm companies with the ammunition they need to communicate critical business decisions, insulate themselves from further targeting, expose wrongdoing, or create community and government alliances.

4. The marriage between intelligence and public relations can set companies and leaders apart, giving them the competitive advantage they need to succeed.

CHAPTER 3

Preparing Your Argument

The Medium Is Always the Message

ROBERT LAIRD
THE DILENSCHNEIDER GROUP

The nature of communications has changed dramatically in the 2000s and 2010s—and that's putting it mildly. The old technology and traditional methods are still around, of course: newspapers, magazines, radio, television, delivering speeches before live audiences, making pitches in person to individuals or small groups, and so forth. But podcasting, texting, social media, videoconferencing, and all the other digital platforms have revolutionized the way we communicate with one another, whether it's one-on-one, before a global audience, or something in between. And you can be sure that even newer technologies will keep coming along, thanks to the driving force of innovative entrepreneurship.

Needless to say, the lockdowns and dislocations caused by the COVID-19 pandemic accelerated the pace of change to warp speed. Seemingly overnight, the verb "zoom" took on a new meaning, just as "Google" has, and that's only one manifestation of the newness of it all. As Genpact CEO Tiger Tyagarajan observed in late 2020, "Our clients have done things in the last five or six months that they thought would take five or six years."

Please realize, too, that not only has the double impact of fast-changing technology and a cataclysmic pandemic transformed the ways in which communicators reach out to target audiences, whether businesses, governments, or individuals. It has also changed the way those audiences receive and react to the messages. It's akin to the scientific rule that says the act of observing a process affects the process. Changing the way a pitch is delivered changes the way it is received.

All these developments have affected how you go about preparing your argument and executing your presentation, whether you are pitching yourself to a prospective employer, selling an organization's services to a potential customer, extolling a company's product, or trying to convince an editor to do a story about one of your clients.

To master these skills, you need to be up to speed on all the new communications technologies and know how to make them work for you. But remember also that certain core principles of communications always apply. The packaging and the method of delivery may be different, but the essential techniques that worked for the pioneers of public relations in the early twentieth century still work today—and will far into the future.

DEFINING "ARGUMENTS" AND "PRESENTATIONS"

Let's pause for a moment and make a distinction between the two terms I just used, "argument" and "presentation," because they relate intimately to these core principles.

Presentations are the end result of a process in which the formulation of arguments comes first. The argument—your thesis, your declaration of what you believe to be true, the point of view you want to convey—comes from analyzing the evidence you've acquired, whether from research, experience, the testimonials of others, or whatever else you have. Preparing the argument is a kind of intellectual exercise because it requires you to sort out the material at hand, think through what is important and what is not, reach your conclusion, and set the goal you want to achieve.

Once you have settled on your argument, you must next decide what is the most compelling and effective way of pitching it to your target audience. That is the presentation part of the process. It means devising specific and persuasive language. It requires concreteness to buttress the argument. Numbers. Quantifiable data. Survey findings. Polling results. Real-life stories with the names and case histories of actual people. Endorsements from credible, respected third parties.

The presentation must be assembled with the time element very much in mind. You may be limited in how many minutes it can last, or you may be required to present for a specified length of time. Disregard such requirements at your peril. Assume they were set for good reasons, and that your failure to observe them could count heavily against you.

Get to the Point, Fast

On the other hand, there may be no fixed time element—you can go on as long or short as you choose. In that situation, let the length of your presentation be determined by the content of your argument. The more there is to say of genuine value, then the longer the presentation—within reason. That means you have to concentrate on your most powerful points. Decide what will really influence your listeners and keep it in. Discard what could be helpful but is not essential. Don't let an open-ended presentation become, in the audience's mind, an endless presentation.

Why concentrate on value? Because in today's high-speed world, audiences have become accustomed to and usually demand short, punchy, to-the-point presentations. Patience runs out fast. The urge to move on to the next thing runs high. Whether you are pitching your case to an audience of one or one thousand, you need to remember the old rule from architecture: less can be more.

That does not mean, though, that you should keep the presentation short by talking fast. In fact, speaking rapidly is one of the last things you want to do. Keep the pace at something like a normal conversation to give the audience time to digest what you're saying, and even slow down a bit for more complicated material. Hamlet's advice to actors was to "suit the action to the word, the word to the action." The same spirit applies when you are pacing your pitch.

Final point: Once you have developed your argument and summed it up in a presentation, then you need an editor. If you are fortunate, that will be a boss, teacher, mentor, experienced colleague, or trusted friend who can review what you have, make comments and suggestions, and, most important, tell you whether it works. Unfortunately, not everyone has the benefit of an independent editor. You may be entirely on your own. In that case, you have to be your own editor.

Triple-Check the Presentation

Far too often in the world of communications, people put a pitch together and think the job is done. Not so. That's only the first step. You need to review it at least three times. In your first review, comb out any errors, such as language that's garbled or clichéd; material that might unintentionally offend the audience; or visual materials that are inappropriate, unattractive, or poorly timed during the presentation.

Second, review the presentation for its effectiveness. Are there passages that drone on too long or are difficult to follow? Is some of the material duplicative? Have you chosen the best case histories to make your point? And above all, are you making the case you want to make? Did you somehow, while assembling your presentation, drift away from the argument that was the whole point of presenting?

Last, after those first two reviews, you need to go over everything at least one more time to make sure the changes you've made haven't somehow created new sets of problems.

Yes, it's a painstaking process. But you need to go into every presentation you ever make confident that you've got everything completely right and that you've left nothing to chance. You're not likely to be given what golfers call a mulligan, another stroke without a penalty. There may be second chances in life, but rarely if ever when it comes to important presentations. One-and-done is the rule. After all, why would a potential employer or prospective client even consider taking you on if you stumble right out of the gate?

All this applies to arguing for anything and everything of importance—a new job, a new client, a new product, a plum assignment, a political candidate. It may also apply to protecting something you already have rather than trying to add something new: for instance, keeping an existing job or holding on to a skittish client. Whatever kind of case you want to make, even in this digital era, when there are so many new methods of delivery, the core principles of communications can never be forgotten or ignored.

DELIVERING THE ARGUMENT

Let's look at the ingredients of effective presentations. Nowadays, the demand is for authenticity, brevity, entertainment, and anything-but-vanilla presentations. The conventional wisdom used to be that the world gives presenters about four minutes to make a favorable impression. That time span is now seriously compressed. Leisurely, rambling openings that seem to say "I've got all the time in the world" invite failure. You must command attention from the start.

One old guideline that does still work is the speechwriter's rule: tell 'em what you're going to say, say it, tell 'em what you've said. In other words, open with a strong, clear statement of what your argument is. Within the first minute or two, the audience should know what you're going to talk about and your point of view on it. Then spell it out, explaining the reasoning underlying your argument and the data, case histories, or other information supporting it—that's the "say it" part. Then summarize it all in concise, punchy language—the "tell 'em what you've said" wrap-up.

It is particularly important to get that last part right, because a strong summary gives the audience a chance to absorb your argument and see how all the information that you've provided leads up to it. Avoid being overly repetitive in your conclusion—you don't want to rehash your entire case—but it is all right to hit the key points, because listeners often need to hear them one more time to fix your presentation in their minds.

Final thought: It's always good to make the absolute last thing you say something memorable—a kind of sound bite that will stick in the listeners' minds. It may be a challenge to the audience's way of thinking, a call to action, a colorful anecdote that illustrates your argument, or just a short, compelling statement such as, "Hire me, I get results," if that's what you've come to say.

KNOWING THE AUDIENCE

Presenting is ultimately all about the audience, not the presenter. You have to know to whom you are going to speak and then fine-tune your presentation to the situation. Those who don't realize this or won't invest the effort to make the event audience friendly are not going to get results.

People who have a keen sense of empathy have a definite advantage in reaching audiences. They can transcend their personal feelings and grasp what it is the audience wants to hear—or sometimes what it doesn't expect to hear, but welcomes once it's been said.

For instance, the audience for Jimmy Kimmel's late-night TV show normally expects a lot of laughs in the opening monologue. Yet one night in 2017, it got something very different—something that made a lot of folks downright teary—when

Kimmel shared the story of his newborn son's congenital heart disease, the emergency surgery he needed, and the nerve-racking treatments that followed.

Kimmel had clearly given a lot of thought to the argument he wanted to make, so he then segued his presentation from the personal to the universal. "If your baby is going to die and it doesn't have to," he said, "it shouldn't matter how much money you make. I think that's something that whether you're a Republican or a Democrat or something else, we all agree on . . . No parents should ever have to decide if they can afford to save their child's life. It just shouldn't happen." The audience burst into applause.

Another aspect of knowing the audience is to ask yourself this question: How is he, or she, or the organization in question, doing? If they've just turned around a bad situation, they will probably want to be recognized for that. If they are entangled in problems, they'll be open to ideas that are offered respectfully. You don't want to imply you know the audience's business better than they do. Instead, you want to identify their pain and address it as someone who has come, not as a know-it-all opportunist, but as a problem solver.

GIVING CONTRARIAN ADVICE

Bear in mind that sometimes organizations have the wrong idea about what their real problem is, and your job is to set them straight. Case in point: United Airlines had a PR disaster on its hands in 2017 when Chicago O'Hare Airport security personnel dragged a sixty-nine-year-old passenger down the aisle and off a plane because United wanted his seat. The incident was captured on phone videos by other passengers, many of whom could be heard screaming at the guards to stop.

After the videos went viral, United's CEO, Oscar Munoz, realized he had to make a statement. But what he said was that the airline regretted "having to re-accommodate some of its passengers." In other words, he thought he had to apologize for inconveniencing a few travelers, not for United's rough treatment of an older man who had done nothing wrong. Munoz made the common mistake in business life of thinking in traditional terms—always keep the customers happy. In doing so, he failed to recognize that this situation was not some minor breakdown in operating procedures, but an enormous breach of conduct, and that the response had to reflect its gravity and deeply personal nature.

It can be challenging to make a presentation in which you tell high-powered executives that they completely misunderstand the problem and must recast their thinking, but the payoff for setting them right can be significant. In United's case, getting the right advice and following it would have averted an immediate, sharp drop in stock price—and a lasting dent in their reputation.

FRESH THINKING

Another kind of presentation that can deeply impress listeners is one that challenges them to break out of their conventional ways of thinking and try something vastly different.

One person who took that route was Pete Frates, who died at the age of thirty-four in 2019 after suffering from ALS (amyotrophic lateral sclerosis, also known as Lou Gehrig's Disease) for seven years. Frates decided that the fundraising for research into a cure for ALS was too workaday and unimaginative, so in 2014 he launched a drive that made ALS research national news: the Ice Bucket Challenge.

The challenge involved getting people to volunteer to have a bucket of ice water poured over their heads. At first glance, it seemed like a wacky idea, but it went viral, and thousands of people signed up to get soaked, including scores of celebrities. One of the most memorable volunteers was Oprah Winfrey, who agreed to take the Ice Bucket Challenge live on her TV show. At the crucial moment, she announced in a perfectly calm voice, "I'm ready now"—and then let out a horrified scream as the bucket was dumped on her, a vivid reminder of what was being endured on behalf of a good cause. At the end of the year, between $160 million and $220 million had been raised for ALS research, and *Sports Illustrated* named Pete Frates as its "Inspiration of the Year" award winner.

Your presentation probably won't require such an outsized proposal as the Ice Bucket Challenge. But one of the questions you need to consider when you are formulating your argument is whether the person or the organization to which you are presenting might need new ideas and fresh ways of responding to its challenges.

HUMILITY AND AUTHENTICITY

Among the qualities many successful presenters display are a sense of humility and authenticity. They realize that their life achievements are not theirs alone, but were enabled by the support they've received from those who have helped them along the way. That self-awareness keeps them connected to reality, restrains any inclination to get boastful or take too much credit, and makes their presentations far more credible and impactful.

Sometimes the presentation is all about expressing one's sense of humility and gratitude to others. Take, for example, the statement Serena Williams made to the press after she had won her twenty-third Grand Slam singles title, the most by any tennis player, male or female, in the modern era. Known as one of the game's fiercest competitors, Serena had every justification for taking personal pride in her victory. But instead she dedicated it to her sister Venus. "I really would like to take this moment to congratulate Venus," Serena said. "She's an amazing person. There's no way I would be at 23 without her . . . She's the only reason that I'm standing here today." Small wonder that Serena Williams commands so much respect as a person as well as an athlete.

Closely related to humility is authenticity. Great presenters do display confidence, but they never let that verge over into becoming cocky or arrogant. They convey their authenticity by speaking from a place of personal conviction, but one that is free of egotism.

One of the best presenters of the modern era is Elon Musk, who has an extraordinary record of turning skeptical audiences into converts. According to one analysis, he is particularly effective at putting across his vision for the future because he uses verbs in the present tense. Not "they will be," but "they are." Not "is going to come," but "is now." That seemingly simple change in how he deploys his verbs conveys strong convictions and real authenticity.

KEEPING IT SIMPLE

Dense is dumb. That's a shorthand way of saying that presentations have to be accessible and that complexity is not the way to achieve that goal. Avoid long passages full of numbers or heavy-duty data—save all that for a fact sheet or some other handout or download. Look for shorter, more direct ways to say things. English is a wonderfully flexible language and almost always offers a quicker, simpler way to express thoughts.

Shun clichés and pointless phrases such as, "As I was saying . . ." and "Okay, then." Never tell the audience, "Let me be honest with you." Those are just more wasted words, and they imply you haven't been honest before. Avoid what's called "throat-clearing": wordy introductory passages that don't actually convey any ideas but only lead up to your message. Go directly to the point.

Storytelling is a great way to get complex points across in an easy-to-follow way. Sheryl Sandberg, the COO of Facebook, is a master of using personal stories and anecdotes to convey her ideas. In her book *Lean In*, for example, she writes about the salary negotiations before she joined Facebook. She was inclined to take the first offer she got, but her husband convinced her to make a counterproposal, which led to a much better offer. A seemingly simple story, but it puts across in a powerful way her argument that women in the business world need to "lean in" to improve their status and pay.

MIRRORING

A basic sales tactic is mirroring the prospect. Do this judiciously—you don't want to come across as insincere or inauthentic. But if, for example, you know the audience members have conservative social values, then there is no harm in being conservative in details such as your dress, allusions, graphics, and language.

Mirroring also means making your presentation responsive to the audience's reactions. To do this successfully, keep it loosely structured. The problem with a set-in-stone system such as PowerPoint is that it's not configured to keep adjusting to the audience's mood. Slide decks are fine when people have come to listen and learn, when you are the lecturer, the teacher.

Let me quote some instructive language from the 2007 *AMA Handbook of Public Relations* to explain that point: When you are making a pitch—when you are trying to sell yourself or your services or your organization—"it's usually better to have talking points, perhaps with an easel, a blank flip chart, and a Magic Marker. In that way, key material can be reinforced visually, depending on whether the audience indicates that it finds the material compelling.

"Mirroring is the most effective way to enhance any presentation or interview. By getting in sync with the decision makers, the speaker creates the space to present persuasive facts, examples, personality traits, and proposed solutions."

THAT'S ENTERTAINMENT

Audiences like to be entertained, even during serious business meetings. Needless to say, making a pitch that includes entertaining elements can be chancy—some listeners may not be amused. But you can minimize that risk through the use of irony: using words whose meaning is the opposite of what is expected. Irony can create a sense of emotional distance and provide the audience with a feeling of detachment and control, which in turn can create instant rapport with the presenter.

For example, you might comment on the surprising conduct of someone everyone is talking about: "That was like learning your marriage counselor is getting divorced." Or describe the bungling of a rival company as "about as impressive as a police station getting robbed."

Irony has the ability to disarm by looking at things in a clever, unexpected way. The audience becomes less guarded and more trusting.

TAKEAWAYS

1. Technology + pandemic = communications transformation. PR professionals are reaching out to audiences in new ways. Audiences are receiving and reacting in new ways.

2. *Plus ça change, plus c'est la même chose.* Another way of saying that, no matter how much transformation there is, the same core principles of communications always apply.

3. Solidly based arguments—based on research and information—are the foundation of all successful presentations.

4. If you don't know who you want to reach, you will reach no one. Your audience(s) must be defined, not guessed at.

5. The medium is still the message. Without properly choosing how your message will be delivered, you have only a random chance of reaching your audience(s).

6. Time is not necessarily on your side. Whether for in-person or on-screen presentations, if you take too much time (or space) to make your argument, you may lose your audience(s). On the other hand, timing is everything. The pacing of your delivery must be top of mind.

(continued)

7. Your presentation needs an editor. Your arguments must be vetted, your presentation critiqued. You have colleagues to ask, right, even if they're virtual? If not, then you must be your own editor, and a perfectionist at that.

8. Practice makes perfect. Never present an untested argument. Never make an unrehearsed presentation. And yes, your mirror counts as rehearsal space.

9. Don't be afraid to be yourself. Let your personality come through.

CHAPTER 4

Words That Work

The Role of Language and Polling in Public Relations and Policy*

FRANK LUNTZ

I t's hard to be an effective advocate and participant in the world of public relations when simple, common messaging is so toxic and the communicators so venomous. George Orwell wrote almost seventy-five years ago that "the English language is in a bad way." Well, he should see it now. Our civil discourse is no longer civil. We speak to incite, not inform. We don't debate; we denounce. Too many of us are too angry to listen, learn, or—God forbid—lead. We *should* be appalled at the

---

* Portions of this chapter previously appeared in Frank Luntz, "No Wonder America Is Divided: We Can't Even Agree on What Our Values Mean," *Time,* October 26, 2018, https:// time.com/5435825/divided-america-values-language-meaning/ and in Frank Luntz and Brian C. Castrucci, "Political Division Is Dangerously Defining Our COVID-19 Conversation," *The Hill,* December 17, 2020, https://thehill.com/opinion/healthcare/530554-political-division-is -dangerously-defining-our-covid-19-conversation.

rampant harshness that pervades public discourse—particularly on the political and policy side of public relations.

The greatest threat to America's future isn't Chinese expansion or a nuclear Iran. The real threat . . . is us. Our greatest strength historically—that "We the People" share a common goal, idea, and even a national dream—is now a glaring weakness, as we stretch and fray the ties that once bound us together.

Welcome to the Era of Indignation.

As Alexander Hamilton taught the fledgling nation though the *Federalist Papers* 220 years ago, democracy is designed for debate. The essence of politics *is* division because issues of life, liberty, and the pursuit of happiness matter. We forget that Hamilton, Madison, and even Jefferson weren't always so civil, and it's hard to imagine today how a vice president would ever challenge a treasury secretary to a duel, but our Founding Fathers were engaged in the birth of a free and independent nation back then, not battling over food stamps or foreign aid. It isn't just healthy, it is *essential* to argue and disagree on pressing issues with those who see the world differently than you do. That's at the core of what makes America, America. The problem is that we are now weaponizing words.

We resent those who label us, even as we do it unthinkingly to others. The Left is "stupid." The Right is "evil." We've become a nation of insult comics, but there's nothing funny about what we say, or what we mean. Ask people how they feel, and they'll tell you "forgotten" and "ignored." We resent elites who have a platform, so we seek to tear it down. The mission of too many practitioners is to use words to elicit emotional pain, the same pain that has been building up for so long inside the people they wish to influence.

Today, too many Americans view those who disagree with them as enemies rather than mere opponents—as genuine threats to what we individually hold most dear. Everyone wants to "be understood," but no one wants to "try to understand." The pithy put-down is preferred to information, explanation, and education. Thank you, Twitter.

But the challenge to the effective art of public relations is even more dire, as we are increasingly unable to agree on common meanings for common words.

For example, I asked a focus group of Democrats and Republicans in Orlando, "Is America exceptional?" Almost all of the Republicans said yes, along with half of the Democrats. Good news, right? A starting point! Agreeing on "exceptional" means that we have at least *something* in common.

Wrong. We *think* we agree, but we don't.

Your responsibility as public relations practitioners, and my job as a pollster, is to dig deeper, to understand what "exceptional" really means. Otherwise, it's just a word—an empty vessel. As it turns out, the same word means very different things to very different people.

To Republicans, "exceptional" is a full-throated rallying cry, delivered with a fist in the air. It means that we are the best—that shining city on a hill, a beacon of hope. The greatest nation in the world; an example for other nations to follow.

To Democrats, "exceptional" does not mean that we are greater compared to other places, because lots of other places (and people) are also great. It means there are things about America that they love—freedom, opportunity, individual rights—that make America great, but not necessarily great-er. The difference between the definitions—and the implications that difference carries—is vast.

As the PR industry has come to realize the hard way, common words no longer have common meaning—even when we think they do. To paraphrase (or mangle) Churchill, we really are two different Americas, divided by a common language. We can't agree on common words. We can't agree on common goals. It feels like a divorce proceeding, where both spouses are fighting over who gets to keep the house . . . which, in this case, just happens to be a nation that we all share. The difference is, neither side is moving out. We're going to have to find a way to make it work. Together.

So what does this all mean to the world of public relations?

Too many Americans have only two approaches when someone disagrees with them: either offend them or unfriend them. All too often, thanks to social media, it's offend and *then* unfriend.

For PR executives, social media has become a booming profit center, with endless vehicles to spread their endless messages. But social media separates us from the *very* real consequences of our words. It desensitizes us. De-*humanizes* us. No one stops to consider how the person on the other end of the app might feel. We say things to people online that would risk a slap across the face in the real world. And in the absence of that risk, we become reckless.

Worse still, this phenomenon of carefully curated newsfeeds is creating echo chambers everywhere that are silos—bunkers—impenetrable to reason and empty of empathy. Think about it: How do you educate your audience to your client or their point of view if no one is listening? How do you change minds that are already made up? No less a figure than Mark Zuckerberg has acknowledged the challenge, yet even he is unclear about how to respond to it.

We are living through yet another Me Generation moment. The intellectual curiosity that once propelled the country has been replaced by a myopic perspective. The problem: social media has democratized and diffused communication at *exactly* the same moment as we demand to be heard. Google Analytics shows that we are ever more likely to use "I" and "me," rather than "we" or "us." So, is it any surprise that we are losing sight of *how* to talk to each other?

In today's hypersensitive world, experts are often dismissed and facts have evolved from *stubborn* to *subjective*. Any fact introduced by the "other side" is hand-waved away as biased, misleading, or self-serving. The ad hominem attack reigns supreme. Even something as simple as counting people at a presidential inauguration is now open for debate, despite clear photo evidence.

But if we can't even agree on facts or photos, how can we ever have a productive public discussion? When does this merry-go-round stop? It stops when we truly, finally, start *listening* to each other. When we "do the hard thing," as John Kennedy said, and when we "lower our voices . . . that we might learn from one another," in the words of his rival Richard Nixon. If they can find common ground, anyone can.

I'm best known for live digital research, where participants use a handheld remote device to express their agreement or disagreement with a speaker on a word-by-word basis. We measure reactions on a 0 (awful) to 100 (perfection) scale. Anything over a 70 is good, and over an 80 is great. It works splendidly for presidential debates, State of the Union Addresses, town halls, live interviews, and more.

In my ongoing research to understand the craft of message dissemination, one of the most impactful statements was from Nebraska senator Ben Sasse in 2017:

> *We have a risk of getting to a place where we don't have shared public facts. A republic will not work if we don't have shared facts. I'm the third most conservative guy in the Senate by voting record, but I sit in [Democrat] Patrick Moynihan's desk on the floor of the US Senate on purpose. Because he's the author of that famous quote that you're entitled to your own opinions, but you're not entitled to your own facts. The only way the republic can work is if we come together and we defend each other's rights to say things that we differ about, we defend each other's rights to publish journalism and pieces and things that we then want to argue about.*

By the end of his statement, the dial score was 94 out of 100 among Democrats and 90 out of 100 among Republicans. That represents the top 1 percent of all communication. It scored so well because of the example it set: a Republican senator commending a luminary Democratic senator on a principle that *all* Americans should share. It's a beacon of light for an America darkened by division and distrust. Senator Sasse is one of the few elected officials who talks like this—and perhaps the only one talking *about* it as well.

But the problem remains with our fact-less future: If we can't agree on something so simple, how can we agree on *anything* at all?

And thanks to unbridled cynicism among opinion makers and shapers in the media and academia, the craft of public relations has been reduced to pithy "sound bites" created by "spinmeisters" and uttered by "gun-for-hire flacks."

The problem with that narrative is that it is simply not true. From the icy-cold "bucket challenge" that raised over $160 million for ALS, to the #MeToo and #TimesUp movements that upended casting rooms and boardrooms across America, to Black Lives Matter and its transformation of American society, the art and science of public relations has had a bigger and more positive impact on how we work and live than the journalists who write about it and the academics who criticize it.

It's just not as simple as who, what, where, when, and why. Effective public relations is built on communication that is both credible and impactful. Corporations and organizations have learned the hard way that they can't just say something and have it believed. Conversely, many organizational leaders and the causes they champion have suffered because what they say has no relevance or believability.

With that in mind, let's take a microscope to the most important public relations effort of our time: surviving and overcoming COVID-19. The language behind the coronavirus pandemic (always call it a pandemic—it's seen as more significant and serious) is a perfect case study of applying the power of words to influence public behavior constructively.

Thanks to an innovative way to apply polling to message development, we were able to prove the theory that simply changing the way America's political and public health leaders talk about the pandemic could profoundly inspire the behavior changes needed to help eliminate COVID-19. Using the right words at the right time could restore public trust, improve compliance with public health safety protocols (yes, call them protocols), prevent deaths, and ultimately get our lives and our economy (in that order) back to normal.

To be clear, polarizing, combative rhetoric is what brought our nation to where it was during the pandemic. And until someone applies the skills and talents of public relations to develop the right messaging, we simply will not close the divides that have erupted across every possible demographic and attitudinal fault line. But just as language has driven our divide, so a new lexicon may be our most valuable tool. Our research in December 2020 offered four critical insights about how our leaders could have improved the way they talked about the pandemic and how, in turn, America could have taken the steps required to eliminate COVID-19 in the United States so much faster and earlier—sparing hundreds of thousands of lives.

Here is what we learned and wrote just days before vaccines became available:

First, we need to balance our language between health and the economy. To no one's surprise, Republican voters are much more skeptical of the virus and its impact than Democratic voters or the broader public. Republicans are also much more hostile about the need for additional "lockdowns" (please call them "stay-at-home protocols") and their significant impact on the economy. Only 12 percent of Democratic voters prioritize the national economy over the health and safety of the nation, compared to 51 percent of Republican voters.

We have been stuck debating this false dichotomy between fighting the virus or supporting the economy since the pandemic began. It is a false choice that has failed to serve the interests of either side. We must protect not only our physical, but also our economic well-being. We need to continually balance our language between the economy and health. While health is more persuasive, ignoring economic anxiety ignores the voices of roughly 40 percent of Americans for whom this is their primary concern—in some cases a crippling one. Messages should emphasize that following public health protocols will help to avoid severe limits and restrictions, and that will speed up the return to a healthy, inclusive economy.

Second, it's time for politicians (and politics) to step aside. Political leaders have been dominating the airwaves and the briefing rooms. Yet, despite their best efforts, the words and phrases they've embraced are missing the mark, failing to motivate millions of Americans who still do not realize their lives and the lives of their families are in jeopardy.

The problem is not just what they say but who they are. If you're an elected official, you are immediately tainted. Everyone is watching and listening for some partisan bias. Don't taint the research and science by sharing it through a partisan lens.

Americans trust recommendations from medical and public health officials above everyone else specifically because their opinions are shaped by science, not politics. Thirty-five percent of respondents believe COVID decisions should come from the nation's highest-ranking medical and public health officials, followed by

28 percent who want their state officials to make those decisions. Whenever we can inject local control into the conversation—and mean it—it will bolster our efforts. People simply have more faith in public health experts delivering localized solutions.

Conversely, only 20 percent said they trust elected officials. It would be far better for all of us if they stood in the background and let the experts do their jobs both publicly and privately. And if they must speak, everything they say should be fact based and decidedly neutral, with absolutely no hint of politics.

As for healthcare CEOs, they've made the media rounds championing their corporate successes. It would be far better for them, their shareholders, and all of us if they took a back seat and let their chief scientists and researchers speak for them. The CEOs are seen as about profit. The scientists and researchers they employ are about us.

Third, voters are interested in supporting leaders for acting on COVID. Only 7 percent of swing voters and 11 percent of Republican voters say they would be less likely to vote for a member of Congress who encouraged people to take steps to stop the spread of COVID-19 (on November 27, 2020, shortly before this was written, the US had just confirmed its two hundred thousandth case). Elected leaders must come to together to pass legislation and make funding available to support our nation's efforts to eradicate COVID-19, realizing it will be an electoral boon, not a bust, across the political spectrum.

Fourth, we need to give people a reason to comply with public health protocols beyond the fact that it's good for them. We need to make COVID-19 tangible by individualizing, personalizing, and humanizing the "pandemic" ("coronavirus" does exactly the opposite). Before talking about reopening the economy and schools, start by emphasizing the shared goal of "returning to normal." That's what Americans really want. The economy is about others. Returning to normal is about us.

We also need to speak to the consequences of failure. For example, Democrats (40 percent) and Republicans (35 percent) agree that COVID-19 is highly infectious, and both are compelled by the statement that one infection can quickly grow into an outbreak that could shutter a neighborhood, a community, or an entire city. Everyone wants "a safe and sensible path forward." And while not everyone agrees that proper behavior is a "national duty," the red and blue states share a belief in and commitment to "personal responsibility."

Elected leaders also must follow the guidance that they promote or risk undermining those efforts. Governors, mayors, and other elected officials are not following their own advice by choosing to dine indoors or travel during Thanksgiving.

This hypocrisy is fodder for pandemic skeptics. Eliminating COVID-19 will take sacrifices—remaining distant from family, avoiding activities we enjoy and that are central to our lives—from all of us. To ask this of the American public means that everyone must take personal responsibility. "Do as I say but not as I do" will perpetuate the pandemic and cost lives.

We all have a part to play in eliminating COVID-19, but we will not work together until we have language that brings us together. If we can all incorporate these simple tips, whether we are talking on the nightly news, posting on social media, or meeting a friend for a socially distanced coffee, we will each be doing our part to eliminate COVID-19 and return to normal.

As you can see from this chart of COVID words to use and lose, every public relations effort requires its own lexicon. For COVID-19, it was essential that health and safety lead the messaging because that was the most important public priority, not the speed of treatments or the eventual vaccine. Similarly, any reference to or empowerment of the government would immediately draw a negative reaction from Republicans and conservatives. That explains why "government lockdowns" was so unpopular a term and why it was necessary to promote "public health" agencies rather than "government" agencies. It's not just knowing what words to use. It's also knowing what words to lose.

COVID WORDS TO USE & LOSE

Words to USE	Words to LOSE
the pandemic	the coronavirus
eliminate/eradicate the virus	defeat/crush/knock out the virus
social distancing	physical distancing
an effective/safe vaccine	a vaccine developed quickly
protocols	orders/imperatives/decrees
face masks	facial coverings
essential workers	frontline workers
personal responsibility	national duty
a stay-at-home order	a government lockdown/shutdown
public health agencies	government health agencies

■ ■ ■

The first half of this chapter focused on the interconnected worlds of public relations, policy, and politics, and the myriad challenges facing PR executives trying to navigate the stormy seas of an unmoored population. But an equally powerful challenge to the PR community originates from the business and corporate world, as more and more people reject the morality of profits over people and the vast incomes of the economic elite.

The causes of public frustration are numerous:

- CEOs declaring million-dollar bonuses days after laying off thousands of workers
- Discrimination (age, gender, ethnicity, etc.) in hiring practices that takes a lawsuit to address
- Pages and pages of contracts loaded with hidden fees and/or fine print that no one reads or understands
- Businesses making promises that they have no intention of keeping
- Businesses hiding product errors or glitches from unsuspecting consumers

And thanks to the unholy alliance between camera cell phones and social media, a problem between a single customer and a huge company that would have been covered up a decade ago is now seen by millions almost overnight.

For these reasons, we have spent the last two decades developing a lexicon to help companies navigate the new anti-business environment, minimizing reputational threats and maximizing PR opportunities. Most PR executives do not open their bag of tricks until retirement, but that denies students of public relations the opportunity to see how the profession really operates. The chart below is real. It includes the "21 Words for the 21st Century," a collection of the most impactful words and phrases for almost any business situation.

The Language of Good Business	
Imagine	Peace of mind
Cleaner, safer, healthier	More efficient and effective
Genuine accountability	A problem solver
Real results/Real solutions	Inclusion
Our mission/My commitment	Our first responsibility
Mutual respect	You decide/You deserve
I hear you/I get it	Building a better future
The consequences	You're in control
Together, we can	Fact-based
No fine print/No exceptions, no excuses	Fierce integrity
A meaningful, measurable track record of success	

Of these phrases, there are nine that are particularly powerful and universally accepted:

1. **"Imagine."** The most powerful word in the English language, it communicates endless possibilities. It is also one of the few words that communicates a vision in the minds of everyone who hears it. Ask people to imagine life at perfection and they have as many different visions as there are people—and all of them are accurate because all of them are self-generated. Great PR is both visual and emotional.

2. **"Cleaner, safer, healthier."** Most companies boast about their "sustainable" practices. The problem with that is that it communicates status quo—that the rivers and streams and open spaces will still be around decades from now. But when you tell people that you want "cleanER, safER, healthiER" communities, that says you want to make things bettER.

3. **Inclusion.** This is probably the most controversial recommendation because it represents the single biggest change in language. Every company has a diversity program, but what people truly want is "inclusion." Diversity tells people that someone like them will be represented, but inclusion tells people that everyone is included. Diversity also suggests that there will be winners (the underserved) and losers (white males). With inclusion, everyone wins.

4. **"Fact-based."** With all the accusations about fake news and the political and ideological chasm that has developed, there is a real hunger for the truth. The scientific community has embraced "evidence" as its North Star, but the problem with that term is that it's legalese—evidence for the prosecution and evidence for the defense. A fact stands above evidence. A fact . . . is a fact.

5. **"Peace of Mind."** Most businesses talk about how their products and services give you a sense of "security." But that just means that there's a threat out there from which they are protecting you. If you talk about "peace of mind," that means there are no threats, that you can close your eyes, relax, and not worry.

6. **"A problem solver."** PR executives are learning that the single most important attribute to pitch on behalf of their CEO clients is "a problem solver." It's exactly the opposite of the typical politician, and it's about changing circumstances for the better both individually and collectively. Like the word "imagine," being a problem solver is in the eyes of the beholder—which makes it a universal principle.

7. **"Together, we can."** Ever since Bono created the One campaign, it has been assumed that people want to get behind a single idea, purpose, or cause. The exact opposite is true. The problem with "one" is that people think they have to submerge their personality and/or principles behind a single effort. The reality is that we want to join and unite while still protecting our individuality. That's why "together" is a preferred public relations term.

8. **"No exceptions, no excuses."** The majority of public relations work occurs because clients don't do as they say or as they should. A PR person is then hired to clean up the mess. But when a CEO issues a blanket statement with a "no exceptions, no excuses" declaration, that's the surest way to say "I mean it. I really mean it."

9. **"Mutual respect."** This is the phrase workers most want to hear from their boss and their supervisors. Too often, those in power talk about "tolerance," yet that is considered too minimal by too many people. Similarly, being "valued" sounds too much like you're putting a price tag on the heads of your employees.

■ ■ ■

This chapter has been about the use of public opinion and language in public relations. There is one more essential aspect of PR to explore: the role of the pollster. The work of a good pollster and wordsmith is essential for good public relations. After all, if you don't know what the public thinks, it's pretty hard to promote the three essential attributes of great PR: ideas, influence, and impact. The problem: the polling industry is going through a tremendous upheaval thanks to their inability to measure Donald Trump or his supporters accurately. But it gets even worse. The credibility of political polling over the next decade may have been dealt a fatal blow in the eyes of the public thanks to its failures in 2020. It was incorrect in predicting Donald Trump's margin of loss, incorrect in predicting Democratic control of the Senate, and incorrect in predicting the gains Republicans made in the House of Representatives.

But before venturing further into an autopsy of polling, it's essential that readers understand that polling is not and will never be infallible. Pollsters and those who use polling need to continually educate people about inherent errors in survey research as well as the uncertainty that polls can't detect. Every stakeholder in the political and public relations process—the pollsters themselves, the media, corporate and organizational executives, and even the politicians—needs to do a much better job explaining with easily digestible language how polls are snapshots in time with room for variation and error. In particular, pollsters need to get better at providing the credibility we want, the confidence we need, and the accuracy we deserve in what is perhaps the best—if imperfect—way to measure what the public really thinks.

But even with the faults of polling, pollsters are still essential. When crafting the language to attack, to defend, to promote, or to criticize, listening to people is more important than listening to leaders or the elite. Rebuilding the trust polling has lost with the public starts with humility, honesty, and accountability, which will require time and patience. Our industry needs to reward accuracy and actively seek to learn how we can improve, not summarily dismiss outlier results as partisan hackery. We should hold ourselves to the highest levels of accountability with the public *before* elections occur, not just as a reactionary post-election defense when our polls are off.

There have been an infinite number of essays, analyses, and chronicles about the novel phenomenon of Donald Trump and his supporters, and how the Trumpian rage against political institutions and elites has changed everything. His critique of political polling is particularly harsh. Trump has assailed polls since he descended the golden escalator at Trump Tower, branding them (and media organizations sponsoring them) as tools of the corrupt, elite ruling class that he is fighting against. (Ask yourself: If you are a Trump supporter, why would you ever participate in a process like polling given Trump's claims about the process?)

That's why gauging public opinion accurately is so difficult. Even with the advent of online survey research, it's tougher than ever to get the people you want to answer the questions you need. Many see the institution as rigged and biased—whether it is or isn't—so they will simply refuse to engage. The only way to remedy this is to approach Trump's supporters with absolute contrition and humility. Many polls jump right into the questions without much pretext, identifying themselves as neutral bystanders, or explaining why answering the questions truthfully should be important to them.

That's why I always begin the polls I conduct with an extra paragraph of context right at the start:

Many Americans feel ignored and forgotten. We are grateful for the opportunity to listen and hear from people like you and then share your opinions with elected officials/business leaders who can make a difference in America's future.

Some have criticized this methodology for making the surveys unnecessarily long or seeming inauthentic. To those I say: Be up front that you value and respect participants' voices and perspectives. Explain that their opinion will make a meaningful, measurable impact on their lives and the country, business, or whatever topic you seek to measure.

As for the media, they are also culpable for the mistakes in polling that Americans have endured the last two presidential elections. Not only have their polling units been responsible for many of the incorrect predictions we've witnessed, but their obsession with the "horse race" aspect of the campaign—analyzing who is up and who is down—is malpractice for the national dialogue. One single poll was the basis for an ABC News/*Washington Post* report that said Biden was up 17 points in Wisconsin days before the election, when he actually won by a percentage point! The saturated emphasis on a single poll at a given point in time does not meaningfully educate the public. Rather, the trend in polls over time is what can inform the trajectory of a candidate's performance.

Ultimately, polling is about listening to and understanding the public and the incredible diversity of opinions they hold. Public relations and political polling are imperfect, and their mistakes in 2020 may spell their end. But I am hopeful we can make the necessary changes and find a way to elevate what the public is thinking so their voice can have an impact on making this world a better place for all. This isn't a mea culpa. It's a reflection and a way forward.

And ultimately, public relations requires getting not just the ear of the public but its agreement. For in the end, it's not what you say that matters. It's what they hear.

CHAPTER 5

Preparing the Communications Program

A New Way to Approach a Vital Task

ART GORMLEY
THE DILENSCHNEIDER GROUP

E very chapter in this book is important, but this one—about a disciplined program to tell your story—is absolutely crucial. The approach outlined here is
at the core of delivering results and value to your client—internal (if you're "in
house") or external (if you're with an agency).

When an outside agency or consultant is used to deliver the desired results,
this outline also provides a guide to evaluating the soundness of the plan or program presented to you.

The prerequisites to designing an effective program are defining and understanding your audience, and knowing what will move them to take a desired
action. Because until and unless you do this, you risk wasting time, energy, and

resources. Serious mistakes can ensue. Getting your target right from the outset is well worth the effort.

Over the course of my career, I have worked with many companies, nonprofit organizations, individual entrepreneurs, and other clients who try to reach everyone they possibly can. Such an approach may be the answer if you are aiming at retail consumers, but even consumer audiences can and should be segmented demographically to focus on likely buyers, those that can influence them, and ultimately on the decision makers themselves. Getting directly to the decision maker, if possible, is often the most efficient means of accomplishing the objective.

Let me offer an example of targeting decision makers. I am reminded of a short tale about Jay Pritzker, the man behind Hyatt Hotels, and a billionaire long before it became commonplace. Over the more than thirty-five years Bob Dilenschneider and I have worked together, I have heard him relate the story many times to clients, prospects, and staff. It is an object lesson in focusing on what and who is important.

As the story goes, it took place many years ago, during a taxi ride from Chicago's Loop to O'Hare Airport. Bob is quick to classify Jay Pritzker as one of the smartest businessmen he ever met. On the way to O'Hare, they discussed an opportunity that was to net Pritzker a great deal of money. Bob says he started out "defining" the potential audience—many thousands of people—and talking about how he would go about reaching them.

Back then, on a good day with no traffic, getting to O'Hare could take about thirty-six minutes. By the end of the trip, Pritzker and Bob had narrowed the "audience" to three people. Pritzker did this by asking a series of questions. Who were the *real* decision makers? They were the target.

The two men mapped out a sophisticated plan to reach these three people and, in the next four months, relentlessly followed every step. Pritzker's goal was achieved with almost no wasted effort or expense. Bob has always said that this episode taught him a very valuable lesson about focusing on who and what counts. He has shared the lesson with many.

NOW YOU'RE READY TO DESIGN YOUR PLAN

In preparing a communications program for a client, prospect, or a direct report in a corporate or organizational setting, I recommend that you use the tried-and-true approach that follows. Doing so will help ensure you touch all the bases.

We call the plan **SO SMArTT**, a simple acronym that will help you remember the seven primary elements of the program: Situation, Objectives, Strategies, Messages, Audiences, related Tactics, and Timeline.

There are other points, but these seven mutually supportive areas are the essential elements of any plan or program. I didn't invent them. They have been at the heart of PR planning and execution for many, many decades.

Don't use these elements solely as a crutch. Each element warrants careful thought and consideration. Each should be linked to the other six in a way that supports achieving one or more of the program's objectives.

In the end, the communications program is all about achieving the plan's objectives—a good reason to define these clearly at the outset. So, until the program links all seven elements with no loose ends, you still have work to do.

In the agency business, communications plans are the consultant's stock in trade. Having spent my entire career on the agency side, I've encountered too many so-called communications programs—from competing agencies, I hasten to add—that amount to handing near identical plans to multiple clients/prospects with little more than the names changed.

Lots of agencies do this routinely. Be aware of it, and if you are on the receiving end, judge for yourself how much real thought and effort went into tailoring a proposed program to your organization's specific needs. The program is usually an agency's first opportunity to demonstrate the unique value, creative approach, and sound judgment the account team should bring to an assignment. Judge accordingly. If you are on the client side preparing a program for your direct report, be equally committed to providing a tailored product.

PUTTING THE PLAN TOGETHER USING SO SMArTT PRINCIPLES

Situation

Lead with a simple declarative statement about the overall aspirations of the client, prospect, or organization. This brief statement should capture how the target wants to be to be viewed, perceived, positioned, or distinguished in the minds of those important to its success. Helping achieve these goals is the purpose of your communications plan.

A client or prospect will always know their business far better than you do. That's a given. But the client or prospect may not have a clear understanding of the situation they are facing, be it a challenge or an opportunity. You may have to help clarify the situation. On the whole, though, your role—your expertise—is to provide communications advice and offer solutions.

But to create the right professional impression and demonstrate a thoughtful approach to the assignment, use this section to showcase your grasp of what the client has told you about the situation they face. Replay it for them. Put it all in your objective, third-party perspective, focusing on the communications aspects of what needs to be done to achieve success. Let the client know you understand the desired goal and the issues they face. The client will find this reassuring and gain confidence in your team's ability to get it done.

The same principles apply if you are an organization on the receiving end of a plan, or you are presenting your plan to your organization's internal client. Use the Situation section of the plan to convey a clear understanding of what needs to be achieved and why.

Objectives

Objectives are the central element of any communications program. What do we want to achieve? If we are at point A, as described in the situation, the objectives define point B concisely. It is where we ultimately want to end up.

Program objectives are usually three to five simple declarative statements about what this communications program aims to accomplish. The objectives should be stated in terms of what success will look like. For example: *Establish company/ organization X as the premier source for expert commentary/advice on investing in renewable energy resources.*

Program objectives should be measurable in a way that relates directly to the communications plan being executed. The chosen metric establishes the standard against which your efforts will be measured and judged. For example, this could be one of our metrics: *Take a monthly count of news media mentions of company/ organization X spokespersons providing advice or analysis on the topic of investing in renewable energy resources.*

With a baseline established in month zero, you should be able to demonstrate a steady increase in media mentions over time. If you help your client— internal or external—select and deploy helpful, professional, and *always available* spokespersons, the reporter will call your spokesperson with little or no prodding from you.

Strategies

This is the conceptual framework that you will rely on to achieve the program's objectives. Most plans have multiple strategies. There is some tendency to confuse strategies with tactics. Getting a client media exposure is a tactic. But noting that we will *use management's successful track record to position the company as a leader in its field*—that's a strategy.

Using our renewable energy example, here are some strategies to establish company/organization X as the premier source for expert commentary/advice on investing in renewable energy resources:

1. Mobilize high-profile spokespersons from major environmental groups to endorse company/organization X's great success in directing investment funding to worthy renewable energy projects.
2. Highlight the positive environmental impact, success, and handsome investment returns achieved by renewable energy projects backed by company/organization X.
3. Ensure top management personnel of company/organization X are highly visible and invited to speak at the nation's premier renewable energy conferences.
4. Seek a seat for a top company/organization X executive on the board of a prominent public company that develops major renewable energy projects for the electric utility industry.
5. Arrange for the CEO of company/organization X to attend the Edison Electric Institute (EEI) annual meeting and spend time with a number of the nation's top electric utility executives.

This is by no means a complete list of strategies that could be aligned with the program's objectives. The key to putting such strategies in place rests on ensuring the "ask" represents a sought-after benefit for all parties concerned.

Messages

These are brief, straightforward declarative statements that support the client's positioning. These messages should be integrated consistently into all future communications with key audiences. Statements that do not support a core message dilute or undermine the overall impact of the communications program.

How often must your audience hear a message before they absorb and act upon it? This is often referred to as a message's "effective frequency." In terms of an absolute number, there is much debate on what works best. In researching this point, I found a variety of "rules of thumb," including the "Rule of 7," the "14 Times Rule," and one oft-cited study on effective frequency, attributed to Microsoft, that concluded a message needed to be heard by the listener between six and twenty times before it was acted upon. There were many more iterations, but they all shared one common theme: frequent repetition of a message is essential, and it works.

Another crucial factor in constructing an effective message is the quality of the message itself. What characterizes an effective message? Here, too, a Google search will unearth various answers. In my experience, an effective message shares four traits:

- **Short**
  Be respectful of your audience's attention span. The rules of thumb just cited were written before the explosion of social media. A message needs to be short and written in plain, everyday language. If your message is about to run into a second sentence, think again. A longish message written to showcase your vocabulary skills has little hope of being readily absorbed by your audience. Attention spans have not only gotten shorter, but the volume of messages your audience is exposed to also has grown exponentially. Remember you are fighting for share of mind.

- **Memorable**
  Crafting a truly memorable message is always a challenge. Start by avoiding clichés. Just because you've heard something roll off a spokesperson's tongue countless times does not make it memorable. In time, it becomes background noise to be tuned out and ignored. Think about how your client's work or mission serves the greater good. Challenge your spokesperson to always deliver the message on a personal level. In our renewable energy example, you would prompt your spokesperson to express the client's deep personal determination to promote, finance, and accelerate the transition to renewable energy. Audiences can sense genuine sincerity

and determination. Urge your spokesperson to encourage the audience to empathize with your client's mission. Empathy links your message to an emotion, which helps make it memorable. While it's not possible or appropriate in every instance, consider if there are ways to trigger an emotional response or connection to the message you want to deliver.

- **Positive**

There are always at least two ways to deliver any message—positive or negative. Given a choice, go with a positive message. This is not an exercise in spinning bad news. It is a way of stating what needs to be done in a positive way that brings focus, energy, and—importantly—the right attitude to the message.

Avoid the trap of telling your audience what you will not do. For example, "We will not ignore the tremendous damage fossil fuels do daily to our environment." Compare that with, "We are determined to deliver renewable energy at a scale that is both clean and affordable." In the first instance, we are taking something away from our audience. In the second example, we are providing a competitive clean-power alternative. Which message do you think stands a better chance of resonating with your audience?

- **Relevant**

When was the last time you bothered to read, watch, or listen to a message that wasn't relevant to your needs? Have you sat through a presentation where the presenter was telling you all about watchmaking, when all you wanted was the time of day? I suppose we all have.

There is only one question to ask about a potential message: Is it relevant to the audience I am trying to reach and will it be well received and acted upon?

Forgive the cynicism, but we all live in the world of "what's in it for me?" When you ask your audience to take even a small step to help validate a client's positioning, be prepared to persuade the audience that whatever you are asking them to do also benefits them. In brief, answer the "what's in it for me" question for your audience even before it is asked.

In the next section, we will look at the audiences our alternative energy client needs to reach. But for now, let me leave you with some thoughts about what it takes to create a compelling and relevant message:

1. **Speak the truth:** The truth, as they say, always comes out in the end, so why not start with the truth? If you have any doubts that your message will hold up to public scrutiny over time, avoid that embarrassment. If you have the wrong message, find one that inspires your own confidence. If it does not inspire you, it won't inspire your audience.

2. **Leverage multiple vehicles:** With the explosion of social media, blogs, and the like, the opportunities for message repetition have multiplied. Will the same message fit all available outlets? Not likely. You will have to tailor the message to the medium, but you must preserve its underlying meaning and consistency.

3. **Stick to your talking points:** Do not allow the message to get lost in the medium. Always remember the thought, idea, or action you are trying to elicit, and stay on point. You must be consistent in your positions. Be clear and concise. Don't compromise on key points.

4. **Know your audience:** Relevance is for the audience to judge, not the speaker. All messages must be compelling, timely, and relevant to their target audience. This does not mean you are pandering; your positions and opinions should not be compromised. Keep your focus on your audience and the messages they need to hear.

5. **Consider your critics:** You will not always be surrounded by friends and supporters. It is safe—and wise—to assume that every message you deliver will find its way back into the hands of your worst critics, who will then use your message against you. Proceed accordingly.

Audiences

Name the targets you identified when you started designing this program, in rough order of importance. Remember that, in most instances, the media is not in itself an audience, but rather an effective conduit to those audiences you hope to influence.

When considering your audiences, always keep your plan's objectives top of mind. It is a question of who must receive, believe, share, and act on your message in order to achieve the objectives you initially identified. There certainly are times when your audience may number in the millions. More often, though, the number of decision makers or influencers you actually need to reach and persuade is far smaller. In the Jay Pritzker example, it turned out to be a mere handful.

CASE STUDY

U sing our renewable energy example as a case study, our objective is to position our company/organization as the premier source for expert commentary and advice on investing in renewable energy resources. Compared with marketing a product or service to consumers, the major audiences we need to reach and influence are quite narrow.

Here are four significant audiences that will help us achieve our primary objective, and why:

1. **Environmental news media**

   Concern about climate change, sustainability, and other related topics that fit under the heading of ESG (Environmental, Social, and Governance) issues has fueled an explosion in related coverage, both traditional and social media.

   It is a rare traditional news organization that doesn't have a dedicated reporter, or even a whole news team, covering such issues. Coverage of developments in renewable energy is closely followed by those who invest in renewable energy projects, either outright or through their investments in electric utilities.

   Reporters need knowledgeable, credible, and readily available resources to comment on developments in the field. Making your organization's spokespersons a go-to source for comment on industry developments elevates the organization's name recognition and positions it as the premier source for expert commentary/advice on investing in renewable energy resources.

2. **Industry research analysts and portfolio managers**

   As with the news media, investment firms and institutional investors employ professional teams of research analysts and portfolio managers that specialize in particular industries, such as technology, airlines, or pharmaceuticals. Those who follow electric utilities are your target.

   Globally, there is a societal push toward sustainability and ESG investing. Sometimes characterized as "doing well (financially) by doing good (environmentally)," this puts investments in renewable energy at the forefront of a powerful trend. Creating favorable awareness among those who make or influence these decisions goes hand in hand with positioning your organization as an expert source among investment decision makers.

Several prominent firms have emerged to provide ESG scores that rate and rank individual companies and investment funds against pertinent criteria, such as a company's public progress in reducing its carbon footprint or making a firm commitment to becoming carbon neutral, or—in the case of electric utilities—replacing fossil fuel–fired generation with clean renewable fuels.

This powerful global trend in ESG investing makes your organization's comments on this hot topic worth hearing. Therein lies the opportunity to further your organization's reputation for renewable energy expertise with this key audience.

3. **Utility industry leaders**

Our client wants to be highly regarded by top decision makers in the renewable energy space. This includes those who design, build, and operate solar and wind facilities. The client wants to be seen as an expert advisor and preferred investment partner in financing the considerable cost of these new renewable energy projects.

Public, political, and financial pressures are moving the electric utility industry in the direction of renewable energy. Most major utility companies now accept that there is an important role for wind and solar in the overall energy mix. With a renewed focus on climate change, pressure to move in the direction of renewables will grow, and that represents an opportunity for our client.

This is where a laser focus on decision makers comes into play. The decision to pursue a renewable energy project, which can involve investments of hundreds of millions or even billions of dollars, rests with top management and boards of directors of the nation's largest electric companies. These companies are invariably investor owned and publicly traded, which means the names and affiliations of each of the company's top management team and board members are publicly available. In other words, it is possible to make an actual list of those you want to reach and influence.

Outside contractors will design and build the new wind or solar facility on the utility company's timetable. Given the enormous size of the capital expenditure, utilities often partner with others to spread the risk and share the returns. That is where our client comes in. They want to be seen as industry experts and preferred partners. They are counting on you and the program you create to raise awareness and elevate their reputation as experts and highly successfully investors in renewable energy.

4. Environmental advocates

Today, every major utility company has a dedicated internal team devoted to working with environmental groups with an eye on eliminating conflicts and finding compromises that both sides can live with. Your client will want to cultivate a constructive relationship with environmental groups generally, but particularly those focused on renewable energy.

As an advocate for greater use of renewable alternatives, your client has a story that should align with the goals of these influential groups. Most are nonprofit organizations, and their leadership and members are very dedicated to the group's cause. They aren't in it for the money. The idea here is for your client to be seen as an ally, advocate, and positive influence on the utility sector for the greater use of renewable energy. In other words, your goals are aligned with their goals.

The way to look at environmental advocates is as a potentially favorable influence on your client's reputation within the renewable energy industry. Where to begin identifying the most important of these groups? The US Environmental Protection Agency website has a series of web pages under the heading "Green Power Partnership" (https://www.epa.gov/greenpower). The website says, "As of the end of calendar year 2020, the more than 700 Partners on this list were collectively using nearly 70 billion kWh of green power annually, equivalent to the electricity use of nearly 6.6 million average American homes." That list, therefore, is potentially a great resource.

Stepping away for a moment from our specific example, the lesson here with audiences is to look beyond the usual suspects in the news media to help your client tell its story directly to the audiences that can help them achieve their desired communications objectives. The news media can be an unguided missile: you tell them your story well and in earnest, but you never know with any certainty how they will choose to play it back to the audience you hope to reach.

Related Tactics

Tactics are the actual public relations, media relations, investor relations, and other activities you will employ to deliver the program's core messages and achieve the plan's objectives. Tactics relate back to the communications strategies developed earlier in the plan. If a given tactic does not align with one or more of the plan's strategies, deliver a core message, and support an objective, it doesn't belong here. Either take the tactic out of the plan or modify your objectives, strategies, and messages to accommodate it.

Always presume you will be presenting your plan to a skeptical audience. Any tactic you recommend must fit the plan's internal rationale. Always be prepared to explain and defend how a recommended tactic will help achieve one or more of the plan's objectives.

The success of any plan will depend on its imaginative execution. But in selling your ideas to a skeptical audience, your plan should represent the pieces of a fine watch, which, properly assembled and aligned, will clearly deliver the time of day.

CASE STUDY

Here are some examples of tactics that relate to the renewable energy example cited previously:

1. **Expert commentary**

   Presenting your spokesperson as an expert begins with an analysis of what print, electronic, or social media outlets best reach your intended audience. The *New York Times*, *Wall Street Journal*, and *USA Today* all have sizable audiences, but which of these carries the greatest weight with those decision makers you are trying to influence? In the case of renewable energy, it may instead (or also) be a narrowly focused trade magazine or environmental news outlet focused on climate change. Create a thorough list of media contact points for all journalists that cover your space. Array them in order of the influence they have on your target audience and focus your outreach efforts accordingly.

   When selecting your spokesperson, look for someone with a warm, outgoing personality who media contacts will find easy to like, talk to, admire, and respect. Experts by definition must have the proper credentials. Reporters and editors at high-profile media prefer sources with the right initials after their name (PhD, MD, MBA, etc.). Having the right "school tie" likewise opens doors. A graduate—or, better still, a current or former faculty member—from Harvard, Stanford, Yale, Princeton, MIT, Caltech, and the like confers instant credibility. It depends on the discipline, but an affiliation with a big-name school carries added weight. Long government service—the voice of a former elected or appointed official—also confers recognition and adds greater instant authority to their remarks. Using a current or former industry heavyweight as a spokesperson can add extra value; they are very likely to already have the kind of media relationships you hope to develop.

   Media outreach is tedious but necessary work. It takes persistence, and your spokesperson must offer something unique. Contrary opinions help a journalist tell both sides of a story. But what is even better is solid data on a subject of interest to a reporter's audience—a study, an analysis, or a whitepaper, for instance.

There is one quality that can trump all others: simply being available when a reporter calls on deadline. A spokesperson may get one call back, but they won't get two. If a reporter needs an expert quote to put a story to bed, they will call or text everyone in their contacts file until someone responds. Granted, except at the largest of organizations, spokespersons have other responsibilities, and reporters understand that they cannot always be reached. But reporters *will* remember who saved the day. So, emphasize for your client that members of the media will quickly learn which spokespersons they can count on—*those* are the ones they will call repeatedly.

2. Third-party endorsements

It is important for your renewable energy client to establish a reputation as a recognized expert in their field. Gaining endorsement for your spokesperson's expertise and professional credentials, as just noted, is a basic starting point. But such an endorsement is infinitely more powerful and credible when recognition of their expertise comes from an independent third party. Therefore, look for a noted expert who is already a recognized source for specialty reporters or media that cover renewable energy.

Identify the most frequently cited sources, then help your client create a personal relationship with as many as possible. This might be as simple as sending periodic notes to the targeted expert to support their comments on the subject and offer your client's input. Target an expert whose perspective differs from what your spokesperson brings to the subject. You will want them to view your spokesperson as an ally, not a competitor.

As the relationship deepens, have your spokesperson suggest to the targeted expert that he or she share the spokesperson's contact points with the media. Ultimately, your spokesperson should seek introductions to others in the expert's network of renewable energy supporters. Another way to leverage the relationship may be to ask the expert to let his or her media contacts know your spokesperson can offer a valuable perspective on renewable energy (e.g., its financial impact). To move things in that direction, your spokesperson can remind the targeted expert that increasing reliance on renewable energy is paramount, but the benefits will not be forthcoming unless investors see the financial benefit that flows from their backing a renewable energy project. That is the valuable added perspective your spokesperson brings to the renewable energy story, and it's why the targeted expert should make the introductions.

Relationship building of this kind can take time. But it will help your spokesperson become part of the "club" of experts that media rely on. It will also create other opportunities, like those that follow, to expand your spokesperson's personal network of industry contacts.

3. Speaking Opportunities

Assuming a return to pre-pandemic in-person business opportunities, consider the speaking and networking opportunities that industry and professional conferences can provide as effective program tactics.

Every industry used to (and, we hope, will again) host conferences that gathered industry leaders to discuss the issues and opportunities facing the industry in the period ahead. These meetings feature keynote speakers from the top ranks of their field, as well as speaking and panelist opportunities for you to explore on your spokesperson's behalf. Smart public relations professionals know how to use such conferences as opportunities to create visibility for their client and enhance their spokespersons' reputation as an important player in the space. These opportunities need good advance work, as conference organizers typically began accepting recommendations for panelists and roundtable participants six to twelve months in advance.

Industry media also typically attend these events. Ahead of time, you would have identified reporters your spokesperson has spoken with, singled them out for brief face-to-face meetings, and ensured that your spokesperson was armed with something of interest to reporters.

Another opportunity that in-person conferences present: many companies rent hospitality suites and invite important guests for dinner or drinks. There is plenty of competition here for the most high-profile participants. One way to increase your chances of getting your top invitees to attend your private gathering is to arrange for an industry "headliner" to be your dinner speaker and drawing card.

Let's focus again on our renewable energy case study. For the electric utility industry, the premier event of every year has been the annual gathering of the EEI, which in a year of in-person events would typically host more than four thousand utility industry executives and industry suppliers. For those in the business of investing in and financing renewable energy facilities, it has been a must-attend, multiday event. With typically only a handful of keynote opportunities, EEI also included a number of special sections devoted to different major areas of the industry, with panel discussions, luncheon speakers, roundtables, and so forth on each area of emphasis—all ripe for showcasing your client spokesperson's reputation.

4. Establishing a Web Presence

Saying someone "wrote the book on it" has long meant they were recognized as the foremost expert on a particular subject. Today, however, bound books have largely been replaced by interactive websites as the top information provider and expert resource. In our example, you want your client's website to be the go-to site for information on the benefits—environmental and financial—and value of investing in renewable energy. The website would focus on the superior financial returns that your client's investors have realized from wind and solar projects they helped to finance. As impressive as that is, the information available on the site should go further to support and highlight the environmental and other benefits of renewable energy as the fuel of the future. For instance, ESG concerns and sustainability have become focal points of impact investing, which concerned institutional investors look for as a must-have benchmark before committing capital to a project. To address this point, you might supplement the website with a more compact PDF brochure that makes the same compelling points about investing in the future of clean energy.

Other good programming tactics? Many universities and private institutions have speakers' programs that can be explored for potential opportunities to get your client's message out in a controlled environment. Speeches can be reproduced physically or electronically on the university's or another institution's letterhead or website. The speech, with the university's imprimatur, can be circulated to your client spokesperson's contact lists.

Editorial articles ("op-eds") and letters to the editor represent two additional controlled opportunities to communicate your client's message. Op-eds demand a compelling point of view, often on a matter of some controversy or disagreement, but they get noticed by decision makers. Letters to the editor can comment positively or negatively on a news story, editorial point of view, or position expressed by the publication. There is a lot of competition for space on the editorial page, so there is no guarantee of placement. But I have seen both methods used, even in unpublished form, to communicate with a specific audience (e.g., employees). All that is required is a prominent notation that reads, for example, "As Submitted to the *New York Times*."

This is by no means an exhaustive list of potential communication tactics. Finding new and different ways to communicate your client's message is limited only by your creativity and imagination. The only thing you need to ask is, will this new approach help achieve the program's communications objectives?

Timeline

This section of the plan contains "next steps" to give the client a sense of the order and time frame in which you will execute the tactical elements. Steps can run the gamut from the approximate to the precise: anything from a general statement about timing, to a detailed Excel spreadsheet with a week-by-week schedule of activities.

Firmly stating to a client what steps come next is crucial to closing the sale and getting any program approved. As you present the plan to your client—internal or external—be prepared to tell your audience what you will do to kick this plan off to a fast start. List the first three to five things that will happen immediately after you get a green light to proceed. In terms of the time frame, these should be action steps that you can launch within the first ten days of an engagement.

The activities reflected in your plan should have a cadence. Successfully communicating your ideas is a building process. Allow your audience to visualize the timeline and the path your plan lays out to achieve success. Make sure there are some early milestones that your audience can relate to and look forward to achieving.

Likewise, clarify the order in which the plan should be executed. While many activities can be pursued concurrently and independently, others will need to build on a foundation established by the successful completion of earlier steps. Point out that achieving early success and then building on that success creates a sense of forward momentum that will propel the plan forward.

For instance, in our renewable energy example, before we can expect any prominent environmental groups to endorse the client, we must

- select a qualified, credentialed spokesperson;
- train them to deliver the client's message effectively;
- document the client's successful track record for investing in renewable energy;
- establish a mutuality of interest with the targeted group (e.g., reducing CO_2 emissions); and
- arrange for a suitable introduction to the group by a trusted environmental ally.

Look for ways to compress this process, if possible, but note that building relationships and trust, whether with customers, employees, regulations, media, or potential allies, will take some time.

AND DON'T FORGET

There are two final elements that you can't shy away from if you want your communications plan to be accepted. Call them "brass tacks"—details of immediate practical importance, according to the dictionary definition.

Measurement

This section of the communications program outlines how progress will be measured against the plan's objectives. For example, if the objective is to change perceptions, then measure progress directly, by surveying the target audience, or indirectly, by tracking changes in the views the target audience expresses. Avoid using arbitrary deliverables as a measuring stick. Knowing the number of media hits, completed interviews, program steps accomplished, and so forth is useful, but does not measure actual progress against a given objective.

The Quality of Your In-Person Presentation

Assuming you are presenting your program in person (which may mean via Zoom!), these details are key:

- Do not rely solely on your slide deck. What if it goes down? Rehearse until you know your presentation so well that you can convey the details without any visual aids.
- Plan the presentation and its timing carefully. Do not waste you audience's time or your opportunity to sell your ideas. Factor in enough time for Q&A, a further opportunity to connect with your audience.
- Chemistry counts. If possible, know who will be in the room and the background of each person. Look for something that connects you personally to one or more of the decision makers. Assign speaking roles to all present. If someone on your team has nothing to add to the presentation, leave them home.
- Your audience will be weighing your ideas right along with your conviction and enthusiasm for them, as well as your and your team's ability to achieve the plan's objectives. A good presentation coach will tell you that every presentation is a performance. Keep that in mind as you and your team present your plan to deliver the solution your audience has been waiting for.

TAKEAWAYS

1. The first step in communications planning is to identify your audience. Know what people and groups make up that audience, and what you want them to do.

2. Memorize the simple acronym SO SMArTT so you can easily remember the seven primary elements of an effective program: Situation, Objectives, Strategies, Messages, Audiences, related Tactics, and Timeline.

3. Know the overall aspirations of the client, prospect, or organization. How do they want to be viewed, perceived, positioned, or distinguished in the minds of those important to their success? Helping them to achieve these goals is the purpose of your communications plan.

4. Communications program objectives should be stated in terms of what success will look like. They should be measurable in a way that relates directly to the communications plan being executed.

5. Strategy is the conceptual framework that you rely on to achieve your program's objectives. Most plans have multiple strategies. Take care not to confuse strategies with tactics.

6. Messages are brief, straightforward declarative statements that support the client's positioning. These messages should be integrated consistently into all communications with key audiences. Statements that do not support a core message will dilute or undermine the overall impact of the communications program. Messages should be short, memorable, positive, and relevant.

7. I'll repeat the importance of audience here: all program elements should be frequently checked to make sure they are directed at the proper target.

8. Specific actions and a schedule round out the communications program, along with measurement metrics.

CHAPTER 6

Government Relations

Setting a Public Policy Agenda

———

EDWARD ROLLINS
POLITICAL ANALYST
AND
JONATHAN DEDMON
THE DILENSCHNEIDER GROUP

Why has government been instituted at all? Because the passions of man will not conform to the dictates of reason and justice without restraint.

—Alexander Hamilton

Experience hath shown, that even under the best forms of government those entrusted with power have, in time, and by slow operations, perverted it into tyranny.

—Thomas Jefferson

Whatever your political viewpoint, whether small government or a greater government role, the fact is that government today touches virtually every aspect of our lives. Consider the following:

- The federal government alone has more than 2 million workers. And that does not include 1.4 million in active military service, almost 1 million reserves, and 800,000 postal workers.
- There are some 16 million state and local government workers, including 3.5 million full-time and part-time primary and secondary public school teachers.
- It's estimated that government employees comprise 15 percent of the total workforce.

Government relations means what it says and also suggests: managing an organization's relationships with federal, state, and local governments to mitigate risk and, ideally, create business opportunities.

"Public affairs" is a term frequently used in the same way, but is generally considered a broader category that incorporates government-relations activities with public policy advocacy, public relations, and multiple strategies to affect government decisions.

According to the Public Affairs Council, a leading organization of public affairs professionals, successful government relations and public affairs involve "educating policy makers about issues, alerting clients and senior management to legislative risks and opportunities, and lobbying to ensure that company views are reflecting in policy debates and outcomes."

Needless to say, any successful organization needs to manage its relationships with the government. We will address how to do so successfully.

THE KEY COMPONENTS FOR SUCCESS

A successful government relations program has several key components:

1. Research
   - Issues analysis, prioritization
   - Key leaders, opinion leaders, and influencers

2. Monitoring
    - Legislation
    - Regulatory action
    - Public opinion
    - Media
3. Objectives
4. Strategy (organizing the effort)
5. Messaging
6. Tactics
    - Direct contact with decision makers/lobbying
    - Coalition building
    - Grassroots
    - Communications and public relations
7. Politics and elections—"where the rubber meets the road"
8. Careers in government relations

RESEARCH—ISSUES ANALYSIS, PRIORITIZATION

All organizations need to identify the major issues affecting their organizations and the government's role in addressing them. We could fill an entire book just listing the possibilities, so let us just use McDonald's as an example of the types of potential government issues with which they have had to, and continue to, contend:

- Obesity and health—remember *Super Size Me*?
- Wages for restaurant workers and farm workers
- Animal welfare and husbandry, such as factory farms
- Human rights, such as in China, where the company has some 3,400 restaurants and was a major sponsor of the Olympics there in 2008
- Marketing to children
- Environmental, Social, and Governance commitments

And those are just a start!

What issues pose the greatest governmental, legal, and brand risk? Are there opportunities such as tax credits for R&D, electric vehicles, or a major beneficial infrastructure project?

RESEARCH—KEY LEADERS, OPINION LEADERS, AND INFLUENCERS

Numerous government leaders and entities make major decisions that can affect an organization. These include Congress, executive branch agencies and regulatory bodies, state legislators, governors, mayors, and city councils.

Regarding the federal government in particular, we must always remind ourselves that while there are thousands of people in Washington, DC, with big jobs, big offices, fancy titles, and enormous prestige, only 537 have real power. They are the ones sent here by the voters—the president, the vice president, 100 senators, and 435 representatives. Even members of the Supreme Court, the apex of our third branch of government, are appointed to their lifelong positions by presidents chosen by voters.

Underlying these individuals is a large but important bureaucracy; sometimes for better, sometimes for worse. There are 15 cabinet positions, led by the president's appointed secretaries and confirmed by the Senate. In addition to the cabinet, the US government manual lists 96 independent executive agencies and 220 components of the executive departments.

And while Congress passes laws, it is important to remember that it is the executive branch and quasi-independent federal agencies that develop the rules to implement them.

Rule-making authorities can include cabinet-level agencies such as the Environmental Protection Agency, or independent agencies such as the Securities and Exchange Commission, Federal Trade Commission, and Federal Communications Commission. In many ways, these agencies and the executive branch can be more important in determining a policy than the legislation enacting it.

Typically, then, who should be on the government relations radar? It varies with the issue, of course, but can include:

- The US president, vice president, and cabinet secretaries and departments
- The leadership of key Senate and House committees
- Members of key government agencies and commissions
- Governors and state legislators
- Mayors and city councils
- Third-party experts and influencers on a particular issue
- Special interest groups and nongovernmental organizations

Let's take banks as an example. High on their radar screens would be:

- The Treasury Department
- The chair and ranking members of the Senate Banking, Housing, and Urban Affairs Committee and House Financial Services Committee
- The President's Council of Economic Advisers
- The Financial Stability Oversight Council
- The Consumer Financial Protection Bureau
- Leading economists, academics, think tanks, and former government banking and finance officials
- Lending, housing, economic development, and other advocacy groups

A word about the federal government as it relates to business organizations. At the end of the day, what businesses want from Washington is transparency and a level of certainty so they can develop long-range plans. What they often get, however, is chaos. As decision makers, many business leaders can't understand the inability to get things done.

Most business leaders look at the federal government in Washington, DC, as an entity that can help them a little or hurt them a lot. And unfortunately, business doesn't have many friends in either party. While the Republican Party has historically been more favorable to business, in recent years it has become more populist and anti-establishment.

MONITORING—LEGISLATION, REGULATORY ACTION, PUBLIC OPINION, AND MEDIA

Critical to successful government relations is the monitoring of potential government actions on issues of importance to the organization. This begins with potential legislation at the federal, state, and local levels. As noted, key government agencies and regulatory bodies with rule-making authority can also significantly affect an organization; they need to be monitored as well.

Achieving success in government relations requires a good understanding of public opinion. There are several ways to measure this:

- Numerous weekly polls on a wide variety of topics and issues can be important identifiers of trends and attitudes. Note that in the wake of several recent presidential elections, polls have come under increased criticism for not accurately predicting the winner or the margin of victory. However, there wouldn't be so many polls if they didn't have proven value. Note also that polls represent only a snapshot of opinion at one point in time, which is why political campaigns continue to poll right up until an election. Last, the quality of polls and polling firms varies significantly. Two gold standards are the nonpartisan Pew Research Center and the National Opinion Research Center at the University of Chicago. But there are other good polling firms as well.

- Focus groups are another technique to identify public attitudes. Roughly ten to twenty people are questioned by a moderator on a variety of topics related to an issue. While not quantitative, focus groups can provide deeper insights into views and attitudes than polling, as well as the strength and depth of those attitudes.

- The media also can provide significant insights into public opinion. What topics are getting the most attention? Who are the public opinion leaders on those topics? What are editorial pages and columnists writing about those topics? Obviously they will be different on the *Wall Street Journal*'s editorial pages versus the *New York Times*'s.

OBJECTIVES

It is important, early on, to identify the ultimate objective of your government relations program: to minimize legal and regulatory risk to an organization and/or risk to its brand or industry.

Some examples include:

- Ride-hailing services Uber and Lyft successfully fought a California proposal to make their drivers employees, a move that would have significantly increased the companies' costs.

- The National Rifle Association successfully passed legislation in Congress that shields gun manufacturers and dealers from legal liability when their guns are used in crimes.

- Thousands of American companies have sought waivers from tariffs on Chinese imports in certain industries.

- Boeing had to undertake a multi-year government relations effort to be able to fly its 737 MAX again after it was involved in two major air disasters. It still had to pay $2.5 billion in fines for misleading the Federal Aviation Administration.

STRATEGY

The next and probably most critical step is developing the strategy to achieve your objectives. What specific tactics will you use to reach your goals? How will the strategy be organized between resources inside and outside the organization? Is the right approach to communicate directly with decision makers, or to build a coalition and grassroots efforts? How much will need to be spent, in terms of both dollars and political capital? To what extent does your organization take the lead versus others, such as your industry trade association (if there is one)?

MESSAGING

A critical component to success is having a strong and compelling message. There is much agreement on the key elements to successful messaging. Strong message components should:

- Be simple and memorable. "Just Do It" . . . "Make America Great Again" . . . "The New Deal."
- Be emotionally based, perhaps counterintuitively so—don't be overreliant on logic and facts. Consider a message from the campaign of Ronald Reagan, the "Great Communicator," in his 1984 bid for reelection: "It's morning again in America," which positively compared the first Reagan term with the stagflation of the preceding Carter administration.
- Tap into values shared with the audience. For each sale, online sock and T-shirt seller Bombas donates a pair of socks and a T-shirt to homeless shelters and organizations addressing homelessness. So far, Bombas has donated some 45 million items.
- Speak directly to the experiences of the target audience. Once again turning to Ronald Reagan, in his sole debate with President Carter, he closed by asking, "Are you better off than you were four years ago?"
- Talk about the benefits to the audience versus various features of the proposition: for example, GEICO's "Fifteen minutes could save you 15 percent or more on car insurance" tagline.
- Have a call to action. What do you want people to think and do?

Smart organizations not only create strong messages, but also regularly test them with target audiences and refine them as needed.

TACTICS

Tactics mean doing what you can with what you have.
**—Saul D. Alinsky, progressive community organizer
and political theorist in the '40s, '50s, and '60s
and author of *Rules for Radicals***

As noted, there are a variety of tactics to execute a government relations strategy or program.

Lobbying

One important tactic is lobbying: direct personal contact with decision makers. Its importance can be seen in the fact that there are some twelve thousand registered lobbyists in the US, and some $3.49 billion was spent on lobbying in 2020, a number that has doubled since 2000.

Why so many and so much? Because lobbying works as part of an overall government relations strategy and plan.

Successful lobbyists spend considerable time developing personal relationships with key decision makers and their staffs, in order to access them on important issues and be in a position to present their case.

Lobbyists come in many forms. They can be lawyers, former legislators and government officials, major political donors, trade associations, and advocacy groups, among many others. Companies can have lobbying capabilities within the organization or hire them from a wide variety of outside practices.

A note on what has been referred to as the "revolving door." This term refers to former government officials who become lobbyists on issues over which they previously had control and/or broad knowledge, based on their government work. (Such lobbyists can command high salaries.) In an effort to stem any conflicts of interest, the federal government, as well as many state and local governments, require "cooling off" periods during which such lobbyists may not lobby their former government colleagues. In the case of US senators and senior administration officials, the cooling-off period is two years. Note also that the federal and many state and local governments require lobbyists to register as such.

An interesting side note on lobbying in conclusion. Legend has it that the word was coined by Ulysses S. Grant while president. As he enjoyed a cigar and brandy at the Willard Hotel, one block from the White House, power brokers would try to buttonhole him in the lobby. Hence Grant called them "lobbyists." While that's a good story, the term actually predates the Civil War. It was probably coined to refer to the lobbies outside of legislative chambers where legislators could be approached. The Grant story nevertheless captures the personal and relationship-based nature of much lobbying.

Coalition Building

In addition to lobbying, another successful government relations strategy is coalition building. It involves finding like-minded allies—individuals and organizations with shared views to grow and enhance the power of your position.

One of the most successful coalitions in recent memory is Mothers Against Drunken Driving (MADD). Founded in 1980 by Candace Lightner, whose thirteen-year-old daughter was killed by a drunk driver, the group now has more than three million members and supporters nationwide, and has partnered with major companies and organizations such as Uber and Lyft, Nationwide Insurance, the NFL, the National Alcohol Beverage Control Association, and General Motors, among others. In terms of how successful a coalition can be, since MADD's founding, drunken-driving deaths have been reduced by 50 percent, saving some 370,000 lives through advocacy, education, and passage of tougher state Driving Under the Influence laws.

A subset of coalitions are industry trade associations, which can serve as effective advocates for specific industries with the government. A good example can be seen in the pharmaceutical industry. Prior to the COVID-19 pandemic, the industry had a major reputational problem with high drug prices. Individual companies did not have the resources to fight the issue alone or to halt some bad actors in the industry who were rapidly raising prices. And frankly, they preferred to remain in the background on the issue, obviously while defending their own pricing regimes. Meanwhile, there were calls at both the federal and state levels to address pricing through legislation, regulation, and even price controls.

As a result, the companies used their trade association, the Pharmaceutical Research Manufacturers of America, to launch a major positive awareness and image marketing campaign, "Go Boldly," about the breakthrough medicines the industry was producing.

One can argue about whether the campaign, which spent tens of millions of dollars in advertising and public relations, was a good government relations strategy. Fortunately for the industry, however, the rapid development of COVID-19 vaccines made pharmaceuticals the only major industry to see its reputation rise, moving up 22 points from 32 percent positive at the beginning of 2020 to 54 percent by the fall of 2020.

Grassroots

I decided to become a community organizer . . . Change won't come from the top, I would say. Change will come from a mobilized grass roots.
—Former president Barack Obama

Grassroots tactics are basically bottom-up-based efforts in which large numbers of ordinary citizens are energized and mobilized over a specific issue. They can significantly alter government and political dynamics.

Grassroots tactics are frequently driven by reaction to one or more specific events. Two examples from two very different political perspectives stand out—the Tea Party and Black Lives Matter.

The Tea Party was a conservative, populist social and political movement that believed there was excessive taxation, regulation, and interference in the private sector under President Barack Obama, setting the stage for President Donald Trump. Like Trump, the group also believed in strong immigration controls.

Its official start can be traced to one CNBC correspondent, Rick Santelli, on February 19, 2009, on the floor of the Chicago Mercantile Exchange. Santelli was upset about federal bailouts under Obama to combat the Great Recession, in particular the Obama administration's mortgage relief plan. Santelli said the plan would "subsidize the losers" and suggested a "tea party." The notion quickly went viral on the internet and created a major political movement.

The result was that Republicans in 2010 picked up sixty-three seats in the House of Representatives, taking control, and also ended the Democrats' veto-proof majority in the Senate.

It's important to realize the Tea Party didn't invent populism and distrust of government. That is as old as the nation itself. But the Tea Party did crystallize the feelings of a large number of Americans in a powerful way. Also note that it contained two qualities of a strong message—simplicity and an emotional appeal by tying the point of view to the Boston Tea Party at the beginning of the American Revolution, as a symbol of freedom.

While coming from a completely different political perspective, Black Lives Matter was a bottom-up movement triggered by several incidents in which White law enforcement officers killed unarmed Blacks.

Black Lives Matter was founded in 2013 by Patrisse Cullors (who first used the #BlackLivesMatter hashtag), Opal Tometi, and Alicia Garza following the acquittal of George Zimmerman, a White civilian, for shooting an unarmed Black youth, Trayvon Martin, in Sanford, Florida. Zimmerman's defense used the state's "stand your ground" law.

More recently, the group has focused on law enforcement killings of Black people, including Breonna Taylor in her home in Louisville, Kentucky; George Floyd in Minneapolis, Minnesota; Eric Garner in New York City; Michael Brown in Ferguson, Missouri; and Laquan McDonald in Chicago, among others.

In 2020, following Floyd's murder, major protests erupted and continued in cities across the US. In June, tens of thousands of protestors gathered at the Lincoln Memorial in Washington to protest George Floyd's death in particular.

The movement led to significant initiatives for police reform, such as bans on chokeholds and no-knock search warrants, and focused national attention on institutional racism.

Once again, note the simplicity and emotional component of the message.

Communications and Public Relations

Any successful government relations program has a strong communications component. As Saul Alinsky notes, "It does not matter what you know about anything if you cannot communicate to your people. In that event you are not even a failure. You're just not there."

Successful communications around government relations has several components:

- An emotional appeal to perceived injustice or inequity.
- A demonstration of shared values with supporters. As mentioned, such shared values could range from racial justice to excessive government spending and regulation or weak borders.
- An ability to create significant visibility of the issue in the media. (For more on media, see chapter eight, "Working with the Media.")
- Major events such as marches, sit-ins, and press conferences.
- Opinion pieces in newspapers, editorial board briefings at those papers, and appearances on cable news.
- Endorsements from important third parties such as academics, think tanks, industry experts, and authors. Special interest groups with similar goals are also strong third parties.
- Direct communications with government leaders. For instance, many trade associations have programs where they visit the members' representatives once a year to express their views. However, communication with government leaders has to be far more frequent.
- Regular communications to supporters.
- A strong social media presence. Case in point: Chipotle was quick to embrace TikTok after it was introduced and got an astonishing 240 million views for the first video it put on the platform. The second video got 430 million views. (For more on the use of social media, see chapter nine, "Evolving Best Practices for PR Practitioners.")

Let us close this discussion about the importance of communications with one last quote from Alinsky: "Always remember the first rule of power tactics; power is not only what you have but what the enemy thinks you have."

POLITICS AND ELECTIONS—WHERE THE RUBBER MEETS THE ROAD

Politics ain't beanbag.
—Humorist and writer Finley Peter Dunne quoting
his fictional character Mr. Dooley in an 1895 sketch

At the end of the day, governments base their decisions on elections and the politics leading up to them. Given the stakes, it is no wonder that politics and elections are rough-and-tumble endeavors.

For some expert perspective, we turn to this chapter's coauthor, veteran Republican campaign consultant and political advisor Ed Rollins. Rollins has managed numerous campaigns and served as national campaign director for the successful Reagan–Bush ticket in 1984.

In his book, *Bare Knuckles and Back Rooms*, Rollins notes that "modern campaigns are tough on the people who run them, but they're toughest on the candidates themselves. That's why the once-noble profession of politics has had so much trouble attracting—and keeping—good people."

In Rollins's view, a number of factors have led to this situation, including negative advertising and money. "Unlike any other business, in which you try to convince the consumer your product is superior, the essence of campaigning today is winning by destroying the opponent and being the lesser of two evils," he says. It is why candidates spend so much time and money not only on negative ads but also on opposition research, or "oppo," to dig out the worst about opponents.

Why is this happening? Rollins says, "Because it works." He notes that a successful campaign strategy is to "always fire first" and "define your candidate before your opponent does it to you."

The second key driver of electoral success, for better and often worse, is money.

The 2020 election, which was twice as expensive as the last presidential election cycle, saw nine out of the ten most expensive Senate races ever. In the 2020–21 election for two Georgia US Senate seats, campaigns raised and spent some $1 billion in the races eventually won by the two Democratic candidates.

The greatest contributor to the increasing influence of money in politics is the growth of political action committees, or PACs. While there are various types, two prominent ones are Super PACs and Leadership PACs.

In 2010, the US Supreme Court ruled in the case *Citizens United v. Federal Election Commission* that bans on corporate and union spending on independent political action committees were a violation of the First Amendment of the US Constitution barring government interference in free speech. The decision helped spur the rise and increasing importance of Super PACs. Unlike traditional PACs, Super PACs can raise funds from individuals, corporations, unions, and other groups without any legal limit on donation size as long as they don't coordinate with specific candidates or make contributions to party coffers.

But, of course, even without coordination, it is easy to align with a candidate and his or her views, so non-coordination is a meaningless distinction.

Rollins notes how PACs are playing increasingly important roles in campaigns, especially enabling special interest groups to "affect campaigns as much as the old ward bosses of Boston and Chicago." While many enter politics with high ideals, *realpolitik* often rules the day and wins.

A WORD ABOUT CAREERS IN GOVERNMENT RELATIONS

If government relations sounds like a career for you, the good news is that there are many paths to entry.

Let's begin with college education. Political science, the discipline that deals with systems of governance and political thought and activities, is one obvious choice for those aspiring to be in government or government relations. In addition, there are a number of excellent master's degree programs in public policy and public affairs at leading universities. These include programs such as:

- The Kennedy School at Harvard
- The Princeton School of Public and International Affairs (formerly the Woodrow Wilson School)
- The Goldman School of Public Policy at the University of California, Berkeley
- The Harris School of Public Policy at the University of Chicago
- The LBJ School of Public Affairs at the University of Texas at Austin
- The John Glenn College of Public Affairs at Ohio State University

There are many more. Such programs can provide a strong base of knowledge and tools for analyzing and addressing public issues of import.

Still another academic option is law school. The American Bar Association reports that there are currently almost thirty thousand attorneys in the District of Columbia, giving it the highest per capita ratio in the country. A large percentage of those lawyers are there to work on government issues, which invariably involve the law. Many DC lawyers are registered lobbyists and often appear before Congress and regulatory agencies. Those disputing laws and regulations often wind up in court, giving another advantage to legal training. According to the Congressional Research Service, in 2021, 144 members of the House (32.7 percent) and 50 Senators (50 percent) hold law degrees.

A MAJOR CAUTION: While academic programs and law school can develop important skills and sets of knowledge, there is no better training than being battle-tested in the real world, particularly in politics and elections.

For those interested in a government relations career, in addition to the academic programs just listed, consider:

- Serving on the staff of a federal, state, or local legislator.
- Serving on an executive branch staff. It doesn't have to be the White House, but can be that of a governor, mayor, or the major departments they lead.
- Volunteer for a campaign. There is no better way to understand the nuts and bolts of how our democracy actually works.
- Volunteer for community advocacy groups where you have an interest, such as healthcare, housing, or economic development.

TAKEAWAYS

1. Working in government can be extremely rewarding but also very challenging and complicated. Unfortunately, there are usually no easy answers for most issues. Many brilliant and hardworking people have come and gone trying to address our nation's needs.
2. New York is still the communications capital of the world. Los Angeles is still home to much of the media and entertainment world. But Washington, DC, is where public policy is made, and it provides the financial resources that drive the policies.
3. Working in or with the government, whether at the federal, state, or local level, is truly a noble calling. As Franklin Roosevelt put it: "Let us never forget that government is ourselves and not an alien power over us. The ultimate rulers of our democracy are not a President and senators and congressmen and government officials, but the voters of this country."

CHAPTER 7

The "New" Investor Relations

Transformational Changes in a High-Profile Discipline

NED RAYNOLDS AND ART GORMLEY
THE DILENSCHNEIDER GROUP

Corporate investor relations (IR) is a communications discipline that serves the information needs of a very specific audience, collectively referred to as the investment or financial community, or just simply "Wall Street." IR's principal role is to ensure the investment community has all the financial and operational information it needs to properly value a company's publicly traded shares.

Why is that important? Because the value of a company's shares determines what it costs to raise additional capital to fund its growth, acquire other companies, and incentivize management. Share price is near and dear to the hearts of senior management. It is a key component by which shareholders and a company's board of directors evaluate and compensate management's performance. This last point gives the IR role a high profile within the corporation.

The in-house IR officer or an IR agency consultant will usually work with the company's CEO and chief financial officer (CFO) in preparing or reviewing many of the documents and activities described in this chapter.

So, if you're the IR officer or consultant for a public company, the accurate, timely information that you issue will affect investors' buy and sell decisions. In turn, the securities markets will reward the company's shares with a full and fair valuation—yes?

In principle, yes, but as a practical matter, it's not so simple. And on top of that, investor relations has changed considerably in recent years.

In the pages that follow, we will examine investor relations today and some of the changes that have transformed the way in which companies can best communicate with investors. Current IR trends include the growth of Investor Days, the use of special purpose acquisition corporations (SPACs) for public offerings, and the burgeoning influence of Environmental, Social, and Governance (ESG) factors on investment decisions.

IR'S GOT RHYTHM

As a company's investor relations program continues year in, year out, there's a rhythm to it.

It's based on a formal reporting system referred to as GAAP (Generally Accepted Accounting Principles), overseen and enforced by the US Securities and Exchange Commission (SEC). It requires a number of mandatory financial disclosures from publicly traded companies, including the quarterly reporting of financial information, together with an audited annual report following the fourth quarter.

An annual form 10-K, together with a proxy statement, must be issued to shareholders. The proxy statement apprises them of the annual shareholders' meeting and certain required information, such as about the board of directors and items they will be asked to vote on by proxy. They do so by mailing back a card with their choices marked on it or voting their proxy electronically. Shareholders may also elect to attend the annual meeting and cast their votes in person.

Additional required filings also include current reports on Form 8-K, generally filed within four business days of the event that triggers the filing; quarterly reports on Form 10-Q, filed with within forty-five days after the end of each of the first three fiscal quarters; and fourth-quarter financial statements on Form 10-K, generally filed within 120 days after the end of the fiscal year.

The quarterly reports are filed with the SEC, but also issued publicly via news release. Investors anxiously await news of financial results, and stock prices may fluctuate in response. Estimates of expected financial results are published by a variety of sources, and the resulting share price movements often track how well actual results square with expectations.

Most public companies also seek to provide investors with relevant information through investor conference calls immediately following the release of earnings. The investors on those calls are usually professional security analysts with either brokerages or financial institutions. These analysts follow a given company rigorously and write influential research reports for their clients. To gain as much insight into the future as possible, analysts will raise challenging questions for company management. (Therefore, management generally scripts its remarks for those presentations and is also well advised to conduct an advance mock question-and-answer session.)

The lineup of speakers on investor calls varies. It most frequently includes the CEO, who handles the "big picture" aspects of the company's performance, and the CFO, who presents the financial information in detail. Additional operating executives may also be present, depending on the company's current situation. The corporate IR executive usually hosts the call and introduces the company's participants.

HOLD AN INVESTOR DAY

Most public companies traditionally present at a number of financial conferences each year, at the invitation of a financial institution or brokerage firm that follows the company. These tend to be concise presentations (20–30 minutes), including Q&A.

The Investor Day—a fairly recent trend—is an in-person public meeting before both brokerage (sell-side) and institutional (buy-side) analysts who follow the company or its industry. Not all companies convene an annual Investor Day, but most are probably well advised to do so. These tend to be dedicated presentations to showcase the company's full management team and provide a look at each of the company's principal operating units.

(COVID-19 precautions, as this was written, tended to move the formerly in-person Investor Day into a virtual, remote mode. In fact, CIRI, the Canadian Investor Relations Institute, said in a survey released in spring of 2020 that of 26 respondents, 18% had postponed their Investor Day and 12% had changed their event to a virtual format.)

Shrewd managements use the Investor Day to give a comprehensive view of the company and its markets, its product or service lines, its ESG situation (see upcoming section), and a detailed examination of its finances. Presentations usually feature executives in charge of various divisions, R&D, and, of course, finance.

Most importantly, the purpose of the Investor Day is to share management's thinking about where it plans to take the company and build the investors' confidence in a successful outcome. The presentation usually includes a thorough parade of PowerPoint-style slides detailing the company's products/services, markets, market shares, financial plans, and, most important, management's strategic plan to grow the company and improve its profitability. The objective here is to raise investors' appetite for investing in the company's prospects and awarding it a higher valuation.

An Investor Day can run anywhere from two hours to a half-day or more. Calendar-year companies usually hold theirs in the spring, after investors have had a chance to react to the past year's results. Investor Days may be held at company headquarters; large companies with extensive investor followings may want to hold them in New York City. A third option for a company that is announcing a key product innovation or strategic partnership is to hold the Investor Day at the location that is home to that development, and also give investors a tour.

DON'T FORGET BROKERAGE-RUN CONFERENCES

Another important item for many companies are the industry-specific gatherings run by brokerage firms. These can last for several days, with blocks of time in which the invited companies make their presentations to institutional investors invited by the brokerages and answer questions from them.

Companies should look at these conference presentations as opportunities to broaden the base of sophisticated investors familiar with the company's business strategy and future prospects. These appearances are valuable and require essentially the same type of preparation as a quarterly earnings call. Issuing a news release is often advisable, and doing so will be required if fresh material information is part of a company's presentation.

IT'S ALL ABOUT THE FUTURE

Okay—by now you know it's tomorrow that counts for investors. They need to be able to estimate what a company's shares will be worth three months, six months, or a year from now, and perhaps even further, and what kind of dividend (if any) it will be able to pay going forward.

Shrewd company managements help investors make those estimates by issuing what is known as guidance—management's own forecast of the range it expects for future results. Managements usually issue and update guidance when they report quarterly earnings. But does giving guidance also raise the value of a company's shares? And can giving conservative guidance set the stage for a positive "earnings surprise" that will boost the stock's price?

For a complex company with multiple product lines in both US and global markets, there are multiple unknowns that can affect future revenues and earnings. They include demand factors in different markets, competition from others' products, and changes in currency valuations.

Therefore, a company whose performance is linked to multiple variables is often wise to offer several ranges for its revenue and earnings guidance dependent on different scenarios for those underlying factors. If such a company has a winning business model, that level of detail can create additional confidence in the strength and stability of its shares.

TO DISCLOSE OR NOT TO DISCLOSE?

That tricky question can cause major legal problems for company officers and boards of directors. According to Investopedia's entry on the SEC regulation, "Rule 10b-5 covers instances of 'insider trading,' which is when confidential information is used to manipulate the stock market in one's own favor." Here, we are also talking about material information that, if known, would lead someone to buy or sell a security.

Essentially, that means when someone uses material information to trade securities with someone not privy to the same information, they are defrauding the other party to the trade. While case law has varied the enforcement of Rule 10b-5 in recent years, it certainly places limits on when officers or directors of a company with insider information can legally trade a company's securities.

The best procedure for a public company is to have its legal counsel provide managers and directors with guidelines as to when they should and shouldn't trade that company's securities. Avoiding 10b-5 liability also argues for the earliest possible disclosure by a company of pending material information.

ATTEND TO THE MEDIA—INVESTORS DO

Investment recommendations aren't developed in sterile clean rooms. They are made in the real world and influenced by the news and events that affect them.

If a company announces what it says may be an innovative new product line, the investment analysts may be inclined to say: "Sounds good, but let's see if it makes real money."

However, if the *Wall Street Journal*, *Barron's*, or *Forbes* publishes an article about the product line, favorably quoting industry experts and potential customers, then analysts will sit up, take notice, and factor the now widely known information into their investment advice. As professionals, how can they ignore what the rest of the world knows?

Media coverage can have a positive, neutral, or negative effect on a company's shares. Here's how the investor relations person (or their public relations counterpart) should become involved:

1. When a positive development appears exciting, offer a story on it to a news media organization that is likely to have an interest in it. (However, if that development is material to investors, ensure you also issue the news to the media generally.)
2. Have a media specialist at the company or an outside agency do so, if the media relations responsibility lies outside the investor relations office.
3. Assist the media organization in putting the story together, including interviews with company executives and outside experts.

The opposite situation is that a news organization publishes an article that is harmful to the company. That situation requires remedial action and is beyond the scope of this chapter to address in detail. But the solution, of course, is to see that

any faulty information in the media report is corrected, perhaps by seeking coun-
tervailing positive coverage from a different news organization.

GOING PUBLIC

One of the most exciting and challenging tasks for the IR practitioner is "taking a
company public"—selling a large part of a private company to public shareholders.

The initial public offering (IPO) process is exacting and hectic. It involves an
intense sales effort to convince investors to buy shares in a company that until then
had been owned only by company insiders and other private shareholders. The
entire procedure must adhere strictly to SEC guidelines. Among the responsibilities of the investor relations specialist before and during an IPO are drafting news
releases, advising on investor presentations ("road shows"), and ensuring communications are SEC compliant.

The key document in an IPO is the registration statement, or S-1. It is a
detailed compendium of disclosures about the business of the company seeking to
go public. It presents the reasons for purchasing shares in the company making the
IPO, together with the risks in doing so. When filed in preliminary form with the
SEC, that initial registration statement is known as a "red herring."

Next is the sales effort for shares of the company conducting the IPO. The key
element here is the road show, in which the investment banking firm engaged to
assist with the IPO arranges for investors in several cities to attend presentations
where management makes its case for owning its shares. As with already-public
companies' meetings with securities analysts, tough and probing questions can
be expected.

Communications during the IPO process must be tightly controlled. For
example, the SEC may consider statements regarding the growth of the company
or its industry outside the registration statement to be "gun-jumping"—making
offers to sell the new securities before they are permitted.

When approved by the SEC, the registration statement can be distributed to
prospective investors as a prospectus—the official offering statement for the new
shares. It must be given to all who are approached to purchase the new stock.

The day of the offering is an exciting one. Based on feedback from potential
investors, the underwriting syndicate decides on a price, adds the final "pricing
amendment" to the registration statement, and the offer goes off. The market price

of the new securities, once issued, may move up or down considerably from the one set in the pricing amendment. For instance, since the dot-com era in the late 1990s, many high-tech or digital companies have generated great speculative interest ahead of their IPOs, and their share prices fluctuated considerably after trading began.

WHAT'S A SPAC?

That odd-sounding name is short for Special Purpose Acquisition Company. Such a company has no commercial operations, but is formed strictly to raise capital through a future IPO for the purpose of acquiring an existing company.

Also known as "blank check companies," SPACs have existed for decades. In recent years, they have become more popular, attracting name underwriters and investors.

SPACs are generally formed by investors or sponsors with expertise in a particular industry or business sector, with the intention of pursuing deals in that area. In creating a SPAC, the founders sometimes have at least one acquisition target in mind, but they usually don't identify that target to avoid extensive disclosures during the IPO process.

SPAC investors actually have no idea what company they ultimately will be investing in. They must trust management to identify and acquire a valuable company with a bright future. SPACs seek underwriters and institutional investors before offering shares to the public. Managements of SPACs typically have two years to complete an acquisition or they must return the funds invested to investors.

WHAT ABOUT SOCIAL MEDIA?

You'd think that, given the lightning-fast movement of information in the digital media age, social media would have a key role in investor relations. Not so. A survey by the National Investor Relations Institute found that only 15 percent to 18 percent of analysts said they were interested in using social media to engage with investor relations. Likewise, the study found that just 28 percent of IR practitioners were using social media.

Why is that so? Consider the quantity of information professional investors require, versus the brevity of, say, a 280-character tweet. Detail-hungry analysts might prefer to go immediately to the financial tables available online.

Is it possible that investors and analysts could come to trust social media sufficiently to act on a brief social media post issued concurrently with an earnings news release in order to make or recommend an investment decision? At this point, that remains an open question.

WHAT DO INVESTORS CARE ABOUT TODAY?

Until recently, investors were concerned almost exclusively about a company's revenues and earnings lines and where those numbers were headed in the future.

No more.

Today, investors are also becoming increasingly interested in a firm's positive or negative contributions to society, in a process called ESG investing, standing for Environmental, Social, and Governance concerns.

ESG investing integrates those socially responsible factors into investment analysis and decision making. However, the factors also cover a wide spectrum of issues that are also relevant to an investor's financial assessment of a company. So, a company's ability to meet ESG factors may also affect that same bottom line that investors look at first.

According to *Forbes*, ESG can include:

"how corporations respond to climate change, how good they are with water management, how effective their health and safety policies are in the protection against accidents, how they manage their supply chains, how they treat their workers and whether they have a corporate culture that builds trust and fosters innovation."

The term "ESG" was coined in 2005 in a landmark study entitled "Who Cares Wins." According to the most recent calculation, ESG investing is estimated at over $20 trillion in assets under management, about a quarter of all professionally managed assets around the world!

What's more, ESG investing has become big business. At this writing, many large banks and other money managers had jumped aggressively onto the ESG idea as a way to market their services.

ESG also runs parallel to the more general societal trend today to demand socially responsible behavior from business. To see how far we've come, dial back to September 1970, when the legendary economist Milton Friedman wrote an essay for the *New York Times* entitled, "A Friedman Doctrine: The Social Responsibility of Business Is to Increase Its Profits." And contrast that with the Business Roundtable's August 2019 statement redefining the purpose of a corporation as promoting "an economy that serves all Americans." It was signed by 181 CEOs "who commit to lead their companies for the benefit of all stakeholders—customers, employees, suppliers, communities and shareholders."

Because the Roundtable had been considered a bastion of traditional corporate America, that pronouncement received plenty of attention. But the organization's commitment really builds on what is becoming the current thinking of many business leaders.

Here's what some of them have said:

- In his 2020 letter to shareholders, Larry Fink, chairman and chief executive of Black Rock, who frequently discussed altruistic issues with the firm's constituents, wrote, "We are facing the ultimate long-term problem. We don't yet know which predictions about the climate will be most accurate, nor what effects we have failed to consider. But there is no denying the direction we are heading. Every government, company, and shareholder must confront climate change."

- Marc Benioff, chair, CEO, and founder of Salesforce, who embraces the title of "activist CEO," told *Fast Company* that today, "being a CEO means that you're taking care of all stakeholders. That stakeholder return is as much table stakes as shareholder return."

- And Jamie Dimon, chairman and CEO of JPMorgan Chase, who is also chairman of the Business Roundtable, says, "The American dream is alive, but fraying. Major employers are investing in their workers and communities because they know it is the only way to be successful over the long term. These modernized principles reflect the business community's unwavering commitment to continue to push for an economy that serves all Americans."

Further endorsement of ESG principles comes from an unexpected source—the Vatican. The Council for Inclusive Capitalism is affiliated with the Catholic Church and operates under "the moral guidance of Pope Francis." The Council also includes CEOs of several Fortune 500 companies as well as policymakers and the general secretary of the International Trade Union Confederation. The founder of the Council, Lynn Forester de Rothschild, also chair of investment firm E. L. Rothschild, said, "Doing this is not simply a market imperative . . . The capital markets are such a powerful force, that we need to remember that our actions, who we are and what we are, are based on morality and ethics. And so the Holy Father really asks us to put profits in service of planet and people."

What are enlightened companies doing today to let investors know about their ESG commitments? Here are some steps to consider:

- In the annual Form 10-K, include a section summarizing the company's ESG actions.
- Issue an annual Sustainability Report, as a number of companies today are doing, especially those with environmental vulnerabilities.
- Weave material on ESG compliance into earnings news releases and periodically include reports on ESG actions in quarterly earnings presentations.

TAKEAWAYS

Is investor relations for you? For someone interested in the financial side of business and how the markets value it, a career in investor relations may be attractive. If so, you will need:

1. A thorough understanding of business and financial statements. If necessary, consider taking accounting courses or even an advanced business degree.
2. Communications skills, written and spoken.
3. The ability to handle massive amounts of detail, since the investors who analyze your company have voracious appetites for it.
4. The ability to work quickly and handle the avalanche of information that pours in as the quarterly earnings numbers are calculated.
5. Experience in accounting, financial analysis, or public relations. In many companies, the IR officer comes from the financial ranks or is the chief public relations/communications executive.

Investor relations is a challenging career that's both exciting and demanding. If you decide to pursue it, we wish you well!

CHAPTER 8

Working with the Media

They Are Not the Enemy, but Care Is Required

JONATHAN DEDMON
THE DILENSCHNEIDER GROUP

The goal of working with the media is straightforward: to enhance the awareness and reputation of the business or organization, then manage and/or mitigate negative commentary and perceptions among the audiences important to it.

In the past, there were just three major broadcast networks, a large and rich variety of local print newspapers, local broadcast news, and several wire services like the Associated Press. Today the media landscape is a complex ecosystem— websites, cable TV, streaming, social media, podcasts, search engines, and a plethora of other new media outlets, given how easy and cheap it is to publish online.

Traditional media is still here, of course, but it is increasingly going online and using many of the other media platforms. For instance, reporters for the *New York Times* and the *Wall Street Journal* have Twitter handles and tweet about their stories.

SOME THINGS HAVEN'T CHANGED

In our over-communicated society, the paradox is that nothing is more important than communication.
—Al Ries and Jack Trout, *Positioning: The Battle for Your Mind*

Despite the incredible and rapid evolution in the media landscape, some things haven't changed. The year 1981 will probably seem like ancient history to most of you. Not only was there no World Wide Web or cell phones, but CNN had only just launched the previous year.

In 1981, two marketing experts, Al Ries and Jack Trout, published the landmark book *Positioning: The Battle for Your Mind*. The central idea was that an organization needs to generate a positive share-of-mind by articulating itself in a way that creates awareness, differentiates it, demonstrates its value, and is compelling and authentic. According to Ries, "What's your brand? If you can't answer that question about your own brand in two or three words, your brand's in trouble."

The classic example of successful positioning, according to Ries and Trout, was the rental car company Avis. It was a perennial number two to Hertz. Avis developed the positioning statement, "We try harder." They didn't try to change people's minds, but rather leveraged what everyone already knew and believed in a compelling and authentic way that stuck in people's minds.

The concept of positioning applies all the more strongly today, given the crowded and disparate media environment. However, in working with the media in a non-advertising setting (which was Trout and Ries's background), it's obvious that more than three words are necessary.

MESSAGING

The first step in successfully communicating with the media is preparation. It is critically important to research, understand, and analyze the broad spectrum of media that offer opportunities and potential dangers to your organization. Who do you want to reach? What are the key publications? Who are their reporters and editors? What topics are they covering that are important to your business and industry?

Out of this flows your messaging. What is the unique value proposition of your enterprise? You should be able to convey it in no more than five compelling messages that should be the basis of all communications with the media. It is what some call "the elevator speech," and you should repeat it frequently.

However, messaging doesn't operate in a vacuum. Successful messaging also includes developing the facts and supporting material that credibly support the positioning.

Organizations have possession of and access to a wide variety of data that can support their messaging. This includes market research, market share, revenue and earnings growth, customer satisfaction, and key market trends, to name a few.

In addition to an organization's own resources, third parties—those outside the entity that can support its credibility—are another key component of successful messaging.

THIRD PARTIES

Good journalists are not going to simply accept what you or your organization say. The City News Service in Chicago produced a number of leading journalists, from the legendary Mike Royko to David Brooks of the *New York Times* to investigative reporter Seymour Hersh. The bureau had a saying: "If your mother says she loves you, check it out."

Good reporters are going to talk to others for perspective and to vet the credibility of what you are saying. Third parties can be a range of experts, including think tanks, academics, nongovernmental organizations, respected authors on a topic, and thought leaders in a given field.

For instance, in automotive manufacturing, the Center for Automotive Research and Edmunds.com are frequently quoted on industry trends. In healthcare, the Kaiser Family Foundation and the Cleveland Clinic, a global leader in cardiology, are often tapped by reporters for their expertise. During the COVID pandemic, leading epidemiologists regularly appeared on cable news to discuss the impact of the disease and how to mitigate its effects. Other third parties frequently quoted are financial analysts for banks and asset managers who closely monitor company performance in specific industries, including whether to invest in a specific firm.

THE FRAGMENTATION OF MEDIA AND CONFIRMATION BIAS

We talked earlier about how traditional media has now become a fragmented, complex ecosystem. David Kennedy, a Pulitzer Prize–winning American historian at Stanford University, says that "the fragmentation of the media, as we've seen particularly in the explosion of social media . . . reduces significantly what used to be the authority and the legitimacy of the so-called mainstream media to report the news in objective ways."

While Kennedy is discussing the trend in terms of American presidential politics, it is true for businesses and organizations as well. Adding to the problem, according to Kennedy, is what is known as "confirmation bias." We now are able to identify and actually consume only those media that reflect our existing beliefs.

Do you watch FOX News or MSNBC? They confirm our views of the world. While it was ridiculed at the time, the notion by a senior advisor to former president Trump that there are "alternative facts" is not, in fact, that off base in today's media environment, at least in Americans' perception of facts.

In 2020, Pew Research Center found that roughly 80 percent of Americans say news organizations tend to favor one side when presenting the news on political and social issues, while only some 20 percent say these organizations deal fairly with all sides.

"You combine the psychological predilection for confirmation bias with the hyper-fragmentation of the media. And you have disintermediated the function of the traditional media to create consensus around an agreed body of data or facts," Kennedy says.

Last, he notes that another result of this fragmentation is that trust in all our institutions, not just media, and even in each other has seriously declined.

BEGINNING TO COMMUNICATE SUCCESSFULLY WITH THE MEDIA

Vital to successfully communicating with the media is understanding that their job is different from, and sometimes in conflict with, your job.

While the business communicator's job is to articulate a positive story about the organization, the reporter's job is to find and write about "news." Journalists also generally do not enter their field to become wealthy. Most believe they have a higher calling as seekers and defenders of truth. It is important to keep this perspective of theirs in mind.

That is why it is important to understand the publication, its reporters, and what they have been writing about that relates to your organization. It also is important to gain as much information as you can about the topic in which they are interested for their story, learn their deadline, and find out what they perceive is the "news" regarding your organization.

In doing media interviews, it is also vital to think through why you or a member of your management team is or should be doing the interview. What is your objective in doing so? What do you hope to get out of it? What messages do you want to deliver? It is not simply about answering questions.

MAKING NEWS: SPECIFIC TACTICS

There are many ways to "make news" and gain positive attention for your organization with the media. The best known of these tools is the press release. Not only are press releases important to communicate news about your organization, but they also have legal implications. The Securities and Exchange Commission's Regulation Fair Disclosure (Reg FD) requires publicly held companies to make broadly and simultaneously public any material disclosures—those that could affect an investor's decision about the company. Distributing a press release broadly, generally through one of the commercial electronic distribution companies like *Business-Wire* or PR News Service, fulfills the Reg FD requirement.

There are many other ways to gain positive media attention as well. These include but in no way are limited to:

- Interviews with senior management
- Opinion pieces, or op-eds, in significant publications, where you have complete control of the editorial content
- Speeches that can be reprinted and sent to key media and other influencers
- A press conference (WARNING—Make sure you have major news. There are few things worse than a press conference with no press.)
- Participation in major trade shows and other industry events
- Trade publication outreach
  - These publications, aside from being read within the industry, are also read by reporters covering your industry for major outlets.
  - Many publish editorial calendars for the coming year that outline the specific topics they will cover in given issues, an opportunity you should exploit.
- Investor Days, on which senior management presents to the investment community its strategy, plans, and performance
- Developing and publishing major intellectual capital

INTELLECTUAL CAPITAL

A word on intellectual capital: proprietary information and thought that an organization develops and owns, and that positions it as a leader in its field on a particular topic, trend, or issue. While not measurable in terms of a company's business performance per se (it's a so-called intangible), it does demonstrate the superior thinking of an organization in conceiving and executing its strategies.

Smart organizations generate significant intellectual capital to achieve positive visibility with the media and other audiences important to it. It can take a number of forms:

- Cutting-edge research by the organization
- Industry surveys
- New trends
- Innovative thinking about an issue
- Patents awarded
- Sponsored research with a think tank or polling/research institution
- White papers on a particular topic

For instance, McKinsey surveyed how eight hundred global business leaders envision the future of the workforce due to the acceleration of automation, digitization, and other trends. The outplacement firm Challenger, Gray & Christmas tracks and publishes the number of layoffs in the US each month, positioning the company as the most knowledgeable in its field.

THE COMPANY WEBSITE AND THE MEDIA

The company website is an important information source for journalists. Companies that are effective with the media generally have an easily identifiable tab labeled "News" or "Newsroom." It should contain the following information:

- Recent press releases, prominently displayed, with past releases in an archive section
- A fact sheet about the company
- Key executive bios
- Recent media coverage as appropriate
- Several interesting photos that media can use with a story to enhance its readership

- Contacts for the media at the company
  - These generally should be the communicators who deal regularly with the media.
  - In certain cases, such as academia and think tanks, it may also be appropriate to list key experts and their areas of expertise.
  - However, media still should be routed through the communications department to reach the experts, as media relations personnel should be aware of all ongoing media contact with the company.

SPOKESPERSONSHIP

For many reporters and editors, dealing with corporate communications and a company's media relations department is a necessary evil. Members of the media tend to view an organization's media relations people as gatekeepers. Reporters and editors prefer to talk to senior management instead.

Thus, a key decision for the PR professional involves choosing the spokesperson for an interview or on an issue. Who is the best person in the organization to address the issue? How comfortable are they with media interviews? Are there any potentially troublesome areas of inquiry?

As a rule, the CEO should only be used for major news—to the extent possible, mainly major positive news.

BRIEFING MANAGEMENT

Of course, senior management has other responsibilities! And in some cases, they don't even like the media, whether because of a bad past experience or the fact that they almost never have final control over the story.

It is therefore incumbent on those dealing with the media to prepare senior managers for media interviews. We recommend the following:

- Create a briefing memorandum of no more than three pages.
- Provide information on the media outlet.
- There should be background on the reporter. Most reporters have LinkedIn accounts with bios if their information is not on the publication's website.
- Provide several of the reporter's most recent stories.
- State why the interview is being done. What is the organization's objective in doing so, and what are the key messages it wants to communicate?

- What are the three most difficult questions that could be asked? Decide the answers in advance.
- To assist those senior managers uncomfortable with the media, you may want to hire an external coach familiar with how the media operates for a coaching session that includes interview simulations and crafting of specific answers.

The company communications professional should be present at the interview for any follow-up questions or materials, and to provide further counsel as needed to the manager following the interview.

BRIDGING AND FLAGGING

There are two techniques that may be helpful in regard to communicating successfully with reporters—bridging and flagging.

Bridging is taking the reporter's questions and areas of interest, and connecting them to what you feel are the relevant points about your organization that you want the story to reflect.

However, unlike many politicians who often ignore reporters' questions and simply deliver their talking points, to preserve credibility you need to actually answer the question before bridging. For example:

Question: "Why were your earnings significantly down this quarter?"
Possible Answer: "There were understandable reasons that included the economic effects of the pandemic, investing in protecting employee safety during the pandemic, and the launch of several new products."

Flagging is calling attention to what you believe are the most important points related to the story. Unless it is a major profile, the reporter is not going to use every quote in the story. What do *you* want those quotes to be? Flagging is especially useful at the end of an interview; for instance, "The most important point is that we have gained XX percent market share versus our competitors."

Other Tips

- If a reporter asks a question, they are generally entitled to an answer.
- Speak from the viewpoint of your audience.

- Avoid jargon.
- Speak in headlines. As previously stated, you will only have a limited number of quotes in the story. What do you want them to be?
- If it is a broadcast piece, think about pictures and audio that can be incorporated into the interview to make it stand out.
- Never say "No comment." It is argumentative and looks like you have something to hide. If you cannot answer a question, you should explain why. There can be many good reasons:
  - I don't know, but will get you an answer.
  - It is nonpublic information.
  - It is important competitive information that our competitors would love to see.
  - It involves confidential employee information.
  - I don't wish to speculate.

BUILDING CREDIBILITY AND TRUST WITH THE MEDIA

Effective media relations depends on your credibility and the media having trust in what you say. Credibility and trust are your two most important assets as a communicator. Once they are gone, they are difficult, if not impossible, to rebuild.

Telling the truth will pay long-term dividends in terms of building credibility and trust. However, this does not mean you have to bare your or your organization's soul. You and your company have the right to maintain certain information as proprietary.

Those who achieve their goals with the media do not engage in "spin," however tempting it is to paint a rosy picture based on facts that are actually mixed and more nuanced. Tell the truth and recognize that success in working with the media is a long-term game, versus simply trying to manage one story. There will be other stories.

ESG

In terms of building additional credibility and trust, one area with the media that is rapidly gaining attention, and where a company or organization can tell a positive story, is ESG: Environmental, Social, and Governance practices. It has become an increasingly important metric in a company's overall image.

ESG encompasses a wide variety of issues and practices, among them the following:

- Environmental stewardship, ranging from engaging in sustainable business practices (e.g., recycling) to climate change.
- Strong social values. These can range from racial and gender diversity of management and employees to commitment and actions to help the communities in which the company is located or does business.
- Governance, which can include the independence and quality of the board of directors as well as issues such as strong financial controls and transparency about the business.

As to the growing importance of ESG, Business Roundtable members are the CEOs of the largest US businesses. These people did not achieve their leadership roles by being tree huggers. However, the group's members recently put out a major statement that "the purpose of a corporation is to lead their companies for the benefit of all stakeholders—customers, employees, suppliers, communities and shareholders." As Alex Gorsky, Chairman of the Board and Chief Executive Officer of Johnson & Johnson and Chair of the Business Roundtable Corporate Governance Committee, put it, the Business Roundtable's position "affirms the essential role corporations can play in improving our society when CEOs are truly committed to meeting the needs of all stakeholders."

Note that properly measuring a company's commitment to ESG is still very much a work in progress, but that progress is being made. The World Economic Forum recently published a universal set of "stakeholder capitalism metrics" including ESG indicators and disclosures for financial markets, investors, and society. The metrics were developed by the Forum in collaboration with Bank of America and the accounting/consulting firms Deloitte, EY, KPMG, and PwC to "help companies demonstrate long-term value creation and their contributions to the [United Nations'] Sustainable Development Goals."

DEALING WITH THE NEGATIVE

Invariably, a company or organization will experience bad news, resulting in negative publicity. Possible reasons can include:

- Poor revenue or earnings
- Product recalls

- Consumer health and safety issues
- Strikes
- Plant closures or layoffs
- Attacks by politicians and NGOs
- Accidents causing employee deaths or serious injuries
- Attacks by activist investors questioning the overall company strategy and its management
- Environmental issues
- Worker conditions and sourcing, particularly in the developing world

It is important to acknowledge the facts of the situation versus trying to "spin" them for short-term gain; once again, credibility and trust are your most important assets. And remember that relations with the media need to be viewed as a long-term game. If you spin the facts, then when there is *good* news, will you be believed or trusted?

Several other tips on dealing with a negative media situation:

- Identify how much traction the story is getting. Do not make more of your denial than is warranted, as it creates the equivalent of being hit by a truck and then having the truck back up over you. To the extent possible, make it a one-day story and respond with equivalency—what is needed but not more than the story deserves.
- Articulate bold, positive steps you are taking to fix the problem.
- Don't be argumentative. As longtime Republican political operative Bill Greener aptly put it, quoting others: "Never argue with someone who buys ink by the barrel."
- Don't repeat negative or inflammatory language from the reporter. Even a denial using such language can be repeated as from you in the story.
- A corollary to that is to take the high road. As former first lady Michelle Obama put it: "When they go low, we go high."
- PROTECT THE RECORD. If you make a mistake, correct it. If the reporter makes a mistake, ask for a correction. While few people read the small corrections in newspapers, by getting one released, you will ensure it is recorded in digital space, frequently even in the online version of the story.

Last, recognize that news stories need a villain and that corporations are rarely viewed as being on the side of the angels. Internationally renowned political scientist and management scholar and chancellor of Vanderbilt University Daniel

Diermeier notes in his excellent book, *Reputation Rules*, "Executives operate under the mistaken belief that the public trusts them. But CEOs are among the least trusted professions, just barely ahead of used-car dealers and politicians."

NEW MEDIA

It is no secret that traditional media has suffered major secular decline in the twenty-first century and continues to face major challenges. According to a 2020 Knight Foundation and University of North Carolina study, more than one-fourth—2,100—of the country's newspapers operating fifteen years ago are no longer in business. At least 1,800 communities that had a local news outlet in 2004 did not at the beginning of 2020. Only half the number of journalists working at newspapers ten years ago are doing so today. According to the Pew Research Center, US newspaper circulation fell in 2018 to its lowest level since 1940, the first year with available data. Newspaper revenues also declined dramatically between 2008 and 2018, according to Pew. Advertising revenue fell from $37.8 billion in 2008 to $14.3 billion in 2018, a 62 percent decline.

The internet obviously has been the driving force in this decline, given the low cost of developing a robust website and content and the ease of distribution, such as via email. And while advertising has migrated to the internet, it sells at a greatly discounted rate compared to traditional print newspaper advertising, and Facebook and Alphabet dominate the space.

Yet, there is some good news: the rise of new media, or what some call digital-native news organizations, born on the internet. They include political commentary sites like Vox and The Hill; more general sites like the Huffington Post and BuzzFeed; and specialty sites like Engadget and TechCrunch in technology, MarketWatch and Quartz on Wall Street, or STAT on healthcare.

One positive side effect of the decline of newspapers and newsrooms is that enterprising reporters are creating their own brands. They are developing their own websites and followings for specific topics like nutrition, health, culture, and aging, to name a few. Many have extremely large audiences. Not only do these journalists have their own websites—as well as newsletters, books, blogs, tweets, social media accounts, and podcasts—but, given shrunken newsrooms at major publications, many of the same journalists also write for leading mass-circulation publications and appear on broadcast outlets. They should not be ignored.

WASHINGTON MEDIA GAMES

Washington, DC, has certain rules of its own in dealing with the media. Sources can declare their disclosures to reporters as being "off the record," "background," "deep background," or "not for attribution." General definitions of the terms—which journalists themselves don't specifically agree on—are as follows:

- **Off the record:** This theoretically means that the information you share with a reporter cannot be used for publication in any way.
- **Background:** Usually means that a reporter can use the information you give them but on conditions negotiated with a source—for instance, not being named or quoted directly, but having their job or position generically described. This is sometimes described as "not for attribution."
- **Deep background:** Most journalists would understand this to mean the information you provide will not be quoted or attributed to you at all. The information may not be included in the article but is used by the journalist to enhance his or her view of the subject matter, or to act as a guide to other leads or sources.

While it is important to understand the media's general understanding of these terms, our advice to practitioners is "DON'T GO THERE." You should be comfortable with whatever you say to the media being on the front page of the *New York Times*. There are various interpretations even among journalists of what these terms mean. And if you work for a publicly held company, there is considerable legal risk in providing what might be considered nonpublic information.

All in all, these terms and rules are best left to Washington correspondents and pundits. If for any reason you need to engage on these terms, rather than just being aware of them, state and agree upon the exact ground rules for your comment with the reporter in advance. Otherwise, it might run on page one!

TAKEAWAYS

We can all benefit from having a checklist of key principles in dealing with the media and reviewing it from time to time. Our own list follows, using some of our previously discussed tips:

1. Know why you are doing a media interview. What is your objective? What are the key messages?
2. What is the publication and who is the reporter? Do you know what the reporter has written about recently?
3. Who are the third parties and what is the independent research that can support the organization's comments?
4. Have a robust section for the media on your company website.
5. If the reporter is interviewing senior management, prepare a briefing paper on the publication, the reporter, their most recent stories, and your desired outcome.
6. As part of briefing senior management, identify the three most difficult or concerning questions that could be asked and identify answers in advance. Consider media coaching where appropriate.
7. Talk from the viewpoint of your audience. Focus on their self-interests and use information that will arouse that self-interest.
8. Avoid jargon. Talk in headlines. Unless it is a profile or a major story, you will probably only have two or three quotes in the story. What do you want them to be?
9. If a reporter asks a question, they generally are entitled to a truthful answer. Then bridge and flag.
10. Tell the truth; don't spin. But don't bare your soul and tell everything you know!

(continued)

11. Never say "No comment." It is argumentative and looks like you have something to hide. If you cannot answer a question, you should explain why. There are many good reasons:
    - I don't know, but will get you an answer.
    - It is nonpublic information.
    - It involves confidential employee information.
    - It is important competitive information.
    - I don't want to speculate.
12. Protect the record. Correct misinformation as soon as you can.
13. For broadcast, think about pictures to make the story more interesting. Simply having "talking heads" gets boring quickly.

CHAPTER 9

Social Media

Evolving Best Practices for PR Practitioners

SHEL HOLTZ
WEBCOR

Once a novelty and a source of derision, social media has evolved into a required component of most public relations plans. Using social media, PR practitioners can conduct research, assess reactions to campaigns, target niche audiences, engage with customers and consumers, attract media coverage, build reputations, and address crises.

At the most basic level, any content shared online can be accompanied by an invitation to share the content on the user's social channel of choice. For example, an article about a product feature can include icons of social networks such as Twitter, Facebook, and LinkedIn; clicking those links allows people to share that content in their own networks. At its most sophisticated, PR practitioners can employ social media to engage specific audiences, build one-to-one relationships, and elevate their media relations activities. In between, PR practitioners can

113

recruit influencers to promote (and defend) the brand, ensure announcements are seen by the right audiences, and react speedily to negative reports and posts.

But social media's impact on the practice of public relations reaches far beyond a new set of tools. It has obliterated the news cycle, which has become a 24/7, minute-by-minute phenomenon. Even press releases and web-based media centers now include some degree of social media. While significant announcements and major changes will continue to drive more traditionally deployed PR activities, much of PR has become an always-on phenomenon. Practitioners now work round the clock to identify threats, capitalize on unexpected opportunities, and provide a steady stream of social media content and engagement—supporting an organization or client's reputation and ensuring awareness among target markets.

What are the risks of ignoring social media? As PR measurement maven Katie Paine puts it, if they're not talking about you on social media, you don't exist.

Paine tells the story of shopping for a new laptop. As she explains, she reached out to her sizable online community for recommendations. She researched the leading recommendations they shared with her, made a decision, and bought a new laptop. The next morning, she awoke wondering, "Did Lenovo and HP go out of business?" Because nobody in her community recommended a Lenovo or HP laptop, she did not consider them. If they're not talking about you, you don't exist.

Another consequence of social media is the muddying of the waters between PR and marketing. With both marketing and PR using the same platforms and channels—and even the same accounts—to amplify messages and reach larger audiences, it can be difficult to see where one ends and the other begins. At the very least, social media has elevated the need for PR and marketing to work in concert.

Gone, for example, are the days when a quarterly earnings press release is sent to selected media, which publish articles to their subscribers that are seen by nobody else, ensuring that a glum financial outlook doesn't conflict with an upbeat product introduction. Today, that pessimistic financial statement could be shared by thousands—*tens* of thousands—of people in the market for the new product, who may shy away from a purchase over worries that the company will not be around long enough to provide product support.

And this just scratches the surface of the effect social media has had on the practice of public relations. This chapter provides a broader overview of social media, how PR practitioners can take advantage of it, and how to prepare for the inevitable challenges social media can present.

WHAT IS SOCIAL MEDIA?

At its core, social media describes online platforms that enable anybody to publish and share content or engage in networking.

Of course, there is more to it than that. It is not unusual to hear some pundits proclaim that social media has been with us since the 1990s. After all, anybody can publish a website. Even before the web appeared, anybody could participate in Usenet newsgroups.

Because of these claims, it is important to differentiate between social media and other tools and channels. The key to that distinction is the word "anybody." It is true that anybody can create a website, but it costs money to acquire a hosting account and requires a certain amount of expertise to work in HTML, the coding language of the web. It is equally true that anybody could (and still can) engage in conversations on Usenet. But knowledge of how Usenet works is necessary (and Usenet isn't easy to learn, in addition to being an anachronism to Generation Z).

What, then, are the characteristics of the social media tools that let people publish, share, and connect?

First of all, *they are shared*. The PESO model of communication—introduced by Arment Dietrich CEO Gini Dietrich—includes four types of media: paid, earned, shared, and owned. Social media falls squarely in the "shared" category. In fact, Dietrich describes shared media as social media. The idea is that the owner of a shared service—such as Facebook or Twitter—lets anybody with an account use it, including companies interested in using it for public relations.

Of the issues associated with shared services such as these, the biggest is a lack of control. Despite having produced content on a shared site for years, an organization could find itself at odds with the service after a policy change, design change, or some other action taken by the site's owner. The service could also determine that content a company shared is inappropriate and remove it or even suspend the organization's account.

The one exception to this lack of control is found in blogs, the original social media platform, which *may* be published on an owned website. Most content management systems that companies use to create and maintain their sites include the ability to host a blog. However, blogs can also be created at no cost on shared sites such as WordPress, Tumblr, Blogger, Medium, and Wix.

That leads to the second characteristic of social media tools: *they are free* (or very, very inexpensive). Cost is not an obstacle to using social media (beyond an internet connection and a device such as a computer or smartphone), because they generate income through advertising.

Third, *they are easy to use*. Nobody needs a tutorial to figure out how to share a Facebook post or send a tweet, including brands (although, as we will discuss later, the ability to advertise on social media sites is also available to anybody).

TYPES OF SOCIAL MEDIA

Social media began with blogs but quickly evolved into several distinct categories.

Social Networks

Facebook, Twitter, and LinkedIn are examples of social networks, where people can connect with others and share everything from birthday greetings and vacation photos to celebrations of personal milestones and accomplishments. Each social network has its unique characteristics and focus, and communicators must select the right one for their objectives and to repurpose content if they are sharing across multiple networks. LinkedIn, for example, is focused squarely on business. Twitter limits tweets to 280 characters. You will find journalists and leaders of government and business on Twitter, while Facebook is still known for being home to consumers, though organizations have begun using it, too.

The Rock & Roll Hall of Fame offers an example of an organization using a social network to achieve a measurable objective. The museum wanted to boost ticket sales while increasing brand awareness. Its social media team observed its own frequent use of Facebook Messenger, leading them to develop a messaging strategy that began on its Facebook page. There, visitors found a "Get Started" button; clicking it initiated a Messenger chat, which enabled team members to respond to questions and comments. Through this direct engagement with the public, the museum grew its audience 81 percent and boosted ticket sales 12 percent.

Media-Sharing Networks

Media-sharing networks are designed primarily to allow users to share media (such as photos, video, and artwork). YouTube and Instagram are prime examples of such networks, while sharing some characteristics of social networks (such as commenting and sharing).

Among the ways communicators can use YouTube, for example, are sharing interviews and creating an ongoing YouTube series. Warby Parker, the eyeglass company, established a dedicated YouTube channel just for customer service. Customers and consumers were able to reach out to customer service through a variety of channels, from email to Twitter. In response to their questions, customer service representatives recorded short videos answering them, then replied with links to the videos. Thus, a single answer to a single question can result in thousands of views of the video. It also puts a real human being in front of the customer (and everybody else who watches the video).

Instagram has emerged as one of the most popular media-sharing sites, leading brands to embrace it by sharing images Instagrammers would be interested in following. Instagram is also home to an army of influencers who (for compensation) will share a company's product with their followers.

The latest media-sharing craze is the Chinese-owned TikTok, where users create and share sixty-second (or shorter) videos. Brands are now sharing their own videos and initiating hashtag challenges (a staple on TikTok); others are taking advantage of videos shared by users. For example, in October 2020, Nathan Apodaca, a laborer at an Idaho potato warehouse, filmed himself skateboarding to work, lip-syncing the Fleetwood Mac song "Dreams" while drinking a bottle of Ocean Spray Cran-Raspberry, and the video happened to go viral (that is, it spread like wildfire, racking up hundreds of thousands of views). Other TikTok users—including *Tonight Show* host Jimmy Fallon and Fleetwood Mac members Stevie Nicks and Mick Fleetwood—shared their own videos of themselves skateboarding, lip-syncing "Dreams," and drinking Ocean Spray juices. Even Ocean Spray's chief executive officer jumped on the bandwagon. Ultimately, Ocean Spray bought Apodaca a cranberry-colored truck for kicking off the trend (he was skateboarding because his truck had broken down), delivered with the truck bed filled with Ocean Spray juice, a gesture that earned its own publicity across multiple channels.

Discussion Forums (or Newsgroups)

Discussion forums allow people to engage in conversation or seek answers to questions about topics of common interest to participants. Such forums predate social media—Usenet dates back to 1980 and bulletin board systems were introduced even earlier—but have benefited from the rise of social media. There are sites dedicated entirely to discussions, such as Reddit and Quora, and social networks that include discussion forums among their offerings (such as Facebook groups).

Discussion forums are ripe for engagement by businesses' representatives. Dell and Cisco Systems both train employee subject matter experts on proper social network behavior, then inform them when an issue has arisen (identified through the companies' sophisticated social media monitoring efforts). Those employees then join the conversation, offering assistance. In one case, a Dell employee determined that the complaints in a newsgroup populated by software developers were legitimate. He explained the situation to the Dell product team, who responded within twenty-four hours by rectifying the situation. The subject matter expert was able to inform the developers in the forum that action had been taken, elevating Dell's reputation for listening and caring about its customers.

Reddit has become a popular forum for engaging directly with users through "Ask Me Anything" (AMA) discussions. The company announces that an executive, product designer, or other employee will be available at a designated time to answer questions. These AMAs, as they're known, can be powerful, earning media coverage and raising the company's profile. They can also be disasters for those who come unprepared; Reddit has a distinct culture and its users have clear expectations.

In May 2020, the staff of the Getty Museum hosted an AMA about the Getty Challenge, an ingenious campaign that inspired people to re-create famous works of art and share the photographs online. One question read, "Do you folks realize this challenge will go on forever?" The response from the Getty staff: "We're cool with that. Even though the artworks could be finite, the recreations (which hail from all over the world) are endless! We're happy for it to continue on forever, especially if it means it gets people to laugh, brings them closer through art, and gets art out into the world for more eyeballs to take interest in." That response was upvoted by Reddit users to the AMA's top spot.

Bookmarking and Content-Curation Networks

Originally conceived as a way for individuals to save online information for later retrieval, these networks have evolved into places where people can discover, save, share, and discuss a host of different media types, from websites to magazine articles. Examples include Pinterest, Pocket, and Flipboard. Pinterest is the most popular of these, leading many companies—notably retailers—to make it easy for people to "pin" headlines and images from their websites.

Pinterest has become a popular site for communicators, where they apply the core of their practice: storytelling, through the use of photos, infographics, and videos. Brand accounts on Pinterest are also home to industry news and media clips, making it easy for others to share them. NBC's *Today* show shared a photo of a cake—along with the recipe to make it—when it achieved the milestone of a hundred thousand Pinterest followers. The social media team behind that decision was well aware that recipes are one of the top categories of content shared on Pinterest. Virtually any content shared on any digital platform can be shared on Pinterest, be they product videos or blog posts. General Electric has amassed more than 22,000 followers for its DIY Science page on Pinterest, where the company shares experiments to try at home.

Flipboard curates content under a variety of categories (technology, design, and entertainment are examples). Users can "flip" content into magazines they set up, which others can subscribe to. Pastaríso Gluten Free Pasta, for example, has set up a Flipboard magazine loaded with recipes, photos, and other content.

Consumer Review Networks

These networks allow people to post reviews of restaurants, products, hotels, attractions, employers, and home improvement providers. Examples include Yelp, TripAdvisor, Angie's List, and Glassdoor. Many other sites include reviews, such as Amazon, where they drive commerce. Reviews have outsized importance to brands, since mountains of research have found that consumers (even in the business-to-business world) trust reviews by people like themselves more than virtually any other information source.

Brands need to monitor reviews in order to identify fakes (a real problem) and respond to legitimate negative reviews. While it is a good idea to respond to all reviews, it is particularly important to address negative ones. A California hospital had accumulated several negative reviews on Yelp. The hospital's communicator began responding, apologizing for the bad experiences and offering to talk in an effort to rectify the situation. In several cases, the patient or family took her up on her offer and even amended their reviews to thank the hospital for listening and acting. Even those responses that did not lead to a contact with the reviewer had a positive impact, since people reading the reviews could see that the hospital was responsive and caring.

Negative reviews can also serve as a source of information about areas for improvement, particularly when multiple reviews address the same complaint.

Blogging and Publishing Networks

Blogger, Tumblr, WordPress, and Medium are among the sites that let people publish multimedia content. As noted earlier, many content management systems that companies use have built-in blogging tools. Blogs provide an outlet for individual creativity. Some bloggers are subject matter experts who share their expertise. Others share political perspectives, write about fashion and food, or simply chronicle their lives (which was the original idea behind blogs, which evolved from online journals—"web logs"). Some social networks also enable publishing, such as articles written on LinkedIn.

As of 2018, Dartmouth College reported that 53 percent of the Fortune 500 had engaged in corporate blogging, the highest its ongoing study has ever revealed. (In 2009, only 22 percent of the Fortune 500 was blogging.) Companies that blog include Microsoft, Samsung (which uses its blog as its official communication channel, posting items about its products, people, and businesses), Marriott International, Prudential, Bayer, the Coca-Cola Company, and Toyota.

Not all blogging is done on an owned blog (that is, a blog over which the company has complete control). Medium is an online publishing platform where anyone can publish content under their own accounts and in "publications," a feature used by the likes of the *Economist*. In 2015, the *New York Times* published an article critical of Amazon's treatment of employees. Amazon's response was a Medium post by Jay Carney, Amazon's vice president of worldwide corporate communications. Dean Baquet, executive editor of the *Times*, posted his response on Medium as well, suggesting that the publishing platform is a valuable tool for timely long-form content.

Niche Networks

Also known as "interest-based networks," these are social networks—with all the same features you will find on one—dedicated to a single topic, such as hobbies, politics, technology, management, books, movies, shopping, raising children, and fashion. Examples include BingeBooks, Last.fm (which aggregates users' cross-platform music listening), Dogster (for dog lovers), Kaboodle (where users share products they've liked), and thirdAGE (health and wellness for women).

Niche networks can also reside on a brand's website. Companies such as Airbnb maintain communities as part of their sites; Airbnb's boasts more than a million members, including guests and hosts. Recent subject lines in the community include "Horrible guests since Pandemic???" and "Building a new vacation home to rent. What would you be sure to do?" That post attracted ten responses, including several with detailed recommendations.

Other niche networks are available on larger social networks. On Facebook, there are thousands of Groups, many created and managed by brands. These are distinct from Facebook Pages, which are controlled by the brand. Rather, Groups are places where fans (and detractors) gather for discussions related directly to the product or service. Consider Instant Pot, the popular pressure cooker, which has about 270,000 followers of its Facebook Page but 2.5 million members of the Instant Pot Community. The brand occasionally posts to the community, but mainly it is community members asking questions and sharing recipes and tips. Even questions that would normally be directed at customer support are answered by members of the community. For example, one user asked why his Instant Pot never seems to come up to pressure. Twenty-seven comments helped him resolve the issue.

The PR value of niche networks should be obvious, with brands engaging with and even hosting their most enthusiastic audiences. Building an enthusiastic community of customers and converting them to fans simply by hosting (and managing) an online community is PR gold.

THE LOSS OF (THE ILLUSION OF) CONTROL

One common brand objection about social media is that they have no control over the conversation on the platforms, where anybody can say anything they want. Many companies lived in fear of a negative tweet from former president Donald Trump that might send their stock price tumbling. Goodyear's share price fell 3.1 percent after the former president urged his followers not to buy its products after inaccurate reports surfaced that the company prohibited workers from wearing

"Make America Great Again" hats. The prohibition was not just on MAGA hats, however; it covered any political expression, a point shared in a post of its own. Before Goodyear corrected the record, however, the shares of one of its competitors, Cooper Tire & Rubber, rose.

It may seem safer to traffic in pre-digital PR tools such as press releases, because of the direct control companies can wield over every word . . . until, that is, the release is distributed, at which point journalists can do anything with them they like. The fact is, companies have never had direct control over their media, only the *illusion* of control.

If you are looking for an example of lost control, consider companies that had no social media presence when a story about the company blew up online. That's what happened to Domino's Pizza in 2009 when an employee shot a video of a colleague deliberately contaminating an order of food. The video went viral, disgusting millions of viewers; the brand was tarnished, with customers wondering if employees at *their* local Domino's were engaging in the same behavior.

The company did not have a Twitter account at the time; it was still considering how it would launch into the social media space, making it harder to take control of the incident. They managed to exercise some control by posting an apology on YouTube and reaching out directly to bloggers writing about the incident. When one of the employees involved (both of whom were arrested and fired) sent an email apologizing and asserting that the tainted food never went to a customer, Domino's shared the email verbatim. Domino's spokesman Tim McIntyre said, "If there is a lesson here, it is to move faster than we did." The way to do that is with active social media channels through which a company can address situations quickly.

It is also possible, with the right channels in place, to change the conversation. One "mommy blogger" began sharing posts about a recently reformulated diaper brand; her children were suddenly experiencing rashes, which she believed could only have been caused by the new diaper. The company did its best to reassure parents that the diaper had undergone rigorous testing before it was introduced to the public, but to little avail as the blogger kept up her attack. A new marketing executive decided to take a different approach. If the subject is diaper rash, she reasoned, let's talk about diaper rash. The company produced a torrent of rash-related content, which defused the situation as consumers saw the company as being helpful instead of defensive.

THE BASICS OF SOCIAL MEDIA USE

Regardless of the social media channel you use for PR, there are guidelines to which professionals should adhere.

Brand Voice

A consistent voice is vital when engaging with social media. That voice also should be consistent with the brand voice employed across other, non-social channels. This does not mean that you should not alter your *tone* based on a variety of factors, such as the channel you are using, the audience you are speaking to, or the situation you are addressing. Rather, your brand voice—which you can also think of as your brand *personality*—is unchanging.

One approach to establishing your brand voice is to list adjectives that reflect your personality. Narrow the list to four or five; these stand as your personality traits, which should always be present in your messaging. For instance, you might wind up describing your organization's personality as confident, caring, optimistic, extroverted, and casual.

Your tone, however, should change depending on the situation. Progressive Insurance provides us with a good example. In 2012, Progressive found itself in the uncomfortable position of defending a driver who had caused the death of a woman covered by Progressive auto insurance. The victim's brother, a comedian, had tweeted, "My Sister Paid @Progressive Insurance to Defend Her Killer in Court." Progressive tweeted its response (poorly), but to make matters worse, the company sent the tweets through its main Twitter account, which used an image of its advertising mascot, Flo. As one publication said, "It doesn't help that Progressive mascot Flo's smiling face is next to each copy-pasted tweet." The company finally got wise and temporarily changed its avatar to its logo. (It is worth noting that Progressive also deleted all of its tweeted responses in a failed effort to erase the history of the incident; users were savage in their response.)

The most successful companies on social media are vigilant about maintaining their voice and adopting the right tone. Wendy's, the fast-food company, is well known for its sense of humor on Twitter. When someone tweeted, "If @ Wendys replies to this tweet, I'll buy everyone who likes it a Baconator." Wendy's responded, "Prove it." On LinkedIn, however, its posts are more businesslike (consistent with the nature of the network), with one beginning, "The Wendy's Company announced today a new community-based giving program to benefit 23 charitable organizations." The voice on each platform is consistent, but the tone changes with the nature of the network.

Two-Way Messaging

Social media is a conversation. Organizations that use it as merely another publishing platform risk alienating audiences. Even worse, they fail to take advantage of the best reason to use social media: to connect directly with the people they want to reach and build relationships with them.

Successful social media is measured most often based on engagement: How many people clicked? Opened a photo? Watched a video? Left a comment? Engagement is far more important than follower count. After all, someone might follow a Twitter account or a Facebook page, then never return. Engagement is a measure of actual interactions between the brand and a customer or prospect.

Put another way, social media is *social*. One study found 45 percent of social media users would unfollow a brand because of too much self-promotion. They would also unfollow if they detected that the messages they see are automated rather than from a genuine person. And about 25 percent of respondents said they expect a response from a brand within one hour of leaving a comment on the brand's Twitter or Facebook page.

Make sure your social media activities are designed to spark the interest and responses of your audience. And be certain that your organization is equipped to respond to inquiries submitted through its accounts.

Authenticity

A public relations agency that specialized in social media was asked by the president of a client company to tweet on his behalf for a few days while he was at a conference. The agency initially refused, arguing that—unlike speeches and shareholder letters—social media demands authenticity. The client persisted; he did not wish to go silent while at the conference but simply would not have time to tweet. The agency finally agreed on the condition that a tweet would appear frequently reminding followers that the agency was handling the account while the president was at the conference. Disclosure made the agency's efforts acceptable.

Authenticity has been a requirement since the earliest blogging days, when "ghost-blogging" was criticized as violating this rule. Regardless of the social channel you use, be honest and forthright, don't fake anything (such as Photoshopped images), and use your real voice. And while it's tempting to copy a competitor's effective social media activities, people can detect the lack of authenticity.

Multimedia

Visual communication has become a vital dimension of social media. Voluminous research has found that photos and video in social media posts achieve higher levels of engagement than text alone. According to one study, video has surpassed blogging as a social media marketing asset. More than 500 million hours of video are watched on YouTube every day; 500 hours of video are uploaded to the site every minute, reflecting people's hunger for video. Meanwhile, Instagram's success is a testament to audience interest in images.

COMPETENCIES FOR SOCIAL MEDIA MANAGEMENT

Social media is a means of communication. This does not mean that communicators automatically have the competencies to manage an organization's social media efforts. Upward of forty competencies have been identified as necessary for various social media activities.

Agencies and in-house communication teams should consider a competency audit to determine those the team already has and those that are missing. These competencies can then be mapped against a social media strategy to determine whether all the competencies required are present in order to execute the plan.

There are only three ways to acquire missing competencies: hire someone who has the required skills, get training for your existing staff, or outsource work to someone with the needed competencies.

Social media competencies fall into four categories. The following is by no means a comprehensive list, and new entries are appearing at a frantic pace. For example, just a few years ago, augmented reality was not a competency to consider; as it has gained steam and social uses for it emerged, it is currently ascending as a social media skill.

The four competency categories, and their associated skills, include the following:

Content Competencies
- Blogging
- Podcasting
- Writing for social media
- Graphics/infographics
- Video production (including knowing the video requirements for each social media channel)
- Content curation
- Coding
- Social visual communication
- Social event management
- Internal (employee) social media

Project Skills
- Search engine optimization (and search engine marketing)
- Blogger/influencer outreach
- Media buying
- Transmedia communication (using multiple channels as part of the same communication effort)
- Digital project management
- Digital/social measurement

Social-Specific Competencies
- Community management
- Social customer service
- Monitoring
- Social software expertise
- Advocacy/ambassador program management
- Wikipedia management
- Metrics
- Mobile communication (e.g., messaging apps)

Center of Excellence Competencies (coordinating social media efforts)
- Social media training
- Content management/strategic planning
- Cross-functional team coordination
- Analytics
- Policy development and management
- Social/digital governance
- Content distribution
- Crisis communications
- Social platform development
- Brand management

PR ACTIVITIES AND SOCIAL MEDIA

So far, we have reviewed several dimensions of social media. Now it is time to connect some of the dots between social media and the day-to-day work of public relations practitioners.

Social Media and Crisis Communications

Today, all crises are social media crises. It does not matter if the crisis emerged through social media or elsewhere; it will find its way there and spread like wildfire (regardless of whether the information people share is accurate).

Research from the Altimeter Group found that 76 percent of social media crises could have been diminished or averted if only the organization had taken appropriate steps before a crisis arose. Those steps include internal education, professional staff, a triage plan, clearly communicated employee policies, identification of relevant influencers, moderation skills, and community guidelines. Only 24 percent of the crises examined were deemed inevitable.

The same principles of pre–social media crisis management apply to a modern crisis. The public remains risk averse: for example, they attach little credibility to business advocates, and emotion (not logic) takes hold of people who feel that the organization's behavior has put them or their loved ones at risk. Organizations still need to respond quickly, accurately, professionally, and carefully. They must be transparent, treat perceptions as fact, acknowledge mistakes, avoid public confrontations, and so on.

What has changed due to social media is the unprecedented speed with which crises erupt and spread, the public's insatiable thirst for news (which, accurate or not, can be found aplenty on Twitter and other social services), and the increasingly porous boundaries between social media and mainstream media. (For example, rather than finding a "man on the street" to interview, many news outlets simply embed tweets shared by someone on the scene.)

Also, anyone can break news. Citizen journalism has become far more common thanks to the news-breaking equipment everyone carries in their pockets: a smartphone, which can record video and audio and share it through a social service before the affected organization or the news media even knows it happened.

This is what occurred during the "Miracle on the Hudson," when pilot Chesley "Sully" Sullenberger landed a plane on the Hudson River. A passenger on one of the ferries that diverted to rescue passengers took a picture with his phone and shared it before the airline or the press was aware that a plane was in the river. There is a video showing the speed with which the nascent Wikipedia entry on the incident was updated in the first two hours as new information emerged. You can watch it here: https://youtu.be/QqyYtWCyIjs.

The use of social media in a crisis has become a requirement for several reasons:

- Social media is increasingly where people go for news and information. During a crisis, online social interaction centers around the "emergency period" of an event, according to a study from the University of Colorado at Boulder.
- Social media enables organizations to update information instantly. This information can be crafted for both the media and the public. When a mass shooting occurred at Fort Hood in Texas, Scott & White, the local hospital chain, was able to notify the public instantly via Twitter that blood donations would be halted at a certain hour; the media used this information to pass the information along via traditional channels.
- Because social media is by nature authentic and human rather than corporate sounding, organizations can show empathy and compassion by employing a human voice.
- Social media produces a permanent record. For example, organizations called to account for their actions can point to messages shared online to validate that they took the correct actions.
- The two-way nature of social media is far more credible than the one-way distribution of information.

Crisis expert Melissa Agnes tells the tale of Emory University's crisis management during the Ebola outbreak. Missionary doctors who had been treating victims in Africa were returning to the United States and quarantined at Emory University Hospital's Serious Communicable Disease Unit, provoking fear that the virus would spread in the US. This led to a flood of critical comments on Emory's Facebook page. Emory monitored the page closely, identifying the key issues that emerged from the conversations, and used them to produce a video FAQ that addressed top concerns and corrected misperceptions. Agnes says, "They also created editorials and other educational materials to help their community truly understand their mission and the caution they were rightfully taking." The hospital's Facebook actions represent just a small part of its overall social media response to the crisis. Overall, the organization's effective use of social media succeeded in minimizing the damage that could have had long-lasting implications for Emory's reputation.

A Platform for Misinformation

Misinformation spreads via social media, often unabated. The leading social media channels—including Facebook and Twitter—have struggled to find a balance between permitting free speech and preventing the spread of both misinformation and hate speech. This requires organizations to amp up their ability to monitor social media, identify harmful disinformation about the organization (or its products, services, people, practices, and partners), and address the misinformation quickly and effectively.

The nature of misinformation is also evolving. Artificial intelligence has enabled people to create videos that appear to feature someone saying things they never said. Known as "deepfakes," these videos promise to create challenges for institutions that must combat the belief that a CEO or other representative said something outrageous, false, defamatory, or otherwise harmful. (There are also positive, legitimate uses for deepfakes. A company could, for example, reproduce a leader's speech in multiple languages, enabling the leader to reach international audiences by appearing to speak a language she doesn't actually understand.)

The deluge of false information also makes it incumbent on organizations to ensure accurate information is easily found. Practitioners will find that producing such information requires more content creation than they are accustomed to; they must also fact-check information, even though it can surface at an alarming rate. The pharmaceutical industry, for example, faces a growing anti-vaccination movement that is founded entirely on misinformation, requiring them to ensure the facts are available online. When a crisis begins to emerge from the anti-vaxxer community, social media can point to these existing resources, thus ensuring that accurate information offsets the bad information, emerges at the top of search engine results pages, and bolsters the organization's reputation.

SOCIAL MEDIA AND MEDIA RELATIONS

Media relations has undergone a seismic change thanks to social media. Some of the key considerations include the following:

- **Twitter**—Despite active user numbers that are far below those of other social media platforms—Twitter doesn't even rank in the top ten, with only about 350 million users, putting it in seventeenth place (number-one Facebook, by contrast, has 2.7 billion)—Twitter has emerged as the dominant channel for journalists and government leaders. One tactic media relations practitioners can employ is to identify the journalists who report on their company's or client's business (use a service such as Muck Rack to find them and their Twitter accounts) and follow them. Be responsive when they ask questions and share useful information in order to build a relationship, which will make it easier to pitch them when you have a story to send their way.
- **Brand journalism**—This term describes articles an organization produces about itself, employing journalistic standards to the reporting. Brand journalism is not meant to replace public journalism (after all, what company is going to investigate its own wrongdoing?). But applying this owned media can (among other things) provide journalists with research material. It is not unusual for articles produced in house to result in external media coverage.
- **Influencers**—As the number of journalists and media outlets declines—particularly in the newspaper world—they are being supplanted by website editors, bloggers, and other influencers, providing a new target for pitches. When the *Encyclopedia Britannica* introduced a service that allowed bloggers to link to its articles without requiring them to become paying subscribers, the company got the word out by reaching influencers in niche communities such as academia, journalism, and library sciences—professionals who had reason to avoid relying on the crowdsourced Wikipedia for encyclopedic information.

- **Social media press releases and newsrooms**—Introduced in 2006 by SHIFT Communications, the social media press release is posted online and incorporates features that make it easy for social media users to spread the news and engage in conversations about it. For example, key sentences can be made ready for tweeting; just a click creates the tweet for the user. The best social media news releases—which usually supplement rather than replace a traditional release—separate key facts and quotes, making it easier for journalists, bloggers, and others to find the elements of the release they will incorporate into their own articles. Images, audio, and video are also made easy to download. Get more information about social media releases here: https://www.shiftcomm.com/insights /social-media-press-release-3-0-2014-edition/.

  A social media newsroom expands on the concept of online newsrooms, which have been around since the mid-1990s as resources for journalists. Social media newsrooms include all the content of a traditional newsroom, but can integrate content from the shared media sites the company uses, such as YouTube, Twitter, and company blogs. These newsrooms also include icons that make it easy for anybody to share content, links to additional information and resources, RSS feeds to your company blog(s), embed codes for videos, and a directory to all social media assets. (Take a look at the Harvard Business School newsroom, which includes links to all the social media accounts of its various elements, such as Twitter accounts, faculty accounts, the *Harvard Business Review*, the Harvard Health Care Initiative, jobs, and many more, including the accounts of special initiatives: https://www.hbs.edu/news/social-media/Pages/default.aspx.)

INFLUENCERS AND AMBASSADORS

We discussed influencers earlier in this chapter, but they are worth examining as a distinct element of public relations in the social media era. Influencers fall into several categories:

- **Mega influencers** are the big names, such as Kim Kardashian and Kylie Jenner, with follower counts in the hundreds of millions and the ability to command large fees to promote a product. A photo of the influencer holding a cosmetic product or wearing a fashion company's clothes can spark interest and inspire sharing that may result in a significant bump in sales. Mega influencers stand out from others because, in all cases, organizations pay them to tap into their followers. (We will discuss pay-for-play in social media later in this chapter.)

- **Macro influencers** tend to earn their fame through means other than Instagram, but are highly desirable as a channel for sharing a company's information. Early social media adopter Chris Brogan, author of several books and a regular on the speaking circuit, has more than three hundred thousand followers. While his posts—and the interests of his followers— are narrower than a mega influencer's, he can still drive traffic to a product or service simply by mentioning it.

- **Micro influencers** have under one hundred thousand followers, but command respect and attention based on the niche in which they engage.

- **Advocates** are individuals who may not command the attention of other influencers, but when their voices combine, they can make an outsized impression. Also known as "ambassadors," they can help or hurt an organization organically, simply by rising up to support or oppose a company's actions or statements. Many organizations invite their most fervent advocates to become official ambassadors, providing them with content they can share or comment on, and boosting the reach of their messages. Employees are also emerging as a source of advocacy, with programs designed to encourage sharing of company content on their personal accounts. Among the reasons why this can be valuable are that employees generally are viewed as more credible than company spokespeople (and even more credible than the CEO, according to the Edelman Trust Barometer), and that they can reach many people not reached by the company's official social media channels.

SOCIAL MEDIA AND BRAND JOURNALISM/CONTENT MARKETING

According to the Content Marketing Institute, content marketing is "a strategic marketing approach focused on creating and distributing valuable, relevant and consistent content to attract and retain a clearly defined audience—and, ultimately, to drive profitable customer action." While content marketing appears to fall in marketing's jurisdiction rather than PR's, the creation of content can serve

PR as well as marketing. (Brand journalism, addressed earlier in this chapter, is one type of content marketing.)

Digital thought leader Neil Patel argues that content marketing needs PR to ensure the work stands out:

> *PR is all about reaching out to the right people. PR pros create and maintain relationships with editors, journalists, and influencers. Content marketing is all about getting attention by telling awesome stories. When you create content that helps or entertains your audience, it gets shared and can even go viral. Combine PR and content marketing and you're putting ready-made stories into the hands of editors, journalists, and influencers. They can give your content the powerful boost it needs to go viral. On top of that, the more quality content you produce, the easier you'll find it is to get the attention of editors. They may even have noticed your content before you reach out.*

PR AND THE STORIES PHENOMENON

In October 2013, Snapchat added a new feature to its app: Stories. Separate from the other posts that Snapchat users shared, content shared via Stories was ephemeral, vanishing in twenty-four hours. It was wildly successful, leading Instagram to adopt the concept and improve on it so much that it became one of its most popular features, eclipsing Snapchat's innovation. Eventually, Stories-like features were added to most social media channels, including Facebook and Twitter.

Communicators have embraced Stories in a big way. Among the uses to which PR practitioners have put Stories are the following:

- Product promotion
- Interviews
- Behind-the-scenes content
- Polls

Earlier, we mentioned augmented reality as a competency that agencies or in-house communications departments may require. Instagram Stories feature AR functionality in the form of filters that brands can pay to create and share, allowing users to add the filters to their images.

PAY-FOR-PLAY

The traditional definition of PR features a wall between it and marketing/advertising. Under this definition, PR is *earned* media, while marketing and advertising are *paid* media, and never the twain shall meet. Social media has upended this concept. Communicators seeking to expand the reach of their social media posts are able to pay to promote the content. (This is why the use of social media marketing tools is a required competency for PR teams.) Promotion of posts usually involves identifying target markets based on geography, age, gender, and interest.

Sponsored content (also known as "native advertising") is another pay-for-play category that holds promise for communicators. (Its origin is the advertorial.) While there are many categories of sponsored content, the best is a work of journalism about a topic that an organization wants covered; the organization either produces the content themselves or has the native advertising department of a media outlet create it. When published in a mainstream media outlet, these articles are clearly designated as sponsored but can attract just as much (if not more) attention than a news or feature article prepared by the editorial staff.

The Netflix series *Orange Is the New Black* provides an excellent example of native advertising. As the series was about to launch a new season, it paid for an article in the *New York Times* that investigated the state of women's prisons in the US. It was as much a work of investigative journalism as any prepared by the *Times*'s journalists, yet it also raised awareness of the show's return.

EXECUTIVES ON SOCIAL MEDIA

Most executives do not use social media as a communication channel, instead delegating the responsibility to the PR, marketing, or social media team. The reasons run the gamut from lack of time to advice from the legal department to avoid social media because of the risk. (Lawyers' jobs are all about minimizing risk.)

This is a mistake. Presidents, CEOs, and other organizational leaders *should* have a social media presence, for several reasons. For one, employees expect to see their leaders on social media. A 2019 study by the Brunswick Group found that 65 percent of employees believe it is important for CEOs to represent their companies online; 60 percent review executive social media accounts before accepting a job offer. (In general, a large percentage of employees follow company social media accounts as a way to stay current with what's going in in the company, further blurring the lines between internal and external communication.)

CEOs are also able to bring a human touch to their brand communications. An established executive social media account can be brought to bear instantly during a crisis.

Most important, though, is that an executive engaging on social media will hear directly from fans and critics, which provides an unfiltered look into the public's reactions to company news and activities. Further, leaders can become influencers, building a fan base that can serve the organization well. Among executives using social media well, look at the accounts of Delta Airlines' Ed Bastian, Hubspot's Brian Halligan, and General Motors' Mary Barra.

OTHER THOUGHT LEADERSHIP

Leaders are not the only company representatives who can serve a company's interests by having a social media presence. Thought leaders are those in the organization who provide insight and guidance to their followers. Once you've identified your organization's thought leaders (which tends to be easy), you can train and assist them in producing content for LinkedIn articles, blog posts, and tweets. This will grow the audience of people who are interested in what they have to say and expand the organization's reputation.

MONITORING AND MEASURING SOCIAL MEDIA

Like any public relations activity, measurement must be a part of any social media campaign or program. After all, without measurement, how would you know your efforts are working? As noted, social media platforms provide metrics that can lead PR counselors to assume they are succeeding, but these metrics actually measure the wrong things. Measuring "likes," for example, may be personally gratifying, but does not let you know whether you have moved someone to action. (Among the user actions that constitute engagement, likes are the least valuable. Much more important are comments, retweets, mentions, and shares.)

A lot of communicators also measure impressions (the digital version of OTS— opportunity to see). Again, the value of impressions is questionable when your communication was designed to produce some kind of outcome. More valuable are traditional PR measurements, such as share of voice and sentiment. Just as marketers measure referrals and conversions from social media, it is important for PR practitioners to identify the outcome they seek from social media activities, choose the metrics that will determine whether those objectives have been met, then measure appropriately.

Monitoring is often lumped together with measurement because it uses some of the same tools. Monitoring social media is part of environmental scanning, a long-standing PR activity through which organizations identify trends, opportunities, and threats by analyzing media reports, regulatory activity, competitive activity, the state of the economy, and other indicators. Adding social media to the mix can provide invaluable insights that were once available only from surveys and focus groups.

Monitoring social media allows organizations to watch online mentions of the brand, its people, products, and other assets, along with any engagement those mentions produce. Monitoring will reveal discussions about the organization in blog posts, tweets and retweets, reviews, and other social media platforms, enabling the PR function to determine how to respond and whether new content is advisable.

There is a wide range of free and paid tools that companies can use to monitor social media. These tools also enable social listening, which is different from monitoring. Monitoring is designed to alert you to a situation that requires a quick response (even if it's just thanking someone for a mention on Twitter), while listening enables you to understand market perceptions in order to inform the approach you take to communication.

TAKEAWAYS

1. Once a novelty and a target of derision, social media has evolved into a required component of most public relations plans. What are the risks of ignoring social media? If they're not talking about you on social media, you don't exist.

2. Social media describes online platforms that enable anybody to publish and share content or engage in networking. These platforms have three key characteristics: they are shared, free, and easy to use.

(*continued*)

3. Social media began with blogs but now comprises a large universe: social networks, media-sharing networks, discussion forums (or newsgroups), bookmarking and content-curation networks, consumer review networks, blogging and publishing networks, and niche networks.

4. Active social media channels can allow companies to address situations quickly, especially crises.

5. The basics of good media relations apply to social media as well. Your "brand voice" needs to be consistent and authentic. Social media is two-way—a conversation that connects you directly with people you want to reach, helping build relationships. Photos and videos are a key part of the conversation.

6. Consider auditing your communications teams to determine what social media competencies are in place, and which need to be created or obtained.

7. Social media can and must augment, and be integrated into, the traditional work of public relations practitioners.

8. As with any PR activity, measurement must be part of any social media campaign.

ADDITIONAL RESOURCES

The impact of social media on public relations cannot be understated and involves far more than a single chapter can deliver. To learn more, the following books can be valuable resources:

- *The New Rules of Marketing & PR* by David Meerman Scott
- *Social Media and Public Relations* by Deirdre Breakenridge
- *The Seven Success Factors of Social Business Strategy* by Charlene Li and Brian Solis
- *Social Media ROI: Managing and Measuring Social Media Efforts in Your Organization* by Olivier Blanchard

- *Trust Agents: Using the Web to Build Influence, Improve Reputation, and Earn Trust* by Chris Brogan and Julien Smith
- *The Social Media Strategist: Build a Successful Program from the Inside Out* by Christopher Barger

CHAPTER 10

Internal Communications

Enduring Themes Focusing on Company Priorities

WILLIAM KEMMIS ADLER
TEREX CORPORATION

M y favorite definition of "internal communications" is that *it is our story*. As an organization, who are we, what are we trying to do, and why? Whether we are a team of five or five hundred thousand, these questions are silently omnipresent, waiting to be addressed. How successful we are in communicating this to our team members will have an enormous impact on our ability to recruit, motivate, and retain a talented workforce, and to achieve our strategic goals so we can compete successfully in the marketplace. If the team isn't working toward common business goals, they will never achieve them.

Internal communication is much more than what leaders tell employees. It is the sum of all team member perceptions about the organization, within the organization. Companies with strong, well-integrated internal communication create a firm foundation on which to interact with employees, so the team can get things done. Conversely, those with inconsistent and unclear internal communication rarely achieve their goals in the long run. Further, internal and external communications inevitably cross-pollinate, so a failed internal program can also impact external perception and ultimately organizational success.

In this chapter we will cover (1) Mission, Vision, and Values; (2) Strategy; (3) Implementation; (4) Channels; and (5) Leadership. The examples are from my professional experience along with insights from respected colleagues with whom I have worked over the years. Their quotes are previously unpublished and were provided for this book.

MISSION, VISION, AND VALUES

Building trust and credibility internally is earned—there's no magic formula. It's about being completely transparent and honest. No hidden agendas. Period. Each of us only has one reputation. Go out of your way to involve other parties and build consensus. This can be time consuming and messy, but the outcome of true collaboration is always worth it.

—Lynne Collins, communications counselor; former communications director at Saatchi & Saatchi

What's our story? CEOs usually have a clear idea of their company's mission, but articulating it is another matter, and expecting employees to absorb it without effort is magical thinking. For the team to embrace and act on top-down messaging, they need to share a common understanding of the company's mission. An internal communication program needs to build upon a widely shared and understood series of interrelated statements that describe Mission, Vision, and Values.

Mission: A short definition of the company, its objectives, and its approach to reaching those objectives. This should define what the enterprise is—its reason for being.

Vision: An aspirational statement about the desired future state of the company.

Values: A list of core values that remain steadfast despite external change or challenges. This is what your company stands for. Values are what makes the mission enduring.

Companies may also communicate their "Unique Value Proposition." This is used especially in a marketing context and spells out what is special about a brand or business.

Mission statements are notorious for being jumbled, pretentious, self-congratulatory run-on phrases that sound as if they were written by a committee, as they often are. A good mission statement is succinct, clear, and free from corporate-speak so the team can relate to and believe in it. For the communicator, the task is to engage at the highest levels of leadership to help shape a coherent, candid, durable statement. This takes time, effort, and a good deal of consensus building.

Often, simple is best. General Electric developed a new mission statement for its Treasury operations in 2014 to help employees understand a complex organization that conducted financing transactions and esoteric risk analysis in a heavily regulated post-recession environment. The senior team met for months, and the explanations they drafted became longer and denser as they listed all of the organization's activities and imperatives. The statement became impenetrable, but the team was determined to keep working until they could plainly describe their mission to employees.

Eventually, former treasurer Kathy Cassidy had an epiphany. She called on her team to stop deliberating and simplify the statement. The result was this gem: *We fund the company and help to keep it safe.*

Similarly, I was on a team at the Reader's Digest Association, now called Trusted Media Brands, that struggled to create statements that were simple yet meaningful as the company was transforming in 2008. After some time, the team whittled long, laborious statements into this clear vision: *We will create the world's largest multiplatform communities based on branded content.*

So, "mission" explains what we're here to do, and "vision" is what we expect to achieve. What guides our behavior as we're going about getting all this done? This is where "values" come in.

Many organizations publish a set of values, and these, too, can sound formulaic, contrived, self-congratulatory, or even ironic. To avoid these pitfalls, the values must mean something important to the company. Terex Corporation created six "Terex Way values" to guide the way leaders and team members conduct themselves: *Respect, Integrity, Improvement, Courage, Citizenship*, and *Servant Leadership*. These values reflect the needs of an organization that is diverse in geography, industries, and types or levels of jobs, as well as the nationality and ethnicity of team members. The words were chosen to reflect the common attributes that Terex team members need to embrace. The team hears about the Terex Way values constantly, from the initial job interview and throughout their tenure. The concepts are referenced in company literature and articles on the intranet. They are cited when team members win an award and discussed during performance reviews. The linkage is so present and obvious that the values are more than mere words, but rather guideposts to live by.

When you create a strong mission or vision statement, or a list of core values, every word should have essential and clear meaning that is important to that organization. After this is in place, you can begin to build your communications program.

STRATEGY

In a world this stressed, immediate, and unpredictable, the role and value of workforce communication has exceptional importance. Employees hear the news first, and they are fully equipped to have intelligent conversations that day with customers, partners, or anyone in their sphere of influence. More than ever, internal communication has to create true believers—clear on the core values and what we stand for, a desire to contribute to the higher purpose of our company and role in the world, and with a genuine belief that they have a voice, and it's heard and respected.

—Mark Harris, global communications advisor, Xero software; retired VP, IBM Consulting; United Press International (UPI)

An organization's communication strategy should support the overall strategy of the enterprise. It must not simply react to events or demands—that results in "noise" and doesn't drive directed action. All communications should be strategic and fit for purpose. Everything you communicate should advance the values, initiatives, and goals of the organization.

Great internal communication supports an organization's goals and delivers through planning. It starts at the top (board of directors, CEO) and aligns with mission, vision, and values. Typically, a communications strategy focuses on elements such as these:

1. Long-term operating plan
2. Annual operating plan
3. Business strategic plans

4. Change management
5. Human resources (HR) initiatives—recruiting, retaining, and developing talent, and supporting engagement, morale, and productivity
6. Diversity, Equity, and Inclusion plan
7. Departmental plans—functions like Finance and Information Technology

Make sure you understand your company's strategic direction. What are the metrics for measuring success? What are the Key Performance Indicators at the corporate, business, and functional levels? The answers will provide insights on where to focus your program.

Informed by the strategic plan, you can start to form your priorities. What is most critical to achieve? What information does your audience need or want? What will motivate them to pay attention? And, perhaps most important, what do you want your audience to understand or do?

At Terex Corporation, we typically have four or five key internal communication objectives for a given year—no more than that. Each is fleshed out in detail, including what success will look like for the objective. The plan should be reviewed throughout the year, especially if there is an opportunity for a midyear review—we call it "Midyear Calibration." This is an opportunity for the communicator to make mid-course corrections, and to make sure he or she is aligned with leadership expectations.

To reach hearts and minds, you'll want to focus intensely on your principal themes. This calls for repetition, especially through communications from your senior-most leader. I have had the good fortune to work for several CEOs who are exceptional at driving home key messages:

- Thomas O. Ryder, who led Reader's Digest Association from 1998 to 2005, used his communications acumen and the power of repetition to begin a global transformation at the firm. He brought with him an appreciation of employee communications honed at American Express, where he had served as president of Travel-Related Services. This was urgently needed at Reader's Digest, where a comfortable legacy culture had left the team ill prepared to compete in the burgeoning digital age. He envisioned how the company could leverage its content online and compete in the new era. As Ryder made his changes, he held regular "Town Halls," staged professionally in a private theater filled with employees. The events were streamed online to team members all around the world—a very early example of a company using such technology—so teams from Australia to Brazil to Poland could all gather, watch, and participate. He also video-recorded updates from his desk and streamed them worldwide. He committed to thoroughly explaining the changes that were taking place in the company, the reasons for them, and the new businesses being launched. "It's axiomatic that clear, consistent employee communication is necessary to create or change a corporate culture," Ryder said, looking back at his program. "However, frequency is vital. I often grew weary of my own messages just about the time they were beginning to register with my colleagues. It's important to repeat the vital messages, over and over, and over again. And again."

- John L. Garrison Jr., chairman & CEO of Terex Corporation, addressed his company's Global Leadership Team in 2019, and behind him was a slide emblazoned with a version of the famous quote by Procter & Gamble's A. G. Lafley: *Transforming an organization requires excruciating repetition and clarity.* "Leaders need to develop clear, consistent communications on what is important to the organization," Garrison said. "Repetition is important, especially in large, multicultural, multi-language organizations. Leaders may think they've communicated because they have said something once or twice or even three times, but communication involves both saying and receiving. The more that we can communicate directly with team members, in multiple formats and channels, the better we can impart the priorities and changes that need to be made."

When Garrison became Terex CEO in 2015, he announced that his top priority was to create a "Zero Harm" safety culture in the workplace. This would be achieved through methodical tracking of safety metrics and steady communications across all channels, including stand-up meetings, digital screens, posters, the intranet, email, and awards programs. Team members are encouraged to spot hazards and report them, and to "pause the job" (halt manufacturing) if necessary. "We start every monthly review, every Board meeting—every gathering of any kind—with a discussion of safety and environment performance. With consistency and repetition, after five years we're starting to deliver better-than-industry norms overall in safety performance. We're still not at Zero Harm yet, so we cannot stop communicating," Garrison said.

For an internal communication program, strategy is the bridge that guides you from concept to execution. Next we will look at how to put plans into action.

IMPLEMENTATION

Effective internal communication is predicated on deeply under-standing not just the requirements of executive leadership, but also the needs of the audience. What are the likely points of resis-tance, skepticism, fear, uncertainty, or lack of knowledge? The effective communicator balances head and heart: she or he speaks to people's need to understand the facts clearly and logically and to their need to be moved, inspired, assured, and motivated. This kind of integrated, balanced communication needs to cascade down the reporting chain and across the organization, allowing employees to hear the information directly from their manager in an authentic manner.

—David Wickenden, retired SVP corporate strategy, AARP; former SVP, FleishmanHillard; UPI

Steps to implement a successful internal communications program include:

- Identify your audiences, program owners, and clients.
- Set realistic goals and timelines.
- Establish a process for approving communications.
- Build the team.
- Apply or develop the channels you'll need (*see next section*).
- Set cadence for key communications.
- Agree on the process and metrics for tracking performance.

From a practical standpoint, you will need to understand who ultimately "owns" internal communication. It may be the CEO, HR, or in some cases marketing or investor relations. Or, you may be part of a larger communications organization that includes public relations, government relations, and so forth. Identify your top stakeholders in the company—think of them as core clients. These would likely include business and functional leaders. Another key department is information technology, given that so many of your channels and tools will be technology based. Your plan should be built to serve these owners and stakeholders.

I place a high premium on establishing an alliance with HR, because their interest and yours coincide most closely. Amy George, SVP and chief HR officer (CHRO) at Terex, said a strong internal communication partner can be of tremendous value to HR, helping them to explain new or changed policies and processes and to build understanding around strategic direction. "A large part of an HR leader's job is to help manage organizational change," George said. "That cannot be done without strong internal communications. If you think about classic change management, some of the key steps are explaining the 'why,' sharing the vision, mobilizing commitment, making change last, and monitoring progress. Each one of these steps requires clear communication to be successful."

Internal communication is like marketing, but your product is ideas—which, if embraced by your audience, can support engagement, morale, productivity, and loyalty. It is imperative to identify your internal targets, starting with the basics like head count, locations, departments, and demographics. In addition to an overall strategy, your plan will ultimately include strategic goals for individual segments within your internal population.

I recommend creating a formal communication plan on how you will reach your audience, reviewed and ultimately approved by your CEO and CHRO. By agreeing on priorities, strategy, and tactics, you will have a clear road map for your program. You and your leadership team will have the same expectations. Events may cause any plan to be reevaluated and updated midstream, but good planning is how all programs should begin.

Start by candidly assessing the current state of your program—is there a legacy internal communication program? Find out which channels have been most or least effective. If possible, survey the organization to get a baseline view, and begin a dialogue that will help you plan an effective and impactful program. This period of analysis should look at each sub-segment of your audience. What are the issues affecting the teams, country by country? Are there issues in factories or call centers, or an outside sales force, all of which are traditionally hard-to-reach audiences? At this point, you will want to understand any mission-critical goals of each business and function within the company.

Now it's time to identify your team. I have worked with small, midsize, and large teams and as a solo practitioner. Teams of any size can be effective if the plan is well implemented and realistic for what the organization expects from you. If your team is small, you can build out with alliances to the businesses or functions for which communication is important, or secure freelance or other external help.

As you develop your program, make sure you understand what is most important to your organization and its leaders. Critically, what is most important to the CEO and CHRO? Make sure that everything relates back to your plan. Focus your resources and attention on what is most critical, and avoid drifting off plan. Any action you take means tacitly deciding *not* to do something else.

"Every communication must link back to the plan or it's not valuable," said Mark Nowlan, retired Microsoft executive and my colleague at PR Newswire in the 1990s. "In your executive's voice, you need a succinct problem statement linked explicitly to the strategic plan, a clear expectation for action, and specific deliverables. This is key to engagement and getting results, whether via one-to-one in person, a talk at an all-hands meeting, or in a written message."

Positioning yourself as a trusted advisor is the key to being taken seriously in communication. You want to be known for impact. You want to *provide* impact. Never fall into the trap of being exclusively an order taker. It is tempting to say "yes" to all requests, but you need to be a strategic player who drives a mission-critical agenda, not simply as a means for getting the story out to the team.

CHANNELS

The foundation of an effective internal communication program has four elements—authenticity, vulnerability, honesty and regularity. Speak from your heart with empathy and humility, and you will have impact.
        —Anthony Harrison, corporate communications leader; former Facebook, Microsoft, The New York Times Company

A channel is any means of reaching your target audience with your message. If you are taking over a legacy program, you may start by using the channels that are functioning well and build from there. You can use online analytics or team member surveys to get a sense of what is working best.

A well-presented intranet is a terrific communications tool. I place a value on providing team members with information in a straightforward manner, with clarity and accuracy. This is a good way to get onto the team's desktops or smartphones with articles, photos, and streamed video, much as team members are accustomed to finding at online news sites. Recently, I have used Bonzai and Microsoft Share-Point Online as intranet platforms.

You can host virtual team meetings using online collaboration tools. You also can email certain announcements and make use of streamed video and multimedia news packages. Other channels include videoconferencing, podcasts, digital signage, kiosks, and recognition and reward platforms. More traditional channels like posters and print newsletters can still play roles. Small-team meetings are an effective channel because team members place a lot of trust in their immediate supervisor. This means you need to keep line managers informed and supplied with communications tools. Everything the team sees during their day is a touchpoint. I like to use multiple channels because everyone has different preferences in how they consume information.

Much of your communication will originate from senior leaders. However, not all communication is top down. Team members may give you feedback or share information among themselves. Viewpoints or consensus can be built holistically, through interaction. Companies used to fear this kind of crosstalk. Today, we look at it as another channel opportunity. This can include online team video collaboration—I use BlueJeans by Verizon and Microsoft Teams—and various types of internal web chats, webcasts, forums, and chat. Microsoft Teams, as well as Slack and Yammer, enable team members to converse among themselves—think of it as corporate social media. There are also countless employee communication apps available that you can discover by searching online.

Companies chart the progress of their communications and team member engagement through surveys, ranging from on-the-spot questionnaires (through platforms like SurveyGizmo and SurveyMonkey) to professionally conducted surveys seeking detailed feedback from the entire organization.

"At Terex we do a comprehensive team member engagement survey every other year," Amy George said. "This allows us to identify global issues that affect team members, as well as local issues that may relate to a specific site. Key to our process is understanding the issues our team members are raising and putting together plans to address them. But what is even more essential is making sure that we communicate throughout the process. This begins with sharing the survey results back out to our team members—thanking them for taking the time to give us their feedback and recapping their comments to let them know that they've been heard. Without this initial feedback, I believe that our team members would grow cynical—feeling like their input was not being considered or taken seriously."

It is important to keep team members updated about progress against the action plans, which encourages them to remain engaged and provide further input as they see action plans unfold.

Your choice of channels depends on the type of communication and audience. Jennifer Sutton, a communications leader and former journalist, does an inspired job of reaching global team members who manufacture for her company, Genie, mobile elevating work platforms. "A little more than half of the workforce does not have regular access to a work computer or a corporate email address," Sutton said. "So, when I think about my audiences, they're divided into three different categories: professional staff who have desk-based jobs; sales and service professionals who travel to visit customers; and team members who spend their day on a factory floor. Within these audiences are different geographies and languages to consider, in addition to the different functional areas where they work. For me, this means finding ways to deliver consistent messages across multiple communications channels that are wide-reaching and high-tech, as well as low-tech but high-touch."

For Genie, reaching shop-floor personnel includes posters in common areas, tabletop informational displays, and a cloud-based digital signage solution that delivers a mix of local and corporate content. Managers are asked to cascade updates to their teams during team meetings. To make sure a consistent message is delivered, Sutton provides supervisors with high-level bullet points.

Another way to reach team members is through corporate social responsibility (CSR), which comprises a company's giving program and team member volunteering. Over the years, I have been able to weave together programs that generate engagement by enabling team members to volunteer and do something together for the community. This becomes even more effective if linked to Diversity, Equity, and Inclusion initiatives to empower nonmajority teams within the population. At GE Capital, working under Eleanor Mascheroni, Managing Director of Communications, we had an annual budget of $6 million in CSR donations that was focused on driving and supporting team member engagement. "Employee communications, when based on truth and authenticity and reality, is even more meaningful when associated with community relations activities that matter to employees," said Mascheroni, today a C-suite strategic communications advisor and board director. "To be recognized for things outside the organization makes the internal environment richer."

Susan Fraysse Russ, who led internal communication and the company foundation at Reader's Digest Association, has developed CSR linkage to a fine art. "When workplace volunteer programs were first introduced, there was a misconception that if you offer employees the opportunity to volunteer, they will choose that over doing their jobs," Russ said. "Instead, it was shown that employees who volunteer are *more* productive overall—a spin on the adage, 'if you want something done, ask a busy person.' And it was proven that employees who volunteer are more engaged in the company's mission overall. The goal of employee communications is to have an informed, engaged, and productive workforce—so it makes perfect sense to align the two functions. Hold a town hall meeting and follow it with a Day of Caring; end your executive retreat with an activity at the local family shelter; or incorporate service projects into your leadership off-site."

Employing the right channel for the audience and task at hand leads to powerful results.

LEADERSHIP

If communications are not candid and transparent, people see through them and management can quickly lose credibility. While certain information cannot always be disclosed, leadership should strive to share as much as possible to keep team members informed. During challenging times, in the absence of information, people make up their own to fill in the blanks and it is often far harsher than the truth. Even when the messages are tough and hard to take, people appreciate honesty. Candor and transparency build credibility and keep team members engaged.
        —Amy George, SVP and CHRO, Terex Corporation

A successful internal communication program is built around enduring themes and focuses on company priorities. Employees want to hear from you, as they yearn for a compelling purpose to rally around. The work relationship is intimate and, for most people, high on their importance list.

"We spend most of our waking hours at our jobs, so our work is one of our absolute primary relationships in life," said Tom Warters, a senior HR leader at The Hartford and formerly with GE Capital. "When you consider it, the economic well-being of our loved ones is attached to that relationship. It is *anything* but casual. Communications is how you build trust, whether it is one-on-one, or through the intranet. Your success will depend on the degree to which those things feel legitimate, honest, candid, and trusted—can I rely on what I see and am being told? Does the message align with what I'm experiencing? All of this is essential."

Team members want to be part of something important, and they look to leaders for inspiration and guidance. Most people who rise to the top of organizations are skilled practitioners of written, video, and in-person communications. Some make it a high priority.

John Garrison, CEO of Terex, for example, is a natural communicator. He issues a team member blog every Monday, fifty-two times a year, and if he visits a manufacturing plant, you may find him 180 feet in the air on a piece of equipment, shooting a selfie video on his iPhone to stream to team members. But not all CEOs are that comfortable with communications. It's up to you to make sure you're around their leadership table, or at least on their calendar, so you can help them leverage their skills and inclinations. Each one of them likely has a communications superpower—you just need to find out what that is!

When GE Capital was selling off assets in 2015, new treasurer Dan Janki was in planning meetings around the clock. HR articulated a growing need for top-down messaging, and Janki mentioned that he would like to do a hallway "stand-up" meeting—but he wanted no fuss or preparation. "Just put up a sign where I should appear and a time, and I'll be there," he told me. I had trepidation, as normally we would prepare. I posted a sign and stacked up some boxed lunches. People were curious and gathered at the appointed time. Janki bounded down the hall and aced his one-hour talk, to the minute. He was riveting. Having discovered that impromptu remarks were Janki's communications superpower, HR and I planned more on-the-fly sessions until everyone on the team had been reached.

At PR Newswire, the late John Williams was key to building a fiercely customer-centric company. I never saw him read from a script, but his talks to the staff were vivid and from the heart. He would shout. He would implore. He would amuse. And he always inspired. His superpower was raw charisma. Similarly, at UPI, I saw CEO Luis Nogales use personal charisma when there literally was nothing but depressing financial news to share with the team during Chapter 11 proceedings. On the darkest days, he would walk through the office, pausing to talk to team members, keeping his shoulders up, using body language to suggest, "Let's keep fighting; let's keep our dignity."

At The New York Times Company in the mid-1990s, James Cutie led a new division formed to build digital businesses and marketing partnerships. His brief was to achieve proof of concept for new media and brand extensions, and to make money for the company. The goal was to do this quickly and quietly in an organization still very much devoted to print. His superpower was communicating in a cerebral, *Times*-like way. Couriers delivered weekly newsletters by hand to each team member, and the package was a gray envelope marked in black letters, "Top Secret." Who wouldn't open that? The mechanism was a bit of a wink, and everyone felt part of something important.

John Patterson, a senior communications advisor and journalist I first met at UPI, reminds us that it is our job to help our leaders communicate effectively. At one point, Patterson wrote for a US senator who was brilliant but, in his extemporaneous remarks, was no friend of concision. "He would wander off the subject and circle around it. He eventually returned to the point, but the journey was interminable and often confusing," Patterson said. "I decided to apply a technique I had used early on to train young broadcast writers. I recorded a few of his rhetorical flights and reproduced them exactly as they were spoken, including the repetitions, the uhs and ahs, the incomplete sentences, everything. Seeing them in print was a revelation to him. I can't honestly say he reformed completely, but the point was made, and it did help him."

Showing leaders their own words can become a "forcing function," according to Tom Warters. "A lot of times, leaders can't separate their choice from the factors they're focused on, and it's only when you show them the communication that they see it from the perspective of someone who had not made the journey with them," Warters said. "It forces leaders to narrow down their options and consider what they really want to say and do. It helps them to think about how they arrived at the decision and how someone might react to seeing it."

TAKEAWAYS

A communicator is a business executive who specializes in the tools he uses to achieve results. He must be every bit the expert in the business, as is his client, or he won't be recognized as a trusted advisor and member of the Leadership Team. Executive communication pros help leaders spot the boulders on the path and move them out of the way—competitive threats, political issues, skill and resource gaps. When communicating with the executive, you'll always have a seat at the table if you articulate how your actions are helping to drive success.

—Mark Nowlan, retired strategic communications expert; formerly Microsoft and SVP PR Newswire

Whether your company has a major initiative or a crisis, its internal communication leadership, strategy, and execution must be flawless. We close this chapter with five real-world case studies.

1. **Fighting a Pandemic**: When the COVID-19 pandemic struck in 2020, Terex faced the challenge of keeping team members safe in factories across the world—including coronavirus hot spots like China, Italy, Germany, the United States, and the United Kingdom. The company kept a steady flow of information to empower the teams to stay safe. "With locations all over the world, we were continually confronted with new situations," said CHRO Amy George. "Communication was key to letting people know what our standard global safety protocols were and what was expected of them. Initially our communications were geared around the safety protocols required for how to return to work safely. But they quickly evolved into tips and best practices designed to keep team members safe no matter where they were. This was important because contact tracing was indicating that most COVID-19 cases were contracted via community spread. We varied our communications as much as possible to keep our team members

(continued)

involved. An example was inviting team members to send in videos of their children demonstrating safety protocols. These proved to be both entertaining and informative."

2. **History's Largest Asset Sale**: When Eleanor Mascheroni was hired by GE Capital to take over Communications in early 2015, she had no idea that within weeks the parent GE would decide to sell most of GE Capital's assets—about $400 billion—and offboard 95 percent of the global staff of 37,500. She inherited a small staff and hit the floor running. The company was determined to treat employees with candor and respect, and to tell them everything that was going to happen. Within two years, the mission was accomplished with almost no disruption. Mascheroni cites highly credible virtual town halls held by GE Capital CEO Keith Sherin, and top-level professional work by her team. "GE was beyond brilliant in addressing the issues right up front, so employees knew they would be fairly treated. It created a foundation of trust. We made the decision early on to take all Q&A, no matter how difficult. We were able to articulate every possible scenario for them—stay, stay for a while and leave, leave with an asset purchaser, or leave immediately. We used every channel: video, microsite, town halls, stand-ups, and emails." One HR colleague gave the program perhaps the best possible compliment: everyone could tell that they were hearing the real story, not one of several competing narratives.

3. **Creative Disruption**: Just before Halloween, Genie communicator Jennifer Sutton was concerned that team members in the manufacturing facilities in Washington State might not have been aware of important changes to the healthcare Open Enrollment process, given that most are not on the intranet or company email. "They do not all arrive at work at the same time, do not have common meetings, and aren't able to schedule time during the workday to attend virtual or in-person Q&A sessions," Sutton said. "The only commonality is that, in each factory, there is a shared break room. This provided the

(*continued*)

basis for a disruptive communications tactic designed to raise awareness and keep Open Enrollment top-of-mind for these employees," she said. The solution: Sutton and colleagues from HR went into the lunchroom dressed in benefits-themed Halloween costumes, including "Nightmare on Benefits Street" (someone who forgot to enroll). The team reverse-trick-or-treated, going around to lunch tables to distribute candy and a handout about the critical need to participate in Open Enrollment.

4. **Dramatic Culture Change**: From 2007 to 2009, the Reader's Digest Association underwent a lightning-fast and all-encompassing global culture change program. The senior team identified four values or attributes that were critical to success—Fast, Accountable, Candid, and Engaged. This became "The FACE Plan," which integrated initiatives around cost reductions, culture change, and growth. Our communications team was charged with making sure every team member understood and got on board with the plan. You could not visit the intranet, walk down the hall, or even look at what was written on the side of your pen (or on your hat or T-shirt) without seeing "The FACE Plan." The attributes were discussed during performance reviews, and the entire employee population was invited to grade leaders on how well they demonstrated the values. This was an example of total blanketing of channels and program integration. The FACE Plan succeeded in changing the fundamentals of the culture.

5. **Embracing the Critics**: In 2014, Tom Warters was serving as GE Capital Treasury HR leader, and after negative employee-feedback surveys he made the decision to invite high-profile critics to join the employee-survey response team. This was not window dressing; the team was empowered to suggest changes and present them to senior leadership for possible adoption. "This sent a signal that we don't want to live in a call-and-response community. I would rather live in a conversation," Warters said. "I don't want to have a fence between our yards and throw things over back and forth; I'd rather take the

(continued)

fence down and let's talk about it. Whether you like it or not, your critics are out there working on your brand. Every day. You owe it to yourself to understand what they are saying. In a lot of criticism there is a grain of truth. If you're confident enough to spend time with your critics and really listen for what could be going on, whether you agree with them or not, some very positive things can happen." In this case, an innovative communications approach led to improved survey results.

A final word on leadership, and this is important: As your organization's internal communicator, you need to be a keeper of the flame of integrity. You are accountable to your boss, your CEO, your CHRO, but also to all the other stakeholders, including your team members. Treat them with respect, which means providing timely and understandable information that they need and can use. You are a conduit, a spokesperson, a news director, and a press secretary. Never be just an order taker, or a propagandist, spin doctor, or censor. Establish yourself as the company's best source for accurate, reliable information. Maintain a reputation for results and credibility, and you will have the best chance of succeeding.

CHAPTER 11

Crisis Communications

Not If, but When

JONATHAN DEDMON
THE DILENSCHNEIDER GROUP

You never want a serious crisis to go to waste.

—Rahm Emanuel

The quote above is from former Chicago mayor Rahm Emanuel, who was President Barack Obama's chief of staff during the 2008–2009 economic crisis and Great Recession. However, similar comments go at least as far back as Italian diplomat, philosopher, and writer Niccolò Machiavelli in Renaissance Florence.

Of course, no one and no organization wants a crisis, but inevitably one will happen.

Crises come in all shapes and sizes, but generally share several attributes:

- They are unexpected.
- They have a strong emotional resonance with a company's key stakeholders, the media, and the public.

- They evolve in unpredictable ways.
- Events seem to outstrip an organization's ability to deal with them.
- They call into serious question the competence and quality of a company's governance and management. For example, Dennis Muilenburg is no longer CEO of Boeing following the 737 MAX disasters.
- They pose extreme, even existential risk to an enterprise.
- They require an outsized and extreme level of communication.

As the late management guru Peter Drucker noted, "Turbulence—for those who still remember a little mathematics—is characterized by unpredictability. It is certain that the unpredictable will happen; but it is impossible to predict where, when or how." So it is with crises.

While no organization can avoid turbulence at some point, it can keep its seat belt fastened and be prepared.

In this chapter you will learn not only how to be prepared, but strategies and tactics for when a crisis actually occurs.

BEING PREPARED

The Team

The first step is to establish a core team that can manage crises effectively right when they occur. The team should include:

- the CEO and/or COO.
- legal counsel.
- public/media relations.

Depending on the nature of the crisis, the team should be expanded to include appropriate senior executives. They could include the following leaders and department heads:

- marketing and sales
- government relations
- human resources/employee relations
- investor relations/the CFO
- international
- supply chain
- plant manager

However, it should not be too large. More than ten people is too large. Identify and notify the core members of the team, and hold a meeting before any crisis occurs.

A word about legal counsel. Counsel can be expected to ably assess the legal risk of the crisis and suggest specific actions to address it. Almost inevitably, the plaintiffs' bar will file lawsuits for millions and even billions of dollars in damages on issues ranging from company products being linked to cancer to violations of securities laws over the nature and timing of disclosure of the issue.

You must realize, too, that there is also what could be called "brand risk" involving a range of organization stakeholders that can be extremely important to the overall strategy. For instance, corporate boycotts over specific company policies, while generally not that successful by themselves, can and do generate significant negative media and public attention that leads to change.

Boycott examples have included Chick-fil-A for its opposition to same-sex marriage, Caterpillar for selling construction equipment to Israel that was used to bulldoze Palestinian homes, and products from South Africa over apartheid.

Two of the most famous boycotts:

- The boycott of Montgomery, Alabama, city buses when Rosa Parks refused to move her seat from a Whites-only section, giving impetus to the young civil rights movement.
- The boycott of grapes led by César Chávez over farmworker pay and working conditions that eventually led to a union contract improving both.

Boycotts demonstrate the need for companies to do the right thing in the first place.

Taking Inventory

Before a crisis hits, the first task for the core team is to take inventory of the type of crises that have occurred in the organization's past and that might occur in the future, given its business.

For instance, for an oil company it could be a major oil spill, such as the *Exxon Valdez* tanker off the coast of Alaska or the *Deepwater Horizon* oil platform explosion in the Gulf of Mexico, causing severe environmental damage and, in the latter case, deaths.

For a food company, it could be contamination of its products, either with a foreign substance or a pathogen such as *E. coli*, necessitating a massive product recall. Perrier's market leadership in mineral water in the US was decimated when trace amounts of benzene, a carcinogen in significant quantities, was found in some of their bottled water.

For a clothing company, it could be a major human rights organization exposing dangerous working conditions or child labor in a developing country. More than a thousand workers perished when a Bangladesh factory producing Nike products collapsed.

The Plan

Using the inventory, compose a written plan—in advance. Make it only a few pages, not a long document that likely will then sit on a shelf. It should include:

- A brief statement to remind those involved in the crisis that the company will address the problem with honesty and transparency, act in the public interest, and have empathy for those affected.
- The core members of the team and their contact information.
- Responsibilities for communications with all key stakeholders, including logistics of those communications. (More on logistics shortly.)
- A system for liaison: information sharing with and input from the board of directors.
- A notice that the group will meet at least once a year to review and update the plan as necessary, looking for potential new clouds on the horizon.
- The company's key brand messages.
- An appendix of contact information for other important stakeholders—employees, customers, suppliers, government officials, and so forth.

Organization and Logistics

As noted, the crisis team needs to have a logistics plan in place for communications—and for everyone to understand it. This should have a number of pieces, including but not limited to:

- The website. There should be at least a page of the latest information on the issue, the company's position, and the ability to send feedback to the company.
- Related to the website, ensure that appropriate security systems have been established to assure nefarious actors aren't able to hack into and alter a company's website or access internal emails.

- How should incoming calls from different audiences be routed?
- Who is in charge of coordinating the various intelligence and feedback for senior management and the board?
- What internal and external resources are available and may need to be brought to bear?

There are many more.

WHEN A CRISIS OCCURS

Monitoring and Gathering Intelligence

When a crisis occurs, the core team and any other appropriate executives should meet to assess the seriousness of the situation.

There should be immediate and ongoing monitoring of reactions, summarized at least daily for senior management. Sources will include:

- social media, given its immediacy and reach.
- incoming media calls, and the nature and tone of the inquiries.
- employee reaction.
- customer reaction.
- any possible government involvement.
- the stock price and Wall Street commentary.

Messaging

While messaging ultimately will depend on the specific situation, the goal should be to assure all affected that the problem is being fixed aggressively and that the company is, as mentioned, responding honestly and transparently, acting in the public interest, and showing empathy for those affected. It also is a generally accepted rule that the best messaging has a strong emotional component versus simply a logical and rational argument.

In addition, while facts certainly need to be marshaled to support the company's messages, generally the media will only use two or three quotes from the company, so the message needs to be concise and to the point.

Finally, given that all or even most of the actual facts may not be known immediately, a "placeholder" statement/message may need to be created from what information is available. Here's an example from Air France when Flight 447 from Rio de Janeiro to Charles de Gaulle Airport in Paris disappeared over the Atlantic, killing all 228 passengers and crew on board:

> *Air France regrets to announce that it has lost contact with flight AF 447 from Rio de Janeiro to Paris-Charles de Gaulle, expected to arrive this morning at 11:15 local time.*
>
> *The flight left Rio on 31 May at 7 pm local time. 216 passengers are on board.*
>
> *There are 12 crew members on board: 3 pilots and 9 cabin crew.*
>
> *The following toll-free number is available*
>
> *In France: 0800 800 812, and + 33 1 57 02 10 55 outside France.*
>
> *Air France fully shares the anxiety and distress of the families of the passengers concerned. The families are being taken care of in a specially reserved area at Paris-Charles de Gaulle 2 airport.*

Here are some additional tips for messaging success:

- Talk from the viewpoint of your audience and to their self-interest.
- Demonstrate concern.
- Avoid euphemisms and jargon. A strike is a strike, not a work stoppage, and an explosion is not an incident.
- Don't speculate.
- Don't be defensive. Do articulate the company's positive response to the issue.
- Talk in headlines.
- Protect the record. Mistakes happen. If you make a mistake, correct it.
- If the media gets something wrong, talk to the reporter and correct it.
- Tell the truth, even if it hurts.
- Don't say "No comment." Reporters generally are entitled to answers to their questions unless there is a reason not to answer them, in which case the reason should be stated to the reporter—personnel information, proprietary competitive information, and the like.
- Don't repeat negative or inflammatory words used by the reporter. They could wind up as part of your quote—"I don't beat my wife."

Responding Appropriately

One of the most important and difficult tasks of crisis communication is deciding how to respond in a way that appropriately reflects the seriousness of the situation.

How aggressively and widely should you respond? It depends. For instance, should the company simply issue a strong statement, or instead make a spokesperson available or communicate even more proactively and aggressively?

The nature of the response is critical, in that you need to address the situation responsibly, but you don't want to pour gasoline on the fire by making the issue larger than it is. Although this often does not succeed, your goal, while demonstrating you are addressing the problem, should be to make the situation a one- or two-day story.

The good news, if there is any, is that the rapidity of today's news cycles means that other major stories may quickly replace yours!

Spokespersonship

One of the most important issues the team will quickly have to address in a crisis is spokespersonship. Who are the people most likely to address a problem, and at what level in the organization?

Spokespersons obviously need to have a strong knowledge of the subject matter and be strong communicators, whether in print or on broadcast. And despite inaccurate and negative stereotypes of what public relations people do, *you should never spin*! Also, the credibility of the spokesperson is critical. Credibility can be lost in an instant and be extremely difficult to regain.

Given the large amounts of communications that are necessary in most crises, the spokesmanship role will likely need to be triaged. For instance, for major customers and media, a senior executive is probably appropriate. For smaller-market media, a public relations person can be used or a written statement issued.

All potential spokespersons should be trained. Numerous companies and consultants specialize in training, particularly with the media. The training should include the most difficult questions a company is likely to face, so that good answers are at the ready. Training sessions obviously should be conducted in advance of any crisis.

Last, as the following section will show, in the age of social media and instant information, how the CEO is positioned and what they say is of special importance. People want to hear from the top.

THE POWER OF THE INTERNET AND SOCIAL MEDIA

The development of the internet has made news and information widespread almost immediately upon becoming available. There are now some 14 billion cell phones operating in the world, with the number expected to climb to almost 18 billion by 2024. Thanks to cell phones, incidents can be documented not only instantly but visually.

Consider the case of Domino's Pizza. On Easter Sunday in 2009, the company learned that two employees in Conover, North Carolina, had posted videos on YouTube that showed one of them sticking cheese up his nose and then putting it on a sandwich that was to be delivered to a customer. His colleague filmed him partaking in other unsanitary acts with the food and uploaded those videos to YouTube as well. The videos immediately went viral, with "Domino's" as a search word surpassing professional media celebrity Paris Hilton for the first time ever. The videos were actually a hoax, but few seemed to care. In addition, like the COVID-19 virus, the story not only spread widely and quickly, but evolved and mutated rapidly.

As Tim McIntyre, vice president of communications at Domino's at the time, noted in a later interview with the *Public Relations Strategist*:

> *What happened in those first 48 hours, from our perspective, is that the story changed. The story took on almost five parts. The first story line was: Somebody's tainting food at Domino's. Then it became: Somebody posted a hoax video starring Domino's. Then it became: What is Domino's doing about it?*
>
> *Then it became the critique of how Domino's handled these rogue employees. And today, the story is: How do brands protect themselves and their reputations in the YouTube era?*

For more on social media, see chapter nine, "Social Media: Evolving Best Practices for PR Practitioners."

SOCIAL MEDIA, FAKE NEWS, AND DISINFORMATION

I've been in two elections. I won them both and the second one, I won much bigger than the first . . . It's a disgrace. It's a disgrace . . . Democrats attempted the most brazen and outrageous election theft and there's never been anything like this. So pure theft in American history. Everybody knows it.
—President Donald J. Trump, at the January 6, 2021, rally in Washington, DC, before his supporters stormed the Capitol. (More than 70 percent of Republicans said in a poll soon after that they agreed with President Trump's contention that he received more votes than Joe Biden.)

A North Carolina man pleaded guilty on Friday to opening fire in a Washington pizzeria that fake news reports claimed housed a child sex ring linked to 2016 Democratic presidential candidate Hillary Clinton. Edgar Welch, 28, of Salisbury, was accused of firing at least three shots from an AR-15 rifle inside the Comet Ping Pong pizzeria in December and pointing the gun at an employee after showing up to investigate the online conspiracy rumors.
—Reuters, March 24, 2017

One of the most difficult aspects of communications in a crisis today is the ability of social media to instantly disseminate not just information but misinformation, conspiracy theories, and hatred. As this book went to press, there was a major ongoing debate over online platforms, their power, and their responsibility for misinformation, false conspiracy theories, and hate groups communicating on the sites.

Social media platforms are trying to address the problem. For instance, Facebook and Twitter both banned conspiracy theories of the group QAnon as well as former president Donald Trump for spreading disinformation and inciting the January 6, 2021, attack on the Capitol.

However, the volume of communication on social media platforms makes policing disinformation challenging. There are 500 million tweets per day, or about 6,000 per second. More than 3.21 billion people actively use Facebook,

Instagram, WhatsApp, or Messenger each month, and 1.82 billion people log on to Facebook daily. Algorithms can help but obviously not completely solve the problem.

Debates are also ongoing over the almost monopolistic power of Facebook and Twitter, along with Google's YouTube, and whether the platforms have gone too far in controlling public discourse. Should private companies have so much control over public debate and comment on social media, and to what extent should they curate and moderate content to control hate and misinformation?

It is a tension that will continue well into the future.

Given these issues, how should companies respond to social media comments in a crisis? Obviously they need to monitor for comments and especially misinformation that needs to be corrected. However, Domino's McIntyre noted that "you might not need the fire hose to put out the candle, but in the social media realm, you might want to have the garden hose handy."

A word of caution. No matter the strength of your argument and actions you take to fight disinformation, many people online are never going to believe you.

USING THIRD PARTIES

Every major poll since the 2020s began has shown a significant decline in trust for institutions, including companies. Internationally renowned political scientist and management scholar and chancellor of Vanderbilt University Daniel Diermeier noted, "In general, people are more likely to attend to negative information than to positive information . . . even when they are faced with contradictory and incomplete evidence."

That is where third parties can help create credibility around a specific situation. Third parties can include scientists, academics, think tanks, opinion leaders, and subject experts on an issue. Who are the leading experts in your industry? What is your relationship with them? How well can they be counted on? If outside experts aren't commenting on your behalf, you can be sure they'll be talking to the media in a crisis.

Once again, a word of caution. The best outside scientific expertise in the world doesn't always win the day. Here is just one example in which there was strong third-party scientific evidence that in the end didn't change behavior. Despite every reputable scientist and medical expert stating that wearing a mask could quickly control the COVID-19 pandemic, many people refused to wear them, seeing them as an infringement on their freedoms, and some even believed the pandemic was a "hoax." This despite the fact that tens of millions of Americans were infected over the course of the pandemic, and hundreds of thousands died.

OUTSIDE INVESTIGATIONS

Another third-party strategy is the independent, impartial investigation; for example, corporate boards of directors hiring outside law firms or other consultants. The objective is to demonstrate the company's commitment to truth and transparency, get to the bottom of the issue, and make recommendations for any changes necessary to protect and assure the public going forward.

For instance, companies have launched these types of independent investigations with outside law firms to investigate claims of sexual misconduct by senior executives. After external lawyers investigated CBS head Leslie Moonves, they found he had engaged in multiple acts of serious, nonconsensual sexual misconduct. He was forced out, then sued by the board for misleading investigators.

Outside lawyers were also brought in to investigate sexual misconduct claims against McDonald's CEO Steve Easterbrook. The lawyers examined Easterbrook's company-issued iPhone 10 and his iCloud account, but did not find evidence of additional misconduct beyond one consensual relationship. But when further allegations emerged, and Easterbrook's emails and communications on McDonald's servers were examined, additional evidence of misconduct was found. In a broader investigation, McDonald's said lawyers ultimately found "dozens of nude, partially nude, or sexually explicit photographs and videos of various women, including photographs of . . . company employees, that Easterbrook had sent as attachments to messages from his company email account to his personal email account."

While certainly not an incident McDonald's is proud of, its statement as a result of the independent investigation is pretty good. In suing Easterbrook to claw back his severance pay based on the additional facts, the company said: "We now know that his [Easterbrook's] conduct deviated from our values in different and far more extensive ways than we were aware when he left the company last year . . . McDonald's does not tolerate behavior from any employee that does not reflect our values. These actions reflect a continued demonstration of this commitment."

A WORD ABOUT SCIENCE—AND CUTTING YOUR LOSSES

As the COVID-19 mask example shows, science can be one of the trickiest aspects of managing a crisis. For example, Bayer's Monsanto faced lawsuits from more than forty thousand plaintiffs alleging its weed killer Roundup caused non-Hodgkin's lymphoma, a cancer of the lymph glands. The company paid $10 billion to settle the lawsuits, despite strong scientific evidence to the contrary. Johnson & Johnson faced more than twenty thousand lawsuits over its talc baby powder. There was one $4.7 billion verdict; while a judge reduced it to $2.1 billion, the company was forced to discontinue the popular product. Once again, there was strong scientific evidence that the product was safe.

These examples raise a point that unfortunately needs to be considered in most crises: business, like life, can be unfair. Companies, despite being on the right side of an issue and doing the right thing, sometimes continue to sustain harm. This is particularly true at for-profit companies, which many instinctively distrust. While you may believe you work for a great company, others do not. Your firm may have to decide at some point to put an end to the issue for the sake of the future—not just its own, but also those of its employees, customers, shareholders, and other stakeholders.

In such situations, the communications, whether regarding a legal settlement or discontinuing a product, will need to be handled carefully to position the decision in the right way and put the issue behind them without arousing fresh debate.

MAKING LEMONADE FROM LEMONS

The end of Rahm Emanuel's quote at the beginning of this chapter, on taking advantage of a crisis, is: "And what I mean by that [a crisis] is an opportunity to do things that you think you could not do before."

Crises, while not sought, can sometimes create opportunities. The gold standard in this regard is Johnson & Johnson and the fatal poisonings related to its pain relief drug Tylenol. Four decades have passed since the tragedy, in which seven people died in the Chicago area after taking cyanide-laced capsules of Extra-Strength Tylenol, the drug-maker's best-selling product. Yet virtually every article on managing a crisis and handling the related communications cites this incident.

As the *New York Times* noted on the twentieth anniversary of the poisonings:

Marketers predicted that the Tylenol brand, which accounted for 17 percent of the company's net income in 1981, would never recover from the sabotage. But only two months later, Tylenol was headed back to the market, this time in tamper-proof packaging and bolstered by an extensive media campaign.

Although Johnson & Johnson spent $100 million on the drug's recall and relaunch, a year later, its share of the $1.2 billion analgesic market, which had plunged to 7 percent from 37 percent following the poisoning, had climbed back to 30 percent.

What set apart Johnson & Johnson's handling of the crisis from others? It placed consumers first by recalling 31 million bottles of Tylenol capsules from store shelves and offering replacement product in the safer tablet form free of charge.

One other example of turning lemons into lemonade. San Francisco 49ers quarterback Colin Kaepernick generated major controversy by taking a knee during the pregame playing of the national anthem, to protest racial injustice and police violence against Blacks. He, and other players who followed suit, were nationally criticized as unpatriotic. Kaepernick has not been able to find work again in the National Football League after his release from the 49ers, despite demonstrating major talent.

Counterintuitively, Nike used Kaepernick in ads as part of its campaign for the thirtieth anniversary of the "Just Do It" slogan. As reported by CNBC, "a #BoycottNike hashtag soon trended on Twitter, and Nike shares took as much as a 3% hit when the campaign was announced. But online sales surged after the ad's release, and the commercial was also met with critical acclaim, winning Nike an Emmy for outstanding commercial." A special athletic shoe featuring Kaepernick sold out its first day.

More recently, Ben & Jerry's ice cream unveiled a mural and billboards in honor of Kaepernick before Super Bowl LV and launched a new ice cream flavor in his name. "As we look back, it's clear that Colin was on the right side of history," said Chris Miller, Ben & Jerry's Head of Global Activism, in a statement. "We wanted to be part of the effort to honor Colin's courage and legacy because we share the same values."

Sometimes you have to think outside of the box—although there is always risk!

TAKEAWAYS

1. Some final words, hopefully of wisdom. Don't panic. Remain calm. Fred Friendly was the producer for the legendary newsman Edward R. Murrow, and later president of CBS News. Referring to a television studio, we recall a quote of his: "You need to keep yourself under control in the control room. There's plenty of built-in tension, and you want others to believe you know what the hell you're doing." Likewise, you want to look like you are in control of events, not the other way around. Whatever the crisis, "This, too, shall pass!"

2. Rome was not built in a day, and neither is image. However, crises can quickly destroy it. In fining Boeing $2.5 billion over 737 MAX safety issues, the US Justice Department said: "Boeing's employees chose the path of profit over candor by concealing material information from the FAA concerning the operation of its 737 MAX airplane and engaging in an effort to cover up their deception. This resolution holds Boeing accountable for its employees' criminal misconduct, addresses the financial impact to Boeing's airline customers, and hopefully provides some measure of compensation to the crash-victims' families and beneficiaries."

3. Before a crisis occurs, what is your organization doing to demonstrate its commitment to the public good, such as positive Environmental, Social, and Governance initiatives? What are the issues your CEO is articulating that will have positive resonance with the public? Do you have a culture of honesty and transparency?

4. Get all the bad information out as quickly as possible. It's not going away on its own, and later can come back to haunt you.

5. When the crisis has passed, do an assessment of what you learned, did well, and did poorly. A famous example of this is the US Army's major study *A Study of Strategic Lessons Learned in Vietnam*, which is now part of the curriculum at the US Army War College.

6. We leave our final words to Domino's McIntyre: "Somebody equated Domino's in the first 24 hours to a grocery store that had 30

(continued)

aisles—and there was a spill in aisle five. They didn't need to mop the whole floor because there was a spill in aisle five. I loved that analogy.

"What was happening, though, is that as we were cleaning up the spill in aisle five, it was leaking to aisles six and seven and four and three. So if anything like this were to happen again and there was a spill in aisle five, I would rope off two aisles to the right and two aisles to the left, and that would be our audience. That would include responding on our Web site a little bit faster, hitting the Twitter community a little bit faster and talking to senior leadership a little bit faster."

7. Good luck with your crisis.

CHAPTER 12

Communications for Private Families

The Fundamentals of Public Relations Apply Here, Too

DR. STEPHEN M. COAN
PHILANTHROPIC ADVISOR

While we all deserve privacy, the term "private families" has another meaning: those possessing great fortunes and significant influence. What kind of fortunes are we talking about? Generally speaking, these families are believed to control more than 50 percent of the world's wealth. Much is written about economic inequality as a social injustice. Private families' measurable possessions and the power that comes with that wealth can foment anger and resentment, controversy and pushback. At the very least, the mere existence of super-wealthy families makes many people uncomfortable.

My priority in this chapter is not to pass judgment on such concentrations of wealth, but to focus on just one issue: effective public relations and communications practices for the wealthy and influential. Public relations is both a business and a mission of sorts, and private families present what are largely unexplored opportunities for people in that business.

Most of my own career has been in philanthropy as both a fundraiser and a member of family foundation boards. In these roles, I have seen firsthand that good communications should be integral to the lives of the wealthy, but often it is not. I have seen individual and family reputations ruined because of poor or nonexistent attention to public relations. In too many cases, wealthy families do not proactively tell their own stories and often let salacious public narratives define who they are and what values they have.

It's been my experience that families that treat their wealth as if it were the assets of an enterprise or a well-run company have a higher probability of (a) not losing those assets and (b) having them fulfill the family's goals. In my world, that's called using *financial* capital. But there are two other essential forms of capital:

- **Human**: the skills, knowledge, and experiences of the families and their members.
- **Social**: the network of relationships that enables families to function effectively in society.

All three forms of capital—financial, human, and social—can be managed and enhanced. But they can also be destroyed by behavior that inflicts reputational damage.

Human beings love stories—aka gossip—about other human beings, especially about the rich and famous. That's why wealthy people have always had to contend with the public's insatiable curiosity about them. Modern technology has become a great enabler of this curiosity. The public craves trivia about the rich—who's marrying (or divorcing) whom, what galas they attend and what they wear, and all the rest of it. There's also the well-intentioned desire to know the stories behind their success, and maybe learn something useful.

MANAGING VISIBILITY

Often the wealth of a family is based on a successful enterprise established by a founding figure. Think of the riches that John D. Rockefeller created when he built Standard Oil, or the fortune that the "Pickle King," H. J. Heinz, established with the food company that bears his name. Those families and others like them have become household names, and the founders' descendants have often gone on to become public figures, whether as owners of sports teams, media companies, or entertainment platforms, or as aspiring politicians. John D.'s grandson Nelson Rockefeller was elected governor of New York four times and served as vice president of the United States for three years; H. J.'s grandson John Heinz was a US senator from Pennsylvania and a potential presidential candidate until his 1991 death in an airplane crash.

Many families whose wealth comes from a foundational business are now significant investors in others' businesses, or bundle others' assets to invest in tandem with them. Many families control more money than some countries do. Others achieve prominence by practicing philanthropy on local, national, and international scales. (Think of the contributions that the Bill and Melinda Gates Foundation has made to raising educational standards and improving world health, among other causes.) Many wield political or governmental power, again on levels from local to global, regardless of whether they hold office. (Think of the attention, both positive and negative, that the Koch brothers, Charles and David, have attracted by supporting libertarian politics and promoting the oil and gas industry.)

The visibility that comes along with these activities must be managed. Visibility can easily become notoriety.

Of course, many private families try to stay private. They avoid public activities and lead low-profile lives, even if their silent influence can be profound. They are all around us; every locality, region, and country has its own set of such people. For every wealthy family's name we know, the evidence suggests there are many more we have never heard of. Even so, because wealth attracts curiosity, *private* families are not immune from the negative consequences of attention. This has always been the case, but the stakes are higher in today's superheated social media environment, especially because the resentment about economic inequality continues to mount.

Visibility, desired or not, managed or not, is one of the chief communications challenges that private families face.

AN OUT-OF-SIGHT MARKET

What is special about the private family market? The size, worldwide reach, and economic clout of these families is considerable. Yet this market is not monolithic, but rather very fragmented—and, like an iceberg, much of it out of sight.

How do you deliver the communications support that private families need? And who does the actual work? Some private families have a public relations person on staff or through their family office, an organization that also handles everything from household management to vacation planning to bill paying. (I'll come back to the subject of family offices later.) Other families depend on the PR departments of the companies they control or the sports teams they own. Some merely task a family member with the responsibility, regardless of qualifications.

Dealing with private families as a communications expert requires a great deal of innovation because, while established public relations methods still apply, new public relations protocols must be constantly invented in real time. That is the challenge—and the satisfaction—of getting in early on this relatively new field.

Private families make up a market in which every public relations discipline can be brought to bear: internal and external communications; crisis management; financial, media, community, and international relations; lobbying; political campaigning; event planning; staffing events; research; and much more. All the lessons in the other chapters in this handbook can be brought to bear with great effectiveness.

In this chapter, I will explore what I see as the challenges of bringing your communications professionalism to this fascinating market. Perhaps you are an employee or a principal of a public relations consulting firm. Perhaps you are an individual practitioner. Perhaps you want to be on a wealthy family's staff. Whatever place you occupy, know that in this marketplace, where legal and financial advice were once the only services these families valued, communications is rising to take its rightful place.

THE ROLE OF FAMILY OFFICES

Let me return to the term "family office," first to explain the special meaning it has in the context of family wealth, and then to explain how public relations professionals come into the picture.

The history of family offices goes back to the late nineteenth century. In what is believed to be the first instance, the Rockefellers decided they needed a private wealth-management advisory firm dedicated solely to their interests. Over time, many other families adopted the practice. But it was the 1980s boom in private family wealth that set off the real growth spurt. By 2020, there were an estimated three thousand family offices in the US, managing somewhere between $1 trillion and $1.2 trillion. According to *Barron's*, the number of firms worldwide is now greater than ten thousand, and they manage upward of $4 trillion.

Family offices come in two flavors: single-family offices that work only for one wealthy clan, and multifamily offices that handle several of them. The services they offer vary from firm to firm and often change over time as clients recognize new challenges or decide on new goals. In general, though, the first and foremost task family offices perform is providing investment advice—they are wealth managers. Beyond that, they may handle a range of tasks, such as making travel arrangements for both business and pleasure, tax planning, handling the payroll for the family's staff (sometimes the family office itself supplies the staff), property management, overseeing charitable contributions, and setting up trusts.

In highly sophisticated family offices, one of the most important functions is managing intergenerational relationships and the transfer of the family wealth down through the years. That might seem routine enough at first glance, but in real life it can present enormous challenges. It is normal, for example, for a family to become quite large by the time it reaches the fourth or fifth generation. As the number grows, individual inheritances and the corresponding influence may become smaller. Not small by the standards of the workaday world, perhaps, but small to someone who can't understand why his or her share of a fortune that was once measured in hundreds of millions is now only a few million. That can be hard to accept for someone with great dreams of wealth and luxury.

And then there are always the family black sheep (yes, they do show up sooner or later) who squander their share of the inheritance and demand more. Managing the fights this inevitably sparks among children, parents, grandparents, siblings, cousins, and so on, is one of the biggest challenges some family offices must deal with—life issues, especially, such as overspending, reckless gambling, multiple divorces, alcoholism, or drug addiction, are variables leading to the disappearance of an inheritance.

Yet another frequent hot potato is managing family relations when a new generation comes along that wants to sell off the family business. The twenty-somethings may feel that too much of the wealth is tied up in tangible goods like factories, offices, or vehicle fleets and want to cash it in with a sale. That is exactly what happened when the Bancroft family, which owned Dow Jones and the *Wall Street Journal*, decided to sell it all to Rupert Murdoch in 2007 for $5 billion.

Sometimes the members of the younger generation want to get out because the nature of the family business offends their values. They believe the factories' smokestacks spew out pollutants, for example, or the company's labor policies seem exploitive, racist, or sexist. (More on this and the public relations challenges it presents later.) Whatever the motivation, the desire to get rid of the very business that has made the family's fortune and perhaps also made the family name can come as a complete and unacceptable shock to parents and grandparents whose lives always revolved around the business. A fight inevitably ensues.

Another struggle may break out if the family member who runs the company decides to skip a generation or two in choosing a successor. Rarely if ever is the generation that is about to be passed over willing to stand by quietly. A variation of this conflict is when the person in charge decides no one in the family is worthy of the leadership mantle and wants to bring in an outsider as the new CEO.

Yet another kind of conflict may arise when the founding figure has grown old in the job but refuses to let go. That can be especially troubling when the creative genius that made him or her so successful long ago is not what's needed to administer what is now a large, complex organization. As the irascible behavior of Henry Ford toward the end of his life demonstrates, a lot of bad decisions get made in such situations. It may be the second generation or perhaps the grandchildren who see the problem and seek to replace the aging boss, but the result is almost always a jarring struggle.

COMMUNICATIONS CHALLENGES

Managing the conflicts that these developments can create is a major family-office challenge. The greater the family wealth is and the better known the family name may be, the more likely it is that such internal conflicts will go public. That is where public relations professionals and communications experts become invaluable allies.

The media love it when rich people are at one another's throats, of course. But beyond the risk of tabloid and social media exposure, there are usually serious consequences involved in these fights. If, for example, the company's reputation is damaged by the bad publicity, uncertainty is sure to follow, workers may see their jobs jeopardized, stockholders may lose value, suppliers may lose business, local communities can lose tax revenues, and entities that have been the recipient of philanthropic donations can be harmed by association. Handling the media in such situations, so that the damage to the family name and the company's reputation is minimized—or ideally, avoided altogether—is a job for communications professionals.

It's not just external media relations that need skillful handling. Internal communications for the family and its company are just as important. There is nothing more upsetting for family members than realizing they've been kept in the dark about important developments. Same thing for employees of the organization. Maintaining clear lines of communication, creating a strong sense of openness and transparency, getting the right information into the right hands at the right time—that's what public relations professionals can do. And that's why they are so essential for family offices and their clients.

By the way, family offices may have communications needs of their own that require expert help. When a Philadelphia-based multifamily office with a "Who's Who" list of clients decided that its wealth-management operations were too stodgy and needed an update, it was concerned that the changes would unsettle many of the families. It called in a major New York public relations firm to help explain the changes. The advice was to set up a carefully scheduled outreach program, including written materials and in-person meetings, to educate the families about the changes and ease them into the new structure. The program—and the changes—came off without a hitch.

LEARNING TO LIVE IN THE OPEN

That last example reinforces the point that public relations is a form of education. Teaching wealthy families how to function in a world in which the privacy they value is under attack is a key role for public relations professionals. Simply put, it is almost impossible in an age of social media to be rich *and* private. Understanding public relations and having an expert available to provide advice is essential. If you were going to lay out this argument to a potential client, it would go something like this.

The public has always had a fascination with the lifestyles of the rich and famous. Part of the appeal is no doubt fantasy—*Maybe I'll live like that one day, too!*—and part of it is bias confirmation—*See how spoiled and selfish they are!* And there is always the schadenfreude when wealthy folks get into serious trouble.

This fascination has taken on a new political edge because of the rising concern over income inequality and its potential threat to democratic institutions. The Occupy Wall Street movement may have lost the energy and determination that once enabled it to take over part of Manhattan's Financial District and capture national headlines. But the movement's mantra ("We are the 99 percent") conveyed a powerful, widely remembered message: that the top 1 percent—a relatively small number of families—controls a disproportionate share of the nation's wealth. And so, even though the Occupy movement is no longer front-page news, the lesson it taught is now baked into the public's mind. Even if you are just part of the top 10 percent, you may be prone to being vilified.

In short, with extreme wealth comes extreme attention. What's more, in the era of social media there is no place to hide. Therefore, managing a wealthy family's reputation and public image requires professional help. The old truism is right: if you don't tell your story, somebody else is going to tell it for you.

FOLLOW THE MONEY

As I mentioned, one of the most common events that calls for the help of public relations practitioners is when a fight breaks out over the disposition of a private family's fortune. For older families, that frequently happens when a new generation begins questioning the sources of the family's wealth or demanding that it be redirected for social justice purposes. (This trend, by the way, is consistent with the reassessment of America's past by people who believe the wrong historical figures have been honored, leading to the removal of statues of Confederate leaders such as Robert E. Lee and the renaming of institutions at many universities.)

One of the most publicized examples of such a family struggle has involved Abigail Disney, the granddaughter of Roy Disney, who was the cofounder along with his brother Walt of the movie studio that bears their name. The issue on which she has been most outspoken is pay equity within the Disney organization. Why, she has demanded to know, are employees at places like Disneyland so poorly paid, when the CEO's compensation is measured in tens of millions a year? "There is nobody on Earth," she has declared, "worth 500 times his median workers' pay." Not surprisingly, the Disney organization has pushed back with a vigorous defense of its pay policy.

Certainly, both sides have arguments to make. This may seem obvious to people who are accustomed to functioning in the public arena. But for wealthy folks with a habit of keeping out of the spotlight, it may be a matter of considerable discomfort. To echo my earlier statement, they must tell their part of the story, or the story will be defined only by one side.

It is vital, therefore, to reach out to potential clients in family conflicts with a well-prepared and convincing pitch to show how you can help them get their case across. And always remember that it's not enough to tell clients that you *get* their side of the argument. You have to persuade them that you have the know-how and the contacts to get that argument into the right hands.

WORKING DIRECTLY WITH FAMILIES

If you are called upon, how do you work with a private family? First, you must know how the family has organized itself and what the hierarchy is. Maybe the founding figure still dominates; such people are sometimes very controlling and often try to run not just the enterprise they created, but also the lives of everyone around them. Maybe there has been an awkward transition of power from the founder to the second generation, and siblings are struggling with one another for ultimate control. In other cases, especially when the family wealth has been spread across multiple generations, there is little clarity or structure. No one is really in charge but everyone thinks he or she holds the reins. That can seriously muddy the communications waters.

Successful private families often treat their wealth just as they would corporate assets. When that is the case, you as a public relations professional need to deal with them just like a corporate client. Lead them toward a mission statement that encapsulates what they are all about. Treat their family name and reputation as a brand. Define the values that underlie the brand, and ensure that every public interaction supports that brand.

Remember that private families, no matter how they are organized, are *families*. And all families, wealthy and not, are unique, idiosyncratic collections of individuals who can squabble, feud, pursue separate agendas, compete with one another, and much more. They can fall apart as easily as they can pull together. Yes, that happens in corporate enterprises, too. But corporate hierarchies have a built-in chain of command that acts as an enforcement agent. This model won't work in families whose hierarchies can be unspoken, informal, changeable—and are frequently ignored by the very people who most need structure in their lives.

All too often in private families, the members delude themselves that they are operating in a kind of democracy where every voice counts. But all too often, a dominating figure is actually the one who makes the decisions. Sometimes it's perfectly clear who the authoritarian is—an assertive patriarch or a strong-willed matriarch. Sometimes it's not so obvious—a member of the younger generation who quietly shapes the family's course, thanks to a shrewder head and quicker tongue than anyone else. Sometimes it's just a bully. In many cases, other family members will accept the situation. They may be intimidated, too disaffected from family affairs to care, or so busy with their own lives that they don't have the time and energy to fight back.

Whoever the real decider(s) may be, you as a public relations specialist need to figure it out and act accordingly. Know where the real power lies.

STICK TO THE FUNDAMENTALS

Let me outline now what I see as the core principles of working with wealthy individuals and families. The first point is that the fundamentals of communications always apply, and they apply with particular relevance to this audience. Those fundamentals are as follows:

1. **Listening**. This is especially important with people who are accustomed to having their words heeded. It does not mean agreeing with everything they say—far from it. But it does mean giving them a chance to express themselves fully, without unnecessary interruptions or commentary. And it means not only listening to the text of what they say, but also cocking a sharp ear for the subtext. For example, does a seemingly mild-mannered criticism of a fellow family member actually express deep-seated anger and resentment?

2. **Openness**. Keep all channels of communication open and working. Whatever it takes, there must be free-flowing exchanges to the greatest extent possible. Be aware that your availability may have to be pretty much 24/7.

3. **Authenticity**. One thing at which the wealthy tend to excel is picking up on phoniness and insincerity—they get a lot of it. You need to be authentic in what you say and do, even if you risk irritating the client. In the long term, honest dealing will get you the respect you need for your advice and counsel to be accepted and acted on.

4. **Patience**. Self-explanatory, but let me add that it does not mean letting problems fester. As a professional, you know that timing is all important to people in the media—they live a life of constant deadlines. So when you are advising wealthy clients, sometimes you'll need to help them understand that, in public relations, you cannot set the timetable

unilaterally—reporters and editors are going to go ahead and file stories and broadcast reports to meet their own needs, not yours or the family's. Haste makes waste, goes the old saying, but in the PR business, it's often fast action that keeps a problem from getting out of hand.

One of the skills you'll need to deploy in working with wealthy clients is explaining the realities of a situation in ways that instruct without insulting. Case in point: In an initial meeting with a potential client, a public relations professional was put on the defensive when the client declared it was pointless to deal with the media because of what he saw as their dishonesty and viciousness. The immediate cause of his anger was the fact that a friend of his, a fellow billionaire, was under attack in the press for some controversial forays into politics and public policy. Knowing the client was part owner of a major-league team, the public relations pro replied, "Look, politics is a contact sport. If you go out on that field, you're going to get hit." The client sighed and said, "Yeah, I guess you're right," and the conversation got back on track.

Another essential in dealing with a private family is getting to know the family story. How was its wealth amassed, what positives or negatives are associated with its creation, how has it been shared, and how has it affected family relationships? This should lead you to understand the family values and culture.

William Faulkner taught us that "the past is never dead—it's not even past." Understanding a private family's past and how that has shaped its present is crucial in understanding its culture and how it will respond to your communications advice.

TAKEAWAYS

Despite the unique challenges of working for wealthy families, certain rules can guide you through the process.

1. Always stick to the fundamentals of communications—listening, openness, authenticity, and patience.
2. Get to know the family history; get to understand its culture.
3. Never forget that however great its wealth, it is still a family, where family dynamics still apply, only writ larger.
4. Treat the family brand as carefully and protectively as you would treat a corporate brand.
5. Pay strict attention to where the power lies—who the real family decider is.
6. Get buy-in on all public relations strategies you develop. Brainstorm ideas first to get input before final decisions are made.
7. Remember that internal communications among family members is just as important as external communications—sometimes even more important.

CHAPTER 13

Going Forward with China

A Guide to Success

VIRGINIA A. KAMSKY AND MICHAEL N. KAMSKY

Ever since Deng Xiaoping launched his reform of the Chinese economy in 1978, we have witnessed the development of a public relations and media industry in China. At the dawn of the People's Republic, media was dominated by the Xinhua News Agency and the *People's Daily* newspaper, both state run. On December 16, 1978, China and the US formally announced the establishment of diplomatic relations between the two nations. Xinhua had a newsstand located on Wangfujing, the main shopping street in Beijing, and on that historic day the *People's Daily* published a "Special Bulletin" printed in red to announce the normalization. You could walk from the Peking Hotel, where most of the few foreigners in the city stayed at the time, down Wangfujing Street and pick up a copy of the "Special Bulletin." A copy of it hangs framed on our office wall today, alongside a picture taken next door to the Xinhua newsstand. This was the media in China in 1978.

Since then, Xinhua News Agency and the *People's Daily* have continued to be important media outlets. But the past forty-plus years have also seen a continued growth and maturing of China's PR and media industry.

To be successful in navigating China's business landscape, it is important first to be sensitive to the nuances of Chinese culture, language, and history; and second, to understand how the media operate. Foreigners must never lose sight of the fact that they are regarded as being in China as guests, and so they must continue to educate themselves on appropriate etiquette and expectations. Equally important, foreigners must remember that the rules of media relations that work in the West do not necessarily apply there. In this chapter, we attempt to describe some of the most important intricacies of operating successfully in China.

HOW CHINESE CULTURE INFLUENCES BUSINESS

A historical system of ethics and morals governs much of the way Chinese individuals interact with one another. The system emphasizes duty, loyalty, filial piety, sincerity, and respect for age and seniority. Deference to authority and to elders, rank consciousness, modesty, moderation in habits, generosity, and avoidance of direct confrontation are all highly valued traits. Group membership is more important than individuality. The actions of the individual reflect not only on that person but also on colleagues in the group.

State-owned enterprises (SOEs) place a real premium on consensus. Matters are often debated until an agreement is reached and a course of action decided upon. Individual group members typically embrace and act on group decisions regardless of their personal views.

While SOEs operate on consensus and process, privately owned companies, particularly technology firms such as ByteDance and Tencent, are different because the only path to such rapid growth is being nimble. That is why we see CEOs of some large Chinese technology companies making unilateral decisions and micromanaging, as one would expect at a start-up. In the management structure of SOEs, there is usually a chairman and a party secretary. The chairman is the one with the strategic vision and in charge of outward communication. The party secretary plays an important role and must approve any new acquisitions or strategic collaborations. State-owned companies and organizations are run by a party committee that is chaired by the party secretary. The chairman would also serve as a member of the party committee and approvals would ultimately be granted on the consensus of the party committee. In some cases, one individual will simultaneously serve as chairman and party secretary. Under the current regulatory climate, the party secretary is, in many ways, more senior than the chairman.

Technology companies in some of the more sensitive sectors, such as traditional or social media, will still experience party influence, even though they may not be government owned. The Chinese government structures its bureaucracy to prevent interconnectedness between party officials and investors or competitors. The government achieves this goal by moving party officials around, either between companies or jurisdictions. Party secretaries will often move after some years at a company or in a city/municipality.

Chinese bureaucracy is strictly hierarchical with well-defined ranks and privileges. Decision making is top down, and personal loyalty is highly valued. Senior Chinese officials are used to acquiescence and command great respect from those around them. When in the presence of high officials, Chinese people are hypersensitive not to do or say anything that will offend or make the official uncomfortable in any way; the officials are acutely aware of such etiquette even when meeting among themselves.

Income inequality in China is significant, and many blue-collar workers find it unfair that certain members of the population have built wealth so quickly. They do not see what characteristics these businessmen have that have allowed them to earn exponentially higher incomes. It is much easier to chalk inequality up to wrongdoing than to merit. People truly believe that the anti-corruption campaign is a tide of change that will bring back more relative equality between the rich and the poor.

Corruption was rampant in the past, but this area is currently a focus for change at the highest level. President Xi Jinping is very focused on anti-corruption. At the outset, Xi empowered Wang Qishan, a former vice premier in charge of trade and investment, to eradicate corruption. Anti-corruption will be an ongoing process. Xi has been credited with making a lot of progress.

A comparable example would be Rudy Giuliani's targeting Marc Rich in 1983, shortly after Giuliani was appointed US Attorney for the Southern District of New York and was eager to make an early splash. Rich invented the spot market for oil and was very high profile. Prosecuting Rich for tax evasion and trading with the enemy was great PR for Giuliani at that time. (Giuliani's PR machine has not been so successful, of course, since he joined forces with former president Trump.)

The situation is largely the same in China, where business owners who are high profile are more likely to face regulatory challenges.

- Face, or 面子 (*mianzi*), the regard in which one is held by others, or the light in which one appears, is vitally important to the Chinese. Causing someone to lose face by putting him down, or failing to treat him with respect, results in a lack of cooperation and often in retaliation. You will also lose the respect of others who are aware of your transgression.

- In China, face cannot only be lost and saved, it can also be given. Doing something to enhance someone's reputation or prestige, such as lauding someone, is an example. However, Chinese often do not say "thank you" when they receive a compliment, but instead brush off what is said as a sign of modesty. They will often say, "This is what I should be doing," rather than accept a compliment for a job well done.

A good opportunity to laud someone is when introducing them to new people. You may have the chance to do this if you attend or convene meetings in China, which often take place over dinner tables with seating for eight or more. To facilitate such introductions, if you are hosting dinner, devote considerable planning to seating arrangements. Invite guests who are interested in meeting one another. Also, seat guests who would be most interested in conversing next to each other. (More on proper Chinese dinner protocol later in this chapter.)

When lauding someone, focus on "name brand" accomplishments more than on personal qualities. Chinese people are highly focused on brand. That is one reason why LVMH has done so well in China. People are branded based on what school they went to and where they live or work. For example, one of Beijing's most expensive office buildings is known as China World Trade Center Tower 3 国贸三期 (Guomao Sanqi). Chinese people have an affinity for schools such as Tsinghua and Princeton. An expensive place to live in Beijing is in the Park Hyatt apartment tower called 银泰 (Yintai). Therefore, even though it may feel crass to us, a good way to laud someone would be to say they attended Princeton, have an office in Guomao Sanqi, and live in Yintai in a big apartment.

MAKING CONNECTIONS

Guanxi (关系), or "connections," is a tit-for-tat arrangement between people who have generally known each other for many years or even decades. *Guanxi* gains you legitimacy and respect that are otherwise difficult to achieve. Chinese people generally expect foreigners to understand *guanxi* and behave according to its rules. The role of having connections, however, has been overplayed because having relationships in the West is not so different from having relationships in China. It takes years to build trust and respect and there are no shortcuts to good relationships. In China, it is important to respect relationships to which a newcomer is introduced by continuing to keep the "friends" who made the connections both engaged and updated. If not, one party will not respond to a newcomer to a relationship, because it would be considered a violation of trust to go around the relationship.

It is vital not to go around people in this fashion. To achieve long-term goals in China, one should adopt a long-term view in handling relationships. For example, say you have been introduced to someone at a meal and want to schedule a follow-up meeting. It is important to ask/notify the person who initially hosted the meal and introduced the parties. When communicating with the new contact in a WeChat group, include the preexisting contact, not only out of respect for the introducer, but also to signal to the new contact that one respects relationships and Chinese culture. Likewise, when asking the introducer whether it is okay to reach out to this new contact, the introducer will usually encourage you to reach out directly. But what they really mean is to keep including them in surface-level communications and group chats used for scheduling meetings. The introducer does not need to be kept in the loop on nuts-and-bolts issues like the content of subsequent meetings. Rather, they want to get credit in their social circles for introducing you to the new contact. It gives the introducer a lot of face to be in contact with foreign companies.

When adding WeChat contacts, it is respectful to offer to scan the new contact's QR code, as opposed to the other way around. By scanning their code, the new contact will receive a friend request that they can later choose to accept or decline. Once you have become WeChat friends with someone, send something friendly like "nice to meet you" or, even better, two handshake emojis or a few smiles. Also, label WeChat contacts in your phone, so you know who they are. You can also add their business card to their profile. Another effective approach would be to add their company and position into their WeChat alias in your contacts. Otherwise, you will end up with contacts like happypug333 and have no idea who they are. WeChat may seem daunting if you have never used it, but it can be learned very quickly, and a colleague can familiarize you with its many uses and the appropriate etiquette when using it. Keep in mind that key legal documents, including approval documents from regulators, contracts, and casual conversation, are all now transmitted through WeChat.

BUSINESS MEETINGS

The pomp and circumstance around Chinese meetings is more significant when meeting with anyone in academia, the nonprofit world, or the public sector. Previous public-sector service carries great importance in China. For example, the bios of meeting participants need to highlight any previous government positions. When it comes to people who are accomplished in other ways, but not financially, show them respect and ensure your behavior reflects a respect for their professions. If they have PhDs, preface their name with "Doctor." If they have a title at a university like vice-headmaster, call them "Headmaster." If someone is a vice governor of a Chinese Bank, address him as "Governor." The only exception would be if both the vice governor and the governor of the bank are present. In that case, address each by their official title. Because of the aforementioned deference Chinese have toward senior officials, your Chinese hosts will treat you with the utmost respect and sensitivity, and will expect to receive similar treatment in return.

At meetings, it is important to formally exchange business cards or to request to add WeChat contacts. You must also exchange mementos without monetary value. For example, chocolates from Switzerland would be a good choice for a Swiss company. While clocks are known in the West as particularly specific to Germany (e.g., a cuckoo clock), never give a Chinese person a clock as a gift, or even a picture or a magnet depicting a clock. The word for "clock" in Chinese is a homonym for "the end" and is used when someone passes away. Also, never give a green cap to a man. Green caps are worn by men whose wives are cheating on them and are anathema as gifts. We recently had a friend give a green hat from his golf club to a Chinese head of a company. The Chinese guest would not accept it, and our friend has been ridiculed since for not understanding Chinese culture. Under current regulations, it is important to avoid giving full and unopened bottles of high-end alcohol to public sector officials.

When it comes to how we present ourselves and how we should be careful about displays of wealth, there are multiple trains of thought. On the one hand, many Chinese businessmen who spend a lot of time with public sector officials will drive inexpensive vehicles. However, when a foreign company visits someone in the public sector, they are also judged by the vehicle in which they show up. In some cases, you might be asked more questions at the gate of an SOE's parking lot if you were to show up in a taxi or a lower-end vehicle from DiDi (China's equivalent to Uber). For these meetings, we recommend cars along the lines of an Audi A6 or a Mercedes E-class. These models are now manufactured in China and are often used by universities and SOEs themselves. They can also be readily ordered through the DiDi app.

It is customary for meeting participants to accompany you to the front door of their offices after a meeting ends. In these situations, you must have a car waiting for them. This is not to show that you readily spend money on expensive transportation. Instead, it conveys that you care enough about the meeting to have organized a reasonably nice car to wait prior to the meeting's conclusion. This practice is a sign of respect for your hosts' time because they will normally see you off at the curb and wave until your car is out of sight. If a car is not waiting at the conclusion of the meeting, then the hosts will wait curbside (even in the cold).

Chinese organizations typically request background information before they agree to formal discussion. You need to provide as much information as possible about yourself and anyone attending with you, and about the topics you wish to discuss. The Chinese side must also have sufficient time to study the request.

In the case of organizing meetings, it is important to avoid being too formal with initial WeChat communication. Send a written introduction only once friendly communication has been established. Voice messages are considered more friendly than written ones and should be between twenty and forty seconds long. It may sound ridiculous, but it is also a good idea to send emojis and animated stickers upon initial communication. Some popular stickers include bunny rabbits saying thank you or handing out flowers.

The Chinese dislike surprises, preferring to make their position clear in advance of a meeting. Before the meeting, make the Chinese side aware of what will be presented, to help prevent a relationship-damaging loss of face. Knowing what will be discussed beforehand also permits the Chinese side to select the proper participants for the meeting.

Because Chinese public sector professionals value formality, dress in formal business attire when meeting with Chinese government entities at their official offices. Men should wear a suit and tie. The Chinese light up when they see foreign businessmen wearing red ties to a meeting. Gold for ties is also good. These colors show respect and understanding of Chinese culture and this is greatly appreciated.

Women can wear any business-appropriate attire to meetings; blue jeans or casual footwear (such as sandals) at government meetings are nonstarters.

Punctuality is considered a virtue in China, so it is important to arrive at meetings early or exactly on time. Guests are greeted upon arrival by a representative and escorted to the meeting room. When a foreign group is late to a meeting, it is considered extremely rude and can negatively affect collaboration. Punctuality is important not only when meeting with SOEs, but also when meeting with Chinese tech and financial companies. It is best to show up to meetings fifteen minutes early. If you invite a Chinese contact to a meeting, they will usually arrive fifteen minutes early, and you should be prepared.

Chinese people generally expect leaders of foreign delegations to enter the room first and in rank order. This avoids confusion. Important guests are escorted to seats, with the principal guest often seated to the right of the Chinese host, the seat of honor. When meeting at a long table, the leader of a delegation sits opposite the number-one person, in the middle of the table, and his delegation fills in alongside of them.

Chinese seldom hold meetings with foreign delegations alone. Staff members are invariably present. Not all the participants are necessarily introduced; those who are not introduced are usually note takers or secretaries. "Secretary" in Chinese is pronounced 秘书 (*mishu*) and literally means "private book." The role of a secretary in China is extremely important and not to be underestimated. The secretary is often considered the "keeper of all secrets" and, in many cases, may influence key decisions. Chinese companies will fill a room with lower-level people who may or may not have any relationship to the meeting content. They are there to make the main meeting participants look more important and often do not talk at all.

Here are some tips for making your first business meetings with Chinese partners a success.

- Remember who holds the floor, and do not interrupt the speaker. This cannot be stressed enough. Sometimes the speaker will pause for a moment. This does not necessarily signal that he or she has relinquished the floor. Wait a few seconds to confirm you can begin your response.
- Chinese people often signal that they understand what the speaker is saying by nodding or with interjections. These do not necessarily signal agreement.

- Never put anyone on the spot during a meeting. Always offer a way out so your counterpart can save face.

- A good interpreter can help you immeasurably in China. When talking through an interpreter, pause frequently and avoid slang and colloquialisms. Although difficult to get used to, always talk to the host, never directly to the translator. Foreigners have a natural tendency to look at and talk to the translator; this should be avoided.

- At the close of the meeting, restate what was accomplished to guard against misunderstandings. Ask for a contact person for future communication.

MEALS

At meals, the Chinese host will sit facing the door, with the most important guest to his or her immediate right. As mentioned, place cards often indicate where one should sit, to help avoid confusion.

At a formal meal, the first activity is the pouring of beverages. Once this is completed—and it can be a somewhat time-consuming process—the Chinese host will open the meal by encouraging everyone to begin eating. After the Chinese host begins eating, only then is it appropriate for you to begin eating. It is considered very rude in Chinese culture to eat before the host starts. This is the case for each course; the foreigner should wait until the host has started each course before beginning.

The first course is usually an array of cold dishes or appetizers. These are generally placed in the center of the table and it is appropriate to take a bite or two of each. At more formal gatherings, each individual is served a plate of assorted cold dishes as a first course.

These cold dishes may include peanuts, walnuts, or pickled cucumbers. Often, the cold appetizers can also include dishes that are the least appetizing to Western palates, such as chicken feet or jellyfish.

It is worthwhile to get food in one's stomach before leaving for dinner—also called pregaming. If you didn't pregame and plan on drinking (see note in the Toasting and Drinking section about deciding to drink), then you'd better eat the chicken feet, because drinking begins before the hot dishes arrive. Drinking on an empty stomach is bad, and this is doubly true with Moutai, an acidic sorghum-based beverage with a 53 percent alcohol content.

There are usually some good hot dishes during the meal, but it is surprisingly hard to eat a full meal at a banquet while carrying on a conversation. If you do not eat enough and you decide to drink, then you will probably get drunker than the other guests.

At some meals, the waiter serves each guest an individual portion of each dish. In other cases, some of the dishes are placed in the center of the table and each person serves themselves. In the latter case, it is a sign of respect for the Chinese hosts to serve the guests at least once or twice. Likewise, when hosting a meal, the hosts should serve the Chinese guests. They will say "no," indicating that you should not be bothered with having to serve, but this really means "yes." Hosts will always insist on serving guests.

Always leave something over on your plate. Not to do so implies you are still hungry. There is usually one dish that everyone wants to eat the most. A common example is ribs. Something expensive like sea slugs, abalone, or soft-shelled turtle may be served to show excess, but most people still prefer eating ribs. Eat the ribs, but don't eat all the ribs. Leave some for the other guests.

Pace yourself. Count on several courses in a formal setting. Your plate will be removed and replaced with a clean one periodically throughout the meal. This is particularly useful if you have left something unappetizing on your plate as you don't have to worry about it staying there throughout the entire meal.

The Chinese hosts will sometimes order something exotic as a test for Western guests. In one year, we have been served rabbit ears, whole songbirds, soft-shelled turtle, chicken feet, camel hump, camel trotters, cockroaches, scorpions, snake, and horns of various kinds. Snake blood has even been put into shot glasses for toasts. It is not a cardinal sin to eschew a particular dish. If you can stomach these delicacies, then call their bluff and pass the remaining portion to them. They will be impressed and find it funny because they probably don't want to eat this stuff either. If you cannot stomach it, that is still fine. It is all in good fun and that is likely the response they are expecting. Just take some of every dish if you possibly can, then push around whatever you do not want to consume and pretend you've sampled it. But never actively decline a dish or drink. And do not suddenly stop eating or drinking in the middle of a meal, lest you make your Chinese hosts feel they have offended you.

- You know you are close to the end of a meal when the fish is served. Fish, pronounced 鱼 (*yu*), is a homonym for 余 and shows that the host wants the guest to be more than satisfied.
- Sometimes a bowl of steamed or fried rice is served at the end of a meal. If you eat the rice, it indicates that your host did not provide you with enough food. One or two chopsticks of rice is okay, but do not eat the entire bowl.
- The end of the meal is signaled by a fruit platter and sometimes a second sweet dish. When the dessert is served, and it is 8:00 or 8:30 PM, depending on whether the meal started at 6:00 or 6:30 PM, be prepared to stand up, say thank you, and leave. The Chinese are early to eat and early to end a meal, and the foreigner should be prepared for a prompt ending to a meal.

When You Are the Host

Make sure your guests are met at the door and escorted to the room. Be present in the room before they arrive so that you can welcome them. Be sure to stand and remain standing until your guests sit. Pay close attention to protocol and don't slight anyone by seating him or her inappropriately. If you are not sure exactly how high someone's rank is, be sure to ask in advance. Following standard seating arrangements is always a good idea.

Lead your guests to the table and help them find their seats. Use place cards to show assigned seats; these should be in English and Chinese if possible. If a senior public sector official is included in a meeting, he or she should be in the seat of honor to the host's right. One should be strategic and understand which Chinese contacts speak English to avoid seating those who don't next to non–Chinese speakers.

Keep a sharp eye on your guests' plates and make sure the plates are kept full of food. Keep serving them, even if they protest.

Toasting and Drinking

Decide in advance whether you will drink alcohol or not and stick to it. Do not start out with Moutai and then switch to a soft drink. If you have a large party, it is considered acceptable to appoint one or more people to be the "designated drinkers" for the evening, but be sure to choose this individual prior to the meal. Chinese consider alcohol an important aspect of any business-related meal, so do not be surprised by the amount served.

It is common for attendees to get very drunk at business dinners. There is a term in China, 一瓶起步 (*yi ping qi bu*), meaning "one bottle to start." It is a badge of honor to be able to consume a whole 500-milliliter bottle of 53 percent Moutai and still be coherent. Some frequent dinner attendees get a lot of practice. There is no pressure to drink at these dinners, and many people are growing more health conscious and declining to drink. But it is all or nothing, so make the decision of whether to drink at the outset. If you don't want to drink, then the waiter will remove your Moutai glass and you won't be offered any for the remainder of the meal.

You will have one glass for a toasting drink (alcoholic) and one for a soft drink (or beer), and you will be served both. You will be served the same drinks throughout the meal and should be prepared to have your drink continuously refilled, so take care which soft drink you chose. The best bet is to request mineral water in order to avoid ten glasses of Coca-Cola or Orange Fanta. Red and white wine are also commonly served at meals. However, you still may be offered Moutai.

A toast by the host will normally be made following the cold appetizers or the first hot course. The host will stand, with an interpreter if necessary, and make some short welcoming remarks. When he or she raises their glass for the toast, everyone clinks glasses and drains a shot of liquor or a glass of wine.

A return toast is customary and expected. The return toast generally takes place one or two courses after the toast by the host. The principal guest should stand, with an interpreter if necessary, raise his or her glass, and make a brief toast. Again, everyone will be included in the toast.

Toasts are common and appreciated. After the two opening toasts, participants from both sides may initiate toasts, with topics such as friendship and cooperation being appropriate. A person may toast the entire table, and the entire table will drink simultaneously, or, generally later in the meal, one person may single out another to drink with him or her.

When toasting someone, hold your glass in your right hand and rest your left hand underneath the bottom. Toast with your glass lower than the other person's; this is a sign of respect.

At a Chinese banquet it is not appropriate to drink alcohol alone. If you wish to take a sip of your drink, it is expected that you will turn to someone at the table and drink a toast with that individual. Beer is often considered a "beverage," not alcohol, and may be sipped without toasting.

Beware of the saying *gan le* (literally, "dry"), which means "bottom's up." Often when drinking Moutai, it is expected that you will drain your glass at each toast. There are many rituals involved in this drinking game. You should lift your glass with both hands; when you have drained it, you demonstrate this to your drinking partner by showing him the dry bottom of your glass. You may even turn the glass upside down on the table or on the top of your head for effect! Take notice of how your Chinese counterpart demonstrates the emptying of his or her glass, and then follow suit.

When drinking Moutai, it is rude to not drain the entire glass when you toast. If you want to drink less, the best way is to pour less into your glass so it may only be half full. Then, when you drain your glass, you will only be consuming the equivalent of half a glass. It is possible to refrain from this game by politely not participating from the beginning. Stopping this kind of toasting once you have started is difficult, as the people who toast you will be offended if you suddenly stop drinking when it gets to be their turn. This is why it is recommended to appoint one or more people as the "designated drinkers" for the evening.

To thank all those who have taken the time to meet with the visiting delegation, it is appropriate for the visitors to host a return meal prior to their departure.

Gift Giving

Gifts are given to show esteem or gratitude. The giver of the gift should hold it with both hands when presenting it to the recipient. Gifts should be presented in red packages, never in white. White is associated with death and funerals in China, whereas red is celebratory and happy. Do not expect your gift to be opened in your presence unless you specifically request it.

Gifts are always presented at the end of a meeting or at the end of a meal and are, in fact, indicators that the meeting or meal has concluded. It would be considered impolite to present a gift at any other time.

It is not uncommon for Chinese hosts to present visitors with gifts. Note that Chinese custom and manners may sometimes require the Chinese to give as a gift something that has been admired. For example, an American visitor to China was quite taken with a set of silver-plated chopsticks used at an official banquet and asked where they could be bought. Ten minutes later, sets of the chopsticks were brought out and presented to everyone in the delegation. Whatever it is that you praise could end up being yours!

Gifts should be symbolic, with no monetary value. When unsure of what to give, a small souvenir is always a safe bet, as is something that symbolizes your country.

Other Social Courtesies

In addition to the specific scenarios outlined above, the following are some other common social courtesies it's important to be aware of.

- The Chinese tend to be formal in introducing, meeting, and greeting visitors. When a new person enters the room and is introduced to you, it is considered common courtesy to stand up to meet them if you are sitting.
- In China, the surname used to always come first in a person's name, but now the practice is mixed, making names confusing. Also, it is becoming more commonplace for Chinese to choose Anglicized first names. The last name is almost always used with a person's title to address someone with whom one is not very familiar. Thus, Mr. Wang Limin, chief of a department, would be called Department Chief Wang. Married women retain their maiden names. Men and women who participate in social functions with foreign guests attend because of their functional positions and usually do not bring spouses.
- The Chinese expect to shake hands upon meeting. Other forms of touching, such as handholding, cheek kissing, or a slap on the back, are not common in initial meetings and are generally avoided between men and women.
- An exchange of name cards is common practice in China, not only at business meetings, but also in other situations. Name cards should always be presented to others with two outstretched hands, one grasping each side of the card, and with the card placed so that the letters or characters are upright from the receiver's vantage point. If applicable, cards should be printed in Chinese on one side and English on the other.

- In social conversation, the Chinese generally make a strong effort to show an interest in the other side's situation, rather than dwelling on their own situation and experiences. The Chinese do not mind being asked personal questions about their family or work and often ask such questions of foreigners. In addition to these topics, questions about the Chinese person's hometown and past experiences can also serve as a means of expressing interest.

- Modesty is important in Chinese culture and, as a result, Chinese often accept compliments in a different fashion than foreigners. Instead of saying "thank you," they tend to protest that they do not deserve the compliment. Another sign of modesty that the foreign guest may experience is that Chinese hosts may say that they have prepared a "simple" meal, while in reality a several-course feast has been prepared.

NAVIGATING THE WORLD OF MEDIA AND PR

The public relations and media climate in China differs greatly from that in the West. In China, the state-run media need to be a key focus; foreign firms should monitor them closely. It is equally important to establish a constructive working relationship with these state-run outlets. Each one employs reporters who specialize in specific areas—for example, industry, technology, and culture—and so multinationals operating in China should be in regular communication with these reporters. This can be done through a PR firm or directly by the company itself. The reporters will measure the success of their careers by their access to background information and substantive content, so it improves media relations to proactively provide content to them.

It is best to focus on the largest news sources in China. Among the leaders of the state media outlets are:

- Xinhua News Agency
- the *People's Daily*
- the *Guangming Daily*
- the *Economics Daily*
- China Central Television (CCTV)

Xinhua News Agency and the *People's Daily* are the most significant state media outlets. The others are also important but often take their lead from these two.

Xinhua represents the government's view on a wide range of issues. Its content is broad based; it covers politics, economics, and culture, among other areas. The *People's Daily* tends to be politically focused. It is written to be easily accessible to the broad masses. In the West, many students of the Chinese language can read the *People's Daily* after a few years of instruction. The *Guangming Daily* is probably the least controversial, since it is centered on the arts and culture, but be aware that the Chinese government focuses on cultural news to help ensure the promotion of what it calls a "harmonious society." The *Economics Daily* concentrates on the economy. It is where to look, for example, for an economic analysis of China's Five-Year Plan.

CCTV is the state-run television outlet in China, and like several other government outlets it offers content that is not viewed as "sensitive." It consists of several channels, each with a different focus. One channel is all news, for example, and another airs popular sitcoms.

In addition to the state-run outlets, there has been a proliferation of new media, including the following:

- **Baidu:** Basically China's Google. After Google itself made some serious missteps and was banned from China, Baidu became the "go-to" source. Its news is accurate and considered to have reliable content on subjects like the economy, politics, and culture.
- **Toutiao:** A news source that is unique in the world because it has an artificial intelligence (AI) platform that recommends all its articles. The AI uses machine learning to understand each user's reading preferences and recommends every article to suit those preferences. That has brought it great success in achieving user engagement. Toutiao is owned by ByteDance, the same company that owns TikTok. ByteDance was founded by Zhang Yiming, an engineer by training and one of China's leading entrepreneurs.
- **Tencent:** A company that leverages connectivity with its own WeChat app.

TAKEAWAYS

To operate in China successfully requires not only a knowledge of business conditions, marketing opportunities, and government policies, but also a sophisticated understanding of Chinese culture and customs. To be a good guest there, it is always important to remember that:

1. China's history is several thousand years old. The Chinese are very proud of that and appreciative of foreigners who come to China with an understanding of their history and culture—not to mention the ability to speak Chinese. That requires great effort, of course, but the rewards are well worth it.

2. The PR and media industries in China are a combination of both the established state media and new, high-tech outlets. It is a combination of the old and the new, with the new media far more technologically developed than anything in the West, such as the algorithm-driven Toutiao. Every executive who understands how the media operate—or who employs a public relations firm that understands it—knows that good communications is an essential part of modern business life. Understanding the media landscape in China is an art unto itself—the rules that apply in the West rarely apply there—so bring a sophisticated game plan with you for the best chance at success.

CHAPTER 14

Cracking the Code of Japan

Ancient and Modern Island Nation

JOSHUA W. WALKER, PHD
JAPAN SOCIETY

Japan is a land of juxtaposition where tradition meets the future—from the world's oldest continuous hereditary dynasty to the remaking of global consumer culture through emojis, precision-built cars, and *Super Mario*. This is one of the most complex, layered markets to understand; its culture, history, and language make Japan not only an island unto itself, but also a paradise of opportunity for those lucky enough to have its abundance revealed.

Japan and Japanese culture represent a unique paradox. Many aspects are insular and exclusive, and the Japanese people often pride themselves on their distinctiveness. Yet they are also voracious consumers of foreign culture, and many parts of Japanese culture have gone global—Japanese cars, sushi, fashion, animation, and video games are known around the world, and in some cases have shaped its pop culture. This tension between globalization and isolation represents over two millennia of Japanese history and culture, something that makes telling the story of Japan, and telling stories *in* Japan as a profession, particularly challenging.

Yet sometimes Japan can serve as the perfect complement or mirror in revealing our own assumptions. Understanding Japan often takes unlearning a Western mindset and adopting a more Zen philosophy.

An example of this contrast: In the West, the gardens of Versailles have classical straight lines and right angles, with broad, clear vistas and gushing, gravity-defying fountains. Versailles conquers nature. Bending from great effort to human design, the natural world conforms to the power of the monarch or state. By contrast, in Japan, the goal is to hide human effort rather than to extol it, and Japanese gardens avoid hard, right angles or unnatural forms. In the gardens surrounding the Chureito Pagoda near Mt. Fuji, there is meaning in invoking nature instead of coercing it. The natural elements are meant to invoke still grander natural elements, as when a rock suggests an island or mountain. Rather than engineered fountains forcing water to spray, gravity alone guides water along simulated rivers, paths of white stone, and pebbles. The entire concept is the awe of nature.

JAPAN'S STORY

Japan has always been shaped first and foremost by its geography. Many compare Japan—an island off the coast of Asia—with Britain's position across from Europe, and there are many similarities in how both island nations balance their relations and alliances. However, looking at the long archipelago of Japan, not from the traditional north–south axis but from a west–east axis, shows Japan as a comprehensive barrier for China and the Asian mainland's outlet to the Pacific Ocean. From this perspective, the history of mainland invasions of Japan, which were all utter disasters and can be counted on one hand, takes on new meaning. The only successful occupation of Japan came not from the mainland, but from the United States after World War II.

As an island nation, Japan has long had to deal with the "Middle Kingdom" of China, through waves of interaction from the golden period of the Heian that imitated the Chinese imperial court and actively imported Buddhism, to the Tokugawa period that banned all interaction with the outside world. Japan transformed itself in the seventeenth century from a divided island of feudal lords to a consolidated nation that came of age in the nineteenth century with surprisingly swift modernization and military victories over the Chinese and Russian empires, leading to an overseas empire of its own. The subsequent way that Japan embraced defeat after World War II, through the American occupation, reshaped its international relations but not its core identity.

Invasions from the sea, as well as frequent earthquakes and natural disasters, have instilled a sense of fatalism in the Japanese, who have learned to bend adversity in the face of disaster. In contrast to America's manifest destiny to settle its West, Japan focused mainly on internal consolidation until the nineteenth century, when it began expanding beyond its own islands in response to the collapse of its neighbors and historic empires.

Periodization of modern Japanese history is typically presented in pre- and postwar terms, with the end of World War II and the collapse of the short-lived Japanese Empire. Within the postwar time frame, historians focus on the American Occupation, marked by General MacArthur's command, and then Japan's transition into the "San Francisco System."

> The defining moment for Japan's post-imperial rehabilitation was when Japan signed the 1951 peace treaty with forty-eight nations in San Francisco, hence the name, formally ending the occupation and aligning itself with the United States for the remainder of the Cold War. Historian John W. Dower is credited with coining this term in his considerable body of work on Japan and reflects on its common usage in his introduction to Postwar Japan as History, ed. Andrew Gordon (Berkeley: University of California Press, 1993).

The strategic parameters of Japan's domestic and international alliances were set by its all-encompassing bilateral Treaty of Mutual Cooperation and Security, which made Tokyo dependent on the United States for all critical foreign and security policies. With American patronage, and without the economic constraints of a full security apparatus, Japan's postwar recovery was rapid, and by the 1970s the country had become an economic power.

Asia's first Olympics, the 1964 Summer Games in Tokyo, was a celebration of Japan's economic miracle, symbolized by the *shinkansen* bullet trains—still the envy of the world today—and modern architecture that rebuilt the capital skyline. It is critical to understand that Tokyo represents the center of almost everything in Japan. Although the spiritual centers of Kyoto and Ise represent minor exceptions with their shrines and temples, the imperial family and symbolic head of the Shinto faith, the Emperor, reside in the heart of Tokyo.

> *In clear contrast to Tokyo's centrality, Washington is the political capital of the US, New York its financial center, Los Angeles a cultural magnet, and San Francisco its tech capital.*

Especially in terms of government structure, which is centered on the Japanese national parliament (called the Diet), the complete domination of the national over the prefectural or municipal offers a more centralized system of governance at all levels. This top-down hierarchical-yet-consensus approach permeates almost all aspects of Japan today.

THE OLYMPIC GAMES

Tokyo was selected to host its second Olympics in 2020, after considerable cost and effort on the part of Japanese prime minister Shinzo Abe, who personally lobbied for it and went so far as to dress up as Mario from the popular Nintendo franchise to welcome the world at the Rio Olympics in 2016. Because Japan is an extremely popular tourist destination—in 2019 it welcomed 31.88 million inbound tourists—the 2020 games were meant to break all records, but of course COVID-19 had other plans.

The coronavirus pandemic delayed the Tokyo 2020 Olympic Games to 2021 and has fundamentally changed our still-evolving landscape. However, like the select group of other elite metropolises that have held repeat Olympics, Tokyo 2020 further burnishes Japan's desire to tell its story on the global stage. Following the Olympics, Japan will host the world again in 2025 at the World EXPO Osaka.

JAPAN'S INTERNATIONAL RELATIONS

Japan's contemporary international relations have been anchored by its security alliance with the US, which in turn has defined its current place in the world. The first Japanese delegation to America, in 1860, was enthusiastically welcomed by New Yorkers and reported thusly by the *New York Times*. Despite immigration restrictions, world wars, financial upheaval, and pandemics, relations between the United States and Japan have endured.

Described by some as America's unsinkable aircraft carrier in Asia, Japan's role has taken on greater importance as geopolitics is increasingly shaped by tensions between the US and China, much as the Cold War was shaped by US–Soviet relations. As the world's third-largest economy, and the immediate neighbor and frontline state to China, together with its long history with the "Middle Kingdom," Japan's role is further heightened. Yet most Japanese relegate these strategic concerns to the government in Tokyo and to the small cadre of diplomatic hands on both sides who have managed the alliance since the end of World War II.

Japan has one of the most singular and distinctive senses of self in the world, so much so that famed Harvard political scientist Samuel Huntington classified the Japanese as the only nation-civilization of its own in his controversial work, *Clash of Civilizations*. A declining population, the lack of naturalization pathways for non-ethnic Japanese (except in highly specialized cases such as sports stars), and low immigration rates all make for a particularly challenging international environment.

The Japanese have seemingly been on a constant search for a past. During the twentieth century, Japan tried to become a military superpower, which worked for a time until it attacked the United States. The next plan was to become an economic superpower under its alliance structure with the US, which also worked for a time. Now many in Japan are wondering what is next. Will Japan become a sustainability superpower as recent leaders have suggested? As we have seen throughout its history, Japan is deeply cosmopolitan while also insular and isolated. That tension has shaped Japanese culture for millennia and will continue to do so well into the future.

UNDERSTANDING JAPAN—JAPANESE LANGUAGE AND JAPANESE-NESS

The Japanese language is one of the most complicated contextual and written structures in the entire world. Japanese is hard to understand unless you know the details of the social context, which is generally assumed. As well, the subtext makes the language particularly difficult for foreigners to understand even if they apprehend the technical dimensions of the language. As a result, a simple

Google translation of Japanese leaves many people more confused; they would have been better served by simply observing without words. The aspect of consensus embedded in the language is particularly important in the functioning of Japanese society.

The reason that Japan has such a complex writing system is largely because it adopted ideographic Chinese characters (*kanji*), which have no syntactical relationship to spoken Japanese. As a result, there are three distinctively different written systems. In English, there are only twenty-six letters. In Japanese, more than two thousand characters are needed to read at a basic level—representing entire words with many different meanings and sounds—plus forty-six *hiragana* characters to connect them, along with forty-six *katakana* characters used for imported foreign words. The amalgamation of characters means that the written form is critical and highly valued, resulting in one of the most literate and print-revering cultures in the world. Everything from the social status and place of the speaker to honorific circularity and deferential respect can be detected from a single word choice.

In the contemporary context, while 140 or 280 characters in an English tweet may constitute a few sentences, the same number can represent entire paragraphs of meaning for the Japanese. The fact that Japanese were some of the earliest adopters of digitization, from personal computers to electronic translations, has led to a more tech-savvy population, which often seems futuristic in application. Yet the Japanese remain, as a population, the lowest adopters of Western social media; by contrast they have the highest newspaper subscription rates in the world.

Television in Japan is ubiquitous and, up until recent digital changes, the public state broadcaster NHK, similar to Britain's BBC or Canada's CBC, ruled supreme. Even as the new generation of Japanese "cuts the cords" in favor of smartphones and streaming platforms, given the highly specialized nature of the Japanese language, these credible broadcasters and their content have an important relationship with their audiences.

Conglomerates drive consumption of both news and entertainment, helping to create entire genres such as unique reality and variety shows that thrive outside of Japan. At the same time, historical samurai dramas captivate audiences along with sci-fi and anime, which has taken off internationally through Japanese film festivals, even though distributors still have not adapted the Hollywood or even Bollywood models of global ubiquity.

Things go best in Japan if everyone knows his or her place and follows the rules. But the Japanese also value consensus, which means that it is awkward to explicitly insist on rules. Thus, many aspects of Japanese culture and language also involve seemingly elliptical ways of saying "No" without ever using an overt negative. The Japanese language structure means that such linguistic moves are rich and subtle—precious commodities in a society that values consensus, and frustrating circles for outsiders trying to get to a specific point in a negotiation. This paradox makes the job of PR professionals even harder.

DECODING PR IN JAPAN: A PRACTICAL ACCOUNTING

Like the Japanese language, which values societal context, Japanese businesses and culture value history and tradition. The *New York Times* recently labeled Japan as an old-business superpower:

> *The country is home to more than 33,000 [businesses] with at least 100 years of history—over 40 percent of the world's total, according to a study by the Tokyo-based Research Institute of Centennial Management. Over 3,100 have been running for at least two centuries. Around 140 have existed for more than 500 years and at least 19 claim to have been continuously operating since the first millennium.*

This respect for longevity, specialization, and tradition often comes at the expense of innovation and start-ups, and also deprioritizes public relations—sometimes viewed as a way to gloss over a lack of quality. Traditionally, PR has been seen in Japan as synonymous with marketing, rather than branding or value generation, thus hamstringing many efforts to tell successful stories. Quality speaks for itself, and having to tell one's own story is not proper for many Japanese.

Against this backdrop, there is admiration for the American way that privileges the image of "cool America," as defined by Madison Avenue and Hollywood. But this admiration is particularly Japanese. Rarely are American campaigns imported directly, even if the products are wildly successful, such as Coca-Cola or McDonald's. Instead, they are adopted and adapted. "Coke Light" has a more appealing name than Diet Coke in Japan, as does the "Teriyaki Burger," which has been extremely successful, even as the Double Cheeseburger and Big Mac remain popular as a taste of America.

Public relations in Japan is a new and evolving field. Even as the world's third-largest economy, Japan represents a cultural and linguistic landscape that, in contrast to nearby business hubs like Hong Kong and Singapore, can mean that global norms of corporate communications do not necessarily apply. Yet Japan's strong cultural influence, especially in pop culture and food (particularly in other Asian countries), adds to the nation's appeal as a gateway for the West into Asia.

Business management in Japan has only recently begun to acknowledge PR as a fully fledged field. For example, the Public Relations Society of Japan is relatively new and quite small, especially in comparison to its American and English-language counterparts. Most Japanese consider PR to be just about advertising, and many still equate it with propaganda.

Unlike the US, Japan is homogenous, with a single language. Within this island nation with a centralized government, there is a general feeling that Japanese can understand each other without the higher context of communication or strategic communications. PR in Japan has developed in tandem with business diversification from globalization and the US, yet the homogeneity of Japan limits the space for PR development. Also, because traditional Japanese newspapers have a subscription rate ten times larger than that of the *New York Times* or other US papers, print ad revenue is extremely high. As a result, the two biggest ad agencies, Dentsu and Hakuhodo, have become extremely strong players in the field.

Dentsu and Hakuhodo are not PR companies in the traditional sense of the word, as they basically buy ads and exert significant influence in mass media the way *Mad Men* portrayed advertising in 1950s and 1960s America. The symbiotic relationship between mass media and these two leaders—developed during Japan's mass-consumption era through selling ads—has resulted in a smaller, less diverse PR market.

Despite the rise of Japan's global multinationals, worldwide PR agencies operating in Japan have generally not had great success; however, they often work with Japanese multinationals outside the country. Domestic PR firms are small. Most Japanese companies continue to rely on Dentsu and Hakuhodo, who in turn often collaborate and partner with global PR firms to service some of Japan's largest accounts.

Legal disclosures involving corporate and economic leaders are generally handled solely by regulatory and finance authorities, not in tandem with PR professionals;

there is a clear incentive to leave things to the local experts, lest the American or Western ways lead people to trouble, whether cultural, legal, or regulatory.

A TIME OF TRANSFORMATION AND OPPORTUNITY

In the 2010s, many global multinationals began opening offices in Tokyo, after decades of running Japanese accounts from their world headquarters. The Japanese business community itself, like its international counterparts, is going through a moment of transformation. Entities ranging from the powerful *Keidanren* Japanese business federation of Fortune 100 multinational companies, to those such as Rakuten and Softbank, have challenged the norms through their business models and unorthodox leaders.

With these changes comes opportunity for public diplomacy in Japan, including new schools for communications and a promising field for the future, including the 2020–21 Olympics and World EXPO 2025. Rather than the exotic "Land of the Rising Sun" of the past, Japan is one of the most comfortably different environments in the world, and businesses are flocking there for the Asian century. Hong Kong and Singapore remain strong competitors, but given Japan's status as the third-largest economy and a strong domestic market—plus its links with the West through its Washington security alliance—Tokyo is becoming one of the fastest-growing destinations for PR professionals.

If we look at the distinction only among PR agencies and PR practitioners in Japan, marketing communication is used for selling services and products; lobbying is used for changing policy, obtaining subsidies, or deregulating government; and storytelling is used for differentiation from mass marketing. Everything is increasingly moving to the digital realm, and the power of social media is beginning to rise along with generational shifts. However, most Japanese are not familiar with the field of PR, lobbying, or storytelling. Even within the communications industry, Japanese may find that there are distinctions without differences. As the American way of doing business and styles of marketing have begun to arrive, those bringing them will encounter many unique features in Japan that require local understanding and partnerships.

There are few resources in English to guide those interested in Japanese public relations, but Dentsu Public Relations compiles an annual handbook titled

Communicating: A Guide to PR in Japan that is packed with insights, making it a must-read for PR practitioners, business managers, and media studies researchers with an interest in Asia.

To reiterate, the Japanese public relations market is unique and can be extremely challenging for overseas companies used to a very different media relations environment. The tried-and-true method of partnering with a Dentsu or Hakuhodo is the most well-trodden path, although it seems there may be more space for change in the future.

JAPAN AS A MIRROR

Japan has oscillated between globalist and isolationist tendencies, making it a particularly difficult country, culture, and language for a foreigner to penetrate. Yet the abundance and benefits of Japan go far beyond its immediate market. The loyalty and "stickiness" of Japanese businesses and customers are legendary—they are the reason why many businesses have thrived for such a long time. Additionally, Japan is like a mirror that clarifies and refines the quality of any enterprise, including storytelling that may have to be adapted and localized.

The benefits to "cracking the code" in Japan and among the Japanese are obvious to all those who have been fortunate enough to do it, but almost impossible to explain to those trying. Like a stroll through a Japanese garden or a hike to the top of Mt. Fuji, it is the journey itself rather than the destination that defines the experience. As PR professionals and professional storytellers set their sights on Japan, a healthy sense of humility, curiosity, and appreciation for Japanese history and traditions will go a long way toward revealing the paradox of this ancient island nation.

FOR ADDITIONAL READING

- Matt Alt, *Pure Invention: How Japan's Pop Culture Conquered the World* (New York: Crown, 2020).
- Dentsu Public Relations, *Communicating: A Guide to PR in Japan,* 8th ed. (Tokyo: Wiley Publishing in Japan, 2018).
- Public Relations Society of Japan, "About PRSJ," accessed June 14, 2021, https://prsj.or.jp/en/.

- Mark J. Ravina, *Understanding Japan: A Cultural History* (The Great Courses, 2015), https://www.thegreatcourses.com/courses/understanding-japan-a-cultural-history.
- Joshua W. Walker, "Shadows of Empire: How Post-Imperial Successor States Shape Memories" (PhD diss., Princeton University, 2012), https://dataspace.princeton.edu/handle/88435/dsp01v405s9415.

TAKEAWAYS

1. Japan is shaped first and foremost by its geography, limited resources, and location as an island off the coast of the Asian mainland.

2. Japan is a natural gateway for Americans and Westerners to Asia, not just because of its geography but also its own cultural influence and history.

3. Do not try PR in Japan by yourself without a deep appreciation for and understanding of the Japanese language, people, and society.

4. Japan is increasingly becoming an island of opportunity, experimentation, and possibility for the future.

5. Japan is a useful mirror in understanding one's own mindfulness, philosophy, and thinking.

CHAPTER 15

Communicating in Canada

Welcome to Canada—Bienvenue au Canada

SARAH L. MANLEY ROBERTSON

Don your favourite touque, grab a pop, and get comfortable on your chesterfield. Let's journey across the 9,984,670 square kilometres (km²)—second in land area only to Russia, with the United States at 9,834,000 km²—that I call home.

Along the way, we'll talk about communications and indulge in a few of our treasures:

- Listen to Drake and Shawn Mendes, Bryan Adams and The Tragically Hip, Rush and Neil Young; Anne Murray, Frank Mills, and Glenn Gould;
- Read Farley Mowat, Wayne Johnson, Nino Ricci, and Lawrence Hill; Robert Munsch and Lucy Maude Montgomery; or Jacques Poulin and Marie Laberge;
- Catch a flick starring Christopher Plummer, Ryan Reynolds, Sandra Oh, Ryan Gosling, or Rachel McAdams.

Explore the history and geography that make us who we are. You'll gain insights to inform your communications approaches to reach the 36,029,245 people who live here with me.

I've watched the notorious Lake Erie undertow at Point Pelee, Canada's southernmost mainland tip, in my hometown, Leamington, Ontario (which is farther south than parts of more than 25 US states). And wondered what the weather was like almost 4,634 km away at Canada's northern boundary, Cape Columbia, Ellesmere Island, Nunavut. I've felt the sting of wind-whipped surf at our most easterly point, Cape Spear, Newfoundland. And wondered what was happening 5,514 km away at our most westerly border, Boundary Peak 187, Yukon.

A PATCHWORK COUNTRY

We're bound by our commonalities. Yet, our history and geography demand we show our unique and vibrant colours. The land itself is a potpourri of 39 terrestrial regions and an estimated 2 million lakes—the most in the world. Our borders enclose more than 52,000 islands and 48 national parks. Our population consists of over 250 ethnic origins or ancestries. More than 1.67 million people in Canada identify themselves as an Aboriginal person (First Nations, Inuit, and Métis). Nearly 1 million immigrants landed at Pier 21 alone between 1928 and 1971.

To me, what makes Canada great is our amalgam of *hybrid traditions, views, and cultures.* It is a posture that at once unites and individualizes. And makes us delightfully eclectic.

We're peacekeepers, yet we've spearheaded the offense in notable battles. Canada completed more than seventy peacekeeping missions between 1947 and 2001, including in Rwanda, Somalia, and Syria; and more recently in the Gulf War, Haiti, and Afghanistan. We played critical offensive roles during World War I in Ypres, Passchendaele, and Dieppe, and our most notable offensive in history saw 14,000 Canadians storm—and take—Juno Beach, Normandy, on D-Day, June 6, 1944. And we back our military through organizations like supportourtroops .com, woundedwarriors.ca, and 1,350 branches of the Royal Canadian Legion.

We endorse the metric system—when we want to. Ask us at what temperature to cook the Thanksgiving turkey in October: we'll give it to you in Fahrenheit. Ask us for the temperature outdoors: we'll give it to you in Celsius—sometimes. When it is hot (our average summer temperature mid-country ranges from 77° to 86°F, or 25° to 30°C), it'll be Fahrenheit because it sounds hotter; when it's cold, you'll get it in Celsius because, well, it sounds warmer and makes us feel better. We still buy 2×4s and describe the fastest cars by their 0–60 speed in miles per hour, while our roads are regulated in kilometres per hour (1.6 km = 1 mi).

> Quick Tip: To do an approximate C-to-F conversation in your head, take the C temp, double it, and add 32—you'll get a close-enough number.

We believe in law and order, yet alcohol smuggling was a popular business in many Canadian coastal and Great Lakes towns during Prohibition, particularly between Windsor, Ontario, and Detroit, Michigan, and along the Saskatchewan–North Dakota border. The Canadian Bronfman family (Seagram's) is known to have done business with the likes of Arnold Rothstein, Charles "Lucky" Luciano, and Arthur "Dutch Schultz" Flegenheimer.

We have our own football league, but 4.33 million Canadians tuned in to Super Bowl LIII.

We're irritated by the stereotypes of how cold it is, yet we embrace our winter sports with gusto. The country boasts almost 300 ski resorts, more than 121,000 km of organized ski-doo trails and 610,000 registered snowmobiles, almost 30 curling organizations and associations, and more than 620,000 registered ice hockey players in the 2018–19 season (our son once believed he'd have his citizenship revoked for not knowing how to skate).

So what? *These idiosyncrasies are important considerations for audience analysis and developing messaging.* For messaging to be effective, the audience must see itself in it: Canadians want the complexity of our collective character—our ethos and history, our heroes, landmarks, and pastimes—reflected.

TIES THAT BIND

While the National Sports Act of Canada acknowledges lacrosse as our national summer sport, you're likely expecting a diatribe on hockey:

- The Canadian women's national hockey team has more wins than losses to the US team.
- The Canadian men's junior team has a record eighteen gold medals.
- Canada has more active players in the National Hockey League than any other country.
- My favourite Canadian players are Darren McCarty, Hayley Wicken- heiser, Bobby Orr, Steve Sullivan, Jonathan Toews, Luc Robitaille, and Sydney Crosby.
- Darryl Sittler (after whom my brother is named) has an unmatched 10-point game.

Instead of writing at length about Ron MacLean and Foster Hewitt (you haven't properly experienced televised Canadian hockey unless you've heard this veteran commentator exclaiming, "He shoots . . . He scores!"), let's turn to an arguably *more* critical bond: our Charter of Rights and Freedoms (The Canada Act 1982).

> "Canadians [are] . . . satisfied with their freedoms-from instead of exploiting their freedoms-to." Peter C. Newman, Canadian author and journalist

Our Charter of Rights and Freedoms reconfirms **English and French as our official languages** and articulates our fundamental freedoms:

a. conscience and religion
b. thought, belief, opinion, and expression, including freedom of the press
c. peaceful assembly
d. association

Our Charter came about not by rebellion or war, but through years of *evolution, debate, consultation, and compromise.*

Canada's first *Bill of Rights* was not part of the Constitution, meaning it could easily be changed and was ineffective in protecting Canadians' rights. Prime Minister Pierre Trudeau committed himself in 1968 to a constitutional bill of rights, and under his leadership, our Constitution (originally the British North America or BNA Act) was patriated from Britain and the 1982 Charter was added.

> *"Canada is the only country in all of the Americas to have gained independence completely without violence, our founders having preferred a more incremental strategy."* Pierre Berton, Canadian historian and journalist

Many elements remain from the BNA Act, which created the Dominion of Canada under the Crown of the United Kingdom of Great Britain and Ireland on July 1, 1867—Canada Day. Her Royal Highness Queen Elizabeth II remains our head of state: when we make our oath of Citizenship, we promise to be loyal to her (and to her successors). And we retain democratic structures like the governor general as the Queen's representative; the Senate of 105 lifetime appointed members; and the House of Commons of 308 elected members allocated by population.

PEACE, ORDER, AND GOOD GOVERNMENT

Many posit that the way we think, act, and behave comes from Section 91, the Peace, Order, and Good Government Clause. The Canadian ethos values the greater good over individual liberty. According to Tommy Douglas, seventeenth premier of Saskatchewan, under whom the continent's first single-payer universal healthcare system was formed:

> *We are all in this world together, and the only test of our character that matters is how we look after the least fortunate among us. How we look after each other, not how we look after ourselves.*

This ethos and history of compromise colours the way we see ourselves: *a middle power comfortable with multiplicity and incremental change.* And it should colour the way you approach communications in Canada.

> *"This is just the way things are in Canada. Authority, rules and proprieties are all hallowed and respected, and that includes traffic lights. Order is accepted as a higher virtue than freedom, security as a greater boon than liberty."* Michael T. Kaufman, *New York Times Magazine* writer

It also shapes how we behave and what we expect during a crisis. During the 1970 "October Crisis," Prime Minister Pierre Trudeau invoked the War Measures Act in response to the kidnapping by the Front de libération du Québec, a militant Québec independence movement, of high-profile political figures James Cross and Pierre Laporte, whom they also murdered. Media questioned P. Trudeau's approach (CBC Archives: *Just Watch Me*, 1970; on YouTube), which significantly expanded police power, allowing for arrests and detention without laying charges and suspending civil liberties; however, opinion polls showed most Canadians supported his actions. He demonstrated leadership. He was calm and decisive. He was accessible to the media. His actions were consistent with his personal repulsion for violence. He was the definitive voice of the crisis.

Another definitive voice, that of Michael McCain, was heard during the Maple Leaf Foods listeria crisis of 2008, during which fifty-seven people were sickened by contaminated deli meats, twenty-two of them dying. As president and CEO of Maple Foods, McCain held a live initial press conference—during which he answered questions until the media had no more (sources familiar say it lasted two hours), instead of cutting them off—and multiple subsequent pressers.

The Maple Leaf Foods case, now a gold standard, holds clues to our *expectations during crisis*:

- make accessible a leader who is directly accountable for decision making, not a spokesperson or corporate statement;
- show authentic humanity and compassion, humility and contrition, eliminating corporate speak;
- make decisions that place the greater good above all and support those actions with data; and
- apologize and accept responsibility; according to experts, McCain's apology (which can be found on YouTube) was unconditional and his assumption of responsibility, unequivocal.

While consulting and collaborating with your Canadian legal counsel is always important—and critical during crisis—Canada is *not as litigious as the US*. According to Canadian corporate lawyers, the punitive damages typically awarded in Canadian civil litigation are insignificant, except in rare, particularly egregious cases. And while class actions against corporations do take place (including against Maple Leaf Foods), these are evolving, with courts beginning to certify a class on a national basis instead of litigating across multiple jurisdictions.

Maple Leaf Foods also offers the gold standard post-crisis. Do not attempt to wipe events from corporate or public memory. Embrace them. Maple Leaf positioned itself as a listeria expert, launching a national listeria education and outreach program.

Within one year, Maple Leaf Foods recovered almost 75 percent of the 30 percent of sales it lost at the height of the crisis. Even with twenty-two listeria-related deaths, the brand remained strong. McCain not only addressed the greater good, he also restored trust.

TRUST AND DISTRUST

Effective communications campaigns reach people where they are; therefore, we must explore trust, specifically, the 2020 "Edelman Trust Barometer."

Large trust gap: The gap in trust between the Canadian informed public and the general population is greater than in any other country (16 points vs. 8 points in the US); meaning, you must target carefully and encourage your organizations to engage with the masses through tangible action—they need to feel cared for.

Canadians are generally trusting: Even the more "distrusting" general population falls into the neutral zone on the Index, and the informed Canadian public is 14 points more trusting than their US counterparts. This means you can approach Canadians from a more neutral or confident stance—as long as you do it with credibly sourced facts.

We trust media (traditional, owned, social, and search engines): Canadians trust traditional media more than people in the United States (by 9 points). This means a carefully constructed, traditional media relations campaign can move the dial. Do not mistake this US/Canada differential for significant trust; the 2021 "Edelman Trust Barometer" showed a trust deficit for search engines, owned, and social media, with only traditional media barely remaining in the trusted category (55%).

Canada/US trust alignment: Canadians and Americans are more aligned; meaning, while you need to customize messages and choose local spokespeople (the 2021 Barometer reinforces this need, showing Canadians look within their community for individuals they trust to address important issues—almost half believe government leaders are purposefully working to mislead them), you can more easily export existing campaign principles. Topics on which we're aligned include:

- a sense of injustice and lack of confidence in the system, overwhelmingly (more than 50%) believing the system is failing us, calling for change, and believing (47%) that capitalism as it exists today does more harm than good in the world.
- a belief that companies should place more importance on stakeholders than on shareholders for long-term success.
- pessimism about economic prospects.
- distrust of societal leaders to address our countries' challenges.

Corporate Canada: Canada is home to more than 2,700 head offices (with more than 50% of them in Ontario and more than 30 of them being multinational, with 14 in the Fortune 500). Canadians strongly believe corporate *CEOs must act to effect societal change and must speak out on societal issues* like diversity, climate change, training for jobs of the future, and ethical use of technology. This fact, combined with Canada's diversity profile and relative population size (about one-tenth that of the US), creates a *communications opportunity for the Canadian leadership of US-based companies operating in Canada.*

Many international organizations place future global leaders as general managers of their Canadian operations as a testing or proving ground. While they are there, demonstrating their competence inside, why not leverage them to build corporate reputation—and their skill set—outside?

Canadians expect these general managers to speak. You need a place to test your messages. So, create thought leadership platforms; train and leverage your executives as media spokespeople; let them address The Canadian Club and The Economic Club of Canada. See what happens. Use the lessons to tweak your messaging for the US audience.

And wherever possible, get them involved in local Environmental, Social, and Governance (ESG) practices and shareholder activism. According to the 2020 "Edelman Trust Barometer" special report on institutional investors, *95 percent of investors expect their firms to intensify the ESG effort, and 80 percent of Canadian firms now screen for diversity and inclusion metrics*—the highest in the world.

Not only do almost three-quarters of Canadians expect companies to take actions that both increase profits and improve communities, but we also tend to buy more often from those we trust.

Trust affects buying habits: According to *Reader's Digest*, 90 percent of Canadians agree that when a product or service's quality and price are similar, we tend to buy from the company we trust more. Most trusted brands in 2020 included Kellogg's, Behr, Shopper's Drug Mart, and Sun Life Financial. Further, they pay more attention to companies they trust and are more likely to remember their advertisements.

Canadian figures we trust: *Reader's Digest* also publishes a list of the most trusted influencers who, notably, are not politicians or business moguls. The 2015 list included journalist Peter Mansbridge, scientist and environmental activist David Suzuki (who also attended my high school), home repair expert Mike Holmes, comedian Rick Mercer, and retired astronaut Chris Hadfield.

> *"Canadians are famously polite. We're a nation of door-holders and thank you-sayers, but we joke about it, too. How do you get 30 drunk Canadians out of a pool? You say, 'Please get out of the pool.'"* Colonel Chris Hadfield, first Canadian to live on the International Space Station.

DIVERSE LANDSCAPE AND CURIOSITIES

As much as good order unifies us, remember our different personalities. Our interests and views are as varied as our landscape:

- New Brunswick boasts the Bay of Fundy's 15-metre-high tides, where over 100 billion tonnes of water rush in and out during each tidal cycle;
- Nunavik features Parc national des Pingualuit and a meteoric crater on the Ungava plateau filled with exceptionally clear blue water;
- Southern Ontario presents majestic Niagara Falls, where 168,000 cubic metres of water per minute cascade down an average of 57 metres from Lake Erie into Lake Ontario.

Diversity is also found in each region's unique landmarks:

- The world's largest hockey stick in Duncan, British Columbia, with a reach of 62 metres, weighing 28,000 kilograms;
- The 3-metre-high beaver in Beaverlodge, Alberta, paying homage to Canada's national emblem;
- Ontario's Big Nickel stands over 9 metres high in Sudbury; the 8-metre-tall Canada Goose in Wawa, Ontario; The Big Apple in Colborne (the world's largest apple-shaped structure, capable of holding 653,800 real apples); the Tomato Tourist Information Booth in my hometown, Leamington;
- The Sign Post Forest in Watson Lake, Yukon, along the Alaska Highway;
- The world's largest cèilidh (KAY-lee) fiddle stands in my current home province, welcoming visitors to Cape Breton, Nova Scotia, with its 18.2-metre height.

While Canada's *unique landscapes and landmarks offer fodder for creative campaigns,* embracing our regional diversity is critical to achieving message penetration. The fact that there is no interprovincial free trade in this country offers some insights into the prevalence of our differences. Even our three groundhogs often have different perspectives. In 2020, Nova Scotia's Shubenacadie Sam predicted a longer winter after seeing his shadow; while in Ontario and Quebec, Wiarton Willie and Fred la marmotte predicted early spring.

DIFFERENCES MATTER

Canada's Aboriginal peoples have perspectives that differ and matter, and it is critical that you seek to understand them. Section 35 of the Constitution Act 1982 declares that Aboriginal peoples in Canada include First Nations, Inuit, and Métis peoples. "First Nations" is a general term encompassing *more than 630 communities, representing more than 50 Nations and 50 Indigenous languages.* It is appropriate to use this term as a general group name provided you are not also making reference to Inuit or Métis members.

Understanding what Aboriginal peoples care about means understanding injustices: the current and ongoing lack of clean drinking water on federal reserves; the widespread killings and disappearances of Inuit, Métis, and First Nations women and girls, including 2SLGBTQQIA people (learn more by reading "Reclaiming Power and Place: The Final Report of the National Inquiry into

Missing and Murdered Indigenous Women and Girls"); and the government and religious authorities' operation of more than 130 compulsory boarding or Residential Schools (which operated into the twentieth century), designed to assimilate Indigenous children into the "dominant" culture by forcibly separating more than 150,000 of them from their families.

In the first half of 2021, the Cowessess First Nation discovered 751 unmarked graves at the site of a former Residential School in Saskatchewan. Weeks earlier, the Tk'emlups te Secwepemc First Nation announced the discovery of the remains of 215 children at a similar former school site in Kamloops, British Columbia. You can learn more by reading the final report of the Truth and Reconciliation Commission. Understanding means educating yourself on these appalling tragedies and working to heal.

Understanding also means learning the views, needs, experiences, and capacities of these communities. It means consulting those who live on reserves under federal jurisdiction as well as those who seek support for their community leaders and agendas while living outside those reserves. It means understanding priorities. It is demonstrated through consultation and co-creation of research, strategy, and initiative implementation, for which financial compensation is often expected.

You may wish to explore the various First Nations education programs offered by Yukon University (https://www.yukonu.ca/programs/all). The more we seek to understand unique challenges, perspectives, and heritage, the more inclusive and localized our solutions and approaches can be.

REGIONAL PERSPECTIVES

Localization is also required across our provinces and territories. For comprehensive appreciation, it is important to work with local public relations experts or agencies (Canada is home to more than twenty major PR firms). To give you a flavour, one that is by no means complete, here are a few examples of regional differences:

Saskatchewan: More than half the population lives outside large centres and is primarily agrarian—not to be confused with lacking financial means or sophistication. The agricultural community is highly sophisticated in their operations, with technological firsts in crop science, plant protein, agricultural equipment, and clean energy, and is strongly influential in public policy.

British Columbia: Canada's top exporter of fish and seafood also relies heavily on tourism, film, mining, and forestry, as well as on the knowledge economy in and around Vancouver. Here, living outdoors is a way of life, people are generally early adopters of innovations that protect the environment (like electric vehicles), and the culture is heavily activist. Uniquely, the seat of government (Victoria) is on Vancouver Island. Just the logistics (helicopter or float plane) of live (post-COVID) meetings with government stakeholders and regulators must be purposefully planned, unlike in Ontario where you can typically take a day trip (at most) or a brisk walk (at least) to reach provincial decision makers. British Columbia is also likely to be found collaborating or aligning with the Yukon, where gold, silver, and ores account for 25 percent of their exports.

Nova Scotia: Highly relationship-focused culture, with the provincial government as the major employer, meaning it has a powerful public relations voice. Issues such as clear cutting, pulp milling, coal mining, and fishing rights concern its residents. Fish, seafood (like Digby scallops and 720 tonnes per year of South Shore lobster), and farm produce are its largest exports.

Newfoundland and Labrador: The country's third-largest fish and seafood exporter delivers snow and queen crab, shrimp, Greenland halibut, and cod, but iron ore and oil from offshore oil fields like Hibernia, Terra Nova, and White Rose are significant economic drivers. It has the highest unemployment rate in the country, relying heavily on federal funding support.

Québec is different.

A DISTINCT SOCIETY

About a third of any given Canada-wide company's business typically comes from "la belle province," and it holds *almost 25 percent of the country's population*. It is important to understand *how* Québec is different. And it is much more than language.

Several laws and regulations on language have been enacted since 1867, including the 1988 Official Languages Act. While New Brunswick is the only officially bilingual province, *Québec is "French First."* Québec's Charter of the French Language regulates product packaging, public signs, posters and commercial advertising, websites, and more. Meaning: When communicating in Québec, remember that these public channels require your creative and your logo to include a "sufficient presence of French"—you may need to add a French language tagline or descriptor.

When developing slogans or creative campaigns, it is not wise to directly translate them—and *do not make the mistake of using an online translation tool*. Instead, employ professional translators who are *certified in Québec or Canadian French*—Parisian French is not the same. Further, *build into your planning timelines* enough days to complete translation and validation, and *implement the English and French on the same day, at the same time*. For a press release, add three working days. For a presentation deck that requires translation of both speaking notes and slides, add seven working days.

Likewise, when developing national media campaigns, it is not enough to simply translate the English press release. *Deploy Québec-specific statistics and data; leverage a Québec-based opinion leader and a spokesperson who speaks Québécois or Canadian French*. Partner with a Québec-based agency who holds relationships with local government stakeholders and regional media.

QUÉBEC'S AND CANADA'S MEDIA LANDSCAPES

To best understand Québec's regional media, let's explore a brief history of the province.

Jacques Cartier claimed present-day Québec City and Montréal for France in the early 1600s. In 1759, the British defeated France on the Plains of Abraham, ending France's empire. Some were not satisfied with the expected integration, asserting that Québec and the Québécois people are a distinct nation. Thus, French Canadian Nationalism was born.

Québec's culture and attitude are heavily influenced by the long history of efforts to secede, including two referendums on sovereignty-association in 1980 and 1995, both of which resulted in narrow "no" votes.

Not only are René Lévesque and Jacques Parizeau key figures in the sovereigntist movement, they are also key influences on Québec's regional media, each holding host, producer, editor, or columnist positions with multiple outlets. Their legacy is a regional media landscape with strong political views.

Aside from some Québec outlets, in general, partisan lines among the five political parties that currently make up our federal parliament are not as clearly drawn in the media here as on US networks like Fox News and CNN.

Québec's local media remains strong despite consolidation. *La Presse*, with increasing online presence, remains the widest-reaching daily; investigative programs like TV-A abound; and the province has more talk radio programs than other parts of the country, where regional presence is declining more significantly. (Our largest national newspaper, the *Globe and Mail*, has limited regional bureau presence. This contraction has significant implications for PR professionals.)

So how do PR professionals reach specific provinces or regions, particularly during crises? As an example of the latter, during the tragic shootings in April 2020 beginning in Portapique, Nova Scotia, and ending one hundred kilometres away in Enfield, first responders and police relied primarily on social media and word of mouth to spread information and instructions to help protect citizens.

For planned campaigns, invest in audio and video news releases, and matte stories. Matte stories can reach over 1,600 community newspapers via services like Fifth Story, for a fee. Community papers are critically important in provinces with highly rural (Saskatchewan, Nova Scotia) and remote (Ontario, British Columbia, the Territories) populations, as well as for highly regulated industries in which paid placements, sponsored content, and direct-to-consumer advertising/advertorials may not be permissible (for example: direct-to-consumer advertising of prescription medications as treatments or cures is prohibited under Health Canada's Food and Drug Regulations).

Our publicly funded broadcaster, the Canadian Broadcasting Company (CBC), while also contracting, remains relatively well resourced, with journalists in over forty Canadian cities plus international bureaus. It is home to key regional news radio, such as *Metro Morning*, which is number one in the Toronto market. It produces podcasts and website content that supplement its radio and television programming. And its evening TV news, *The National*, averages just over one million viewers per night (although Canada's most-watched evening news is *CTV National News* at 1.6 million). It is home to CBCKids, comedy (check out *This Hour Has 22 Minutes*), and investigative programs like *The Fifth Estate*.

While magazine readership is declining, 44 percent of Canadians twenty-one to thirty-four years old and 67 percent of those between fifty and sixty-nine still read print magazines. The leading English magazines (by readership) include *Reader's Digest* and *Canadian Living*, with the top French titles being *Chatelaine*, *La Semaine*, and *L'actualité*. *Maclean's* is our national news magazine.

Aside from the obvious borderless reach of internet news, *the population along the southern Canada–US border is an important consideration.* About 66 percent of Canadians live within one hundred kilometres of it, meaning many of us regularly consume US media, particularly those in larger border towns.

CANADIANS ARE NOT AMERICAN

Despite sharing the world's longest land border, perhaps the greatest consideration is that *we are not American.*

> "We are not Americans who happen to have drawn the worst climate and the best geography; we are a different people." June Callwood, Canadian journalist and founding member of the Civil Liberties Association

We see moments like Thanksgiving (October) and Remembrance Day (November 11) as *solemn observances and not as commercial opportunities.* Since 2010, at least four US-based retailers launched Remembrance Day sales in Canada, which were considered disrespectful.

We're *inventors but not innovators.* Canadians invented the garbage bag (Wasylyk and Hansen), IMAX (Ferguson, Kroitor, and Kerr), the fibreglass goalie mask (Plantes), insulin (Banting and Best), and the square-headed Robertson screwdriver. But we aren't keeping pace with the world on producing innovation. According to the Coalition for Action on Innovation, Canada's productivity falls well short of the US's and has declined since the 1980s. Investment in research and development is limited to academic centres and government labs, and private sector investment is stagnant.

In fact, we stifle our own innovation. The Avro Arrow aircraft was the world's most advanced supersonic all-weather interceptor. But in 1959 our government ceased Avro's work on the Arrow and the Orenda Iroquois engine, destroying the five operational Arrows, all those in development, and all engineering drawings and plans. Its inexplicable termination incited the demise of Canadian aeronautics innovation.

> *"We're the only country on Earth whose citizens dream of being Clark Kent instead of Superman."* Peter C. Newman, Canadian historian and journalist

And we have an abundance of *heroes who aren't always obvious*:

- Terry Fox for his Marathon of Hope, beginning the national cancer-research fundraising effort;
- Hope Swinimer for founding the first privately owned wildlife rehabilitation centre in Nova Scotia;
- Team Canada for their 1972 win over the Soviet national team in the 1972 Summit Series;
- The people of Gander, Newfoundland (population 11,000), who cared for more than 6,500 passengers and crew of 39 planes diverted there from US airspace on 9/11 (and in fact the entirety of Newfoundland and Labrador, which opened their doors to more than 17,000 grounded international air travelers).

In short, we are home to *enough characters and figures to fuel campaigns without inserting foreign (to us) figures* who may not value peace, order, good government, and—above all—the greater good.

I hope your journey across our history and geography has generated insights to inform your strategy and inspire your content.

Perhaps along the way, you took a swig of truly Canadian beer (Moosehead, Caledon Hills, The Banded Goose, Landwash), munched some ketchup potato chips, enjoyed Farley's antics in Lynn Johnston's *For Better or For Worse* comic strip, or sipped a Caesar.

EDUCATION AND PROFESSIONAL DEVELOPMENT

If you're now intrigued enough to further your professional development or build a career in Canadian public relations and communications, there are an abundance of possibilities. With more than twenty major PR firms having offices across

Canada (including multinationals like Argyle, Citizen Optimum, Veritas, and Weber Shandwick), there is plenty of expertise, local knowledge, and resources to help address your needs or pursue a meaningful career.

To locate Canadian firms and experts, use one of these resources:

- Canadian Council of Public Relations Firms: http://ccprf.ca/
- The Manifest: https://themanifest.com/ca/public-relations/agencies
- PRovoke (formerly The Holmes Report): https://www.provokemedia.com/latest/news
- Sortlist: https://www.sortlist.ca/public-relations

You can also find local experts and professional development opportunities through various professional associations, each of which also has their own accreditation and awards programs:

- Canadian Public Relations Society (CPRS): https://www.cprs.ca/
  - CPRS Awards of Excellence: https://www.cprs.ca/Awards/Awards-of-Excellence
- Public Affairs Association of Canada: https://www.publicaffairs.ca/
- Council of Public Relations Firms: http://www.prfirms.org/
- Local chapters of the International Association of Business Communicators
  - IABC Toronto Awards: OVATION Awards, Communicator of the Year, Student Awards (https://toronto.iabc.to/)

And if you're interested in formal education opportunities, Canada is home to several excellent certificate, degree, and postgraduate programs across the country at schools like Royal Roads University (British Columbia), Mount Saint Vincent University (Nova Scotia), Memorial University (Newfoundland), Sheridan College (Ontario), McGill University (Québec), Brock University (Ontario), University of Calgary (Alberta), and my two alma maters: University of Western Ontario and Humber College (Ontario). Wishing you good learning.

TAKEAWAYS

1. To achieve message relevance, it would be a mistake to simply extend an American-made campaign to the Canadian marketplace; and further, to assume that even a Canada-adjusted campaign will effectively reach the nation's population without considering provincial, territorial, and regional differences.

2. Consultation and co-creation with First Nations, Inuit, and Métis are prerequisites on certain issues.

3. Language, while an important factor, is not the only factor making Québec a unique marketplace.

4. Leverage local thought leaders, spokespeople, data, landmarks, celebrities, characters, geographical wonders, and heroes to regionalize your press releases and other materials.

5. Find a Canada-based communications partner for local relationships, perspective, information on regulations, and unwritten expectations.

6. Approach crises with a definitive, authentic voice that is accessible and takes accountability.

7. Respect the peace, order, and good governance we value—it defines who we are as individuals and as a nation, and influences the way we process information.

CHAPTER 16

Public Relations in Higher Education

DONNA CAPRARI HEISER, APR, CFRE,
CHIEF ADVANCEMENT AND EXTERNAL AFFAIRS OFFICER,
AVE MARIA SCHOOL OF LAW

BE A GOOD LISTENER

As a public relations professional, you have chosen to study and practice in the fascinating field of communications. Whether you are serving an institution of higher learning or an organization, what could be more rewarding than being at the center of how people receive and process information, and then crafting a plan to influence them?

In my experience, the first lesson in effective public relations and communications is to become a good listener. As Stephen Covey outlined in his book *The 7 Habits of Highly Effective People*, "Most people do not listen with the intent to understand; they listen with the intent to reply." As public relations counselors, and in our everyday lives, never underestimate the value of listening to understand. Challenge yourself to be an "active empathic listener."

John Morgan, associate vice president for public relations at Quinnipiac University and chair of the Public Relations Society of America's (PRSA's) Counselors to Higher Education, knows firsthand the value of listening: "Listening is so important. One of the most timely faculty placements our University was able to generate began with a conversation with a law professor over coffee at Quinnipiac. In the course of conversation, the professor told me he was from Colorado and one of his areas of expertise was juvenile justice. When Columbine hit, I remembered the professor and contacted him to see if he would be willing to speak to the media. After receiving his approval, I reached out to several media outlets, including NBC's *Dateline*, to make them aware the professor was available to speak with them. NBC sent a driver to campus to transport the professor and me to its New York studio, where the professor appeared on *Dateline* that evening. It's important to 'build a bench' of faculty experts you can call upon when news breaks."

Before a public relations plan can be executed, a press release written, or a social media message posted, we need to listen to the various audiences, or publics, with whom we wish to communicate. As public relations counselors, one of our most important jobs is to try to clearly understand the issue, problem, or opportunity, and then discern the best way to convey information and to gain acceptance. It is vitally important to put ourselves in the mindset of the person or group we are hoping to communicate with and influence. How do they want to receive information? What do they feel the issues are? In their words, "What's in it for me?" It is your job to discern "what's in it" for the person or group you are hoping to influence, and then to develop your plan.

Simply and eloquently put by Robert Dilenschneider, the editor of this book and one of the most distinguished leaders in the public relations industry, "Public relations is the art of influence."

And from *Cutlip and Center's Effective Public Relations*, one of the leading treatises of the public relations profession, "Public relations is the management function that establishes and maintains mutually beneficial relationships between an organization and the publics on whom its success or failure depends" (p. 29). Indeed, you must understand the people you seek to influence before seeking to influence them.

RACE—THE FOUR-STEP PROCESS TO ENSURE SUCCESS!

One of the best ways to begin any public relations plan, and one that I have used since the beginning of my career, is to employ the four-step process of strategic public relations management that includes the following: Research, Analysis, Communication, and Evaluation, known by the acronym RACE. Every successful public relations plan must address each of these issues.

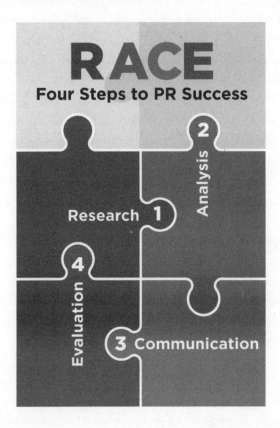

STEP 1: RESEARCH

You might be tempted to eliminate research from your planning because of time, resources, or the desire to move on to Step 3, Communication—the fun part! But don't take the shortcut! Research can be done many different ways. The best research usually involves a formal study with quantifiable and qualifiable outcomes. If you are unable to do this, consider less formal options including focus groups with students, faculty, or community leaders; one-to-one fact finding and meetings; reviews of online forums; blogs and chat rooms; web-based research; trade or education association research; and collegial discussions. Perhaps easiest of all, using SurveyMonkey or a similar platform will quickly and affordably poll your constituents, alumni, students, benefactors, faculty, and board. Craft a list of what issues or questions you need to know before you move on to the next steps of Analysis, Communication, and Evaluation. And don't forget that students or work-study interns can sometimes help to gather the research and conduct interviews for you.

Speaking of evaluation, a solid research plan can serve as the vehicle for evaluation by repeating and analyzing the research upon conclusion of the campaign. How far did you move the needle of influence? Is there a better understanding of the problem? Does the research indicate more or different communications should be employed? Through research, you can identify strengths, weaknesses, opportunities, and threats to your college or university; measure your success; and inform next steps. Without it, you are limited in your understanding of a situation and will be hard pressed to recommend holistic, effective solutions.

STEP 2: ANALYSIS—STRUCTURING THE PLAN

Once you have defined the public relations problem or opportunity through research, the next steps are to establish your public relations goal, then analyze and plan how you expect to achieve it. Are you hoping to gain university-wide acceptance of a new academic program? Or does the board hope to demonstrate how a relocation or merger will result in new opportunities and revenue streams that will allow for future growth? Or perhaps you want to learn how budget cuts to education will impact your public university?

Your goals should address the opportunities and threats you uncovered in your research and should be vetted with all stakeholders. Without a goal that has been endorsed and accepted by the board, president, faculty, and other decision makers, you will not reach a successful outcome. It sounds easy enough, but again, many public relations plans are overly focused on the third step in the process, Communication. A "Ready, Fire, Aim" approach, in which you spend only cursory time on research, strategic planning, and analysis, will not achieve your aim.

If you're short on time or pressed for a quick turnaround, level-set with your stakeholders, make your case for a calculated plan to achieve your goal, and work to ensure buy-in. With a strategic approach born from critical, creative thought, you will be more likely to achieve your goal. This success, in turn, will have the helpful benefit of sending a clear message to the president and board that, for the success of the institution, it is necessary for the public relations strategic advisor to have a seat at the decision-making table.

James Lukaszewski, arguably one of the best crisis management experts in public relations today, explains the importance of strategic thinking and goal setting in his book *Why Should the Boss Listen to You? The Seven Disciplines of the Trusted Strategic Advisor*:

> Have a destination before you start the journey and understand the outcome you seek to achieve before you begin. More good intentions perish for want of a clearly defined destination than for almost any other reason. A focus on the goal tends to reduce the wandering generality tendency and to force people to focus on more meaningful specifics, more meaningful actions that construct the desired outcomes. If the goal is missing, you and the boss are going nowhere. (p. 167)

Known as America's Crisis Guru, Jim shared with me his seminal list of eight tests to pass to demonstrate you have become a trusted strategic advisor, and I've shared them below. Ask yourself if you have what it takes to be considered a strategic partner with your boss.

1. People remember what you say and quote you when you're not in the room.
2. People quote you in your presence.
3. People tell your stories and share the lessons, giving you the credit.
4. People tell your stories and share your lessons as though those stories and lessons belonged to them.
5. Others seek your opinions and ideas, then share their agendas and beliefs with you in the hope of influencing you to influence the behaviors and decisions of others more senior than either of you.
6. The boss asks others to run their stuff by you before running it by them.
7. Meetings are held up waiting for you to arrive to make important contributions or interpretations of current events.
8. The boss calls you first, or early, and speaks to you last.

Mr. Lukaszewski also has some sage advice before you pursue becoming a trusted strategic advisor. He recommends asking yourself:

- Do I have the stomach for the intense, conflict-ridden, and often confrontational environment in which decisions are made at the senior levels of organizations?
- Can I dispassionately assess the strengths, weaknesses, opportunities, options, and threats to the organization from a variety of useful constructive perspectives (more than just the media)?
- What is the real expertise, beyond my area of staff knowledge, that I bring to those who run my organization?
- Will I commit to mastering the seven disciplines of the trusted strategic advisor and harness their power for my success and the success of those I advise?
- How do I credibly and convincingly answer the question "Why should the boss listen to me?"

As a respected author, speaker, crisis management consultant, and chairman of The Lukaszewski Group, Lukaszewski is known as one of the most sought-after strategists in the areas of crisis communication, litigation visibility management, and reputation threats. He is a recipient of the Patrick Jackson Award for Distinguished Service to the Public Relations Society of America and PR News's Lifetime Achievement Award, and is the author of thirteen exceptional crisis communications and management books that have served to inform our profession.

Another challenge in the Analysis stage of your plan is to identify the key publics, or audiences, that you hope to communicate with. It's crucial to tailor your objectives, strategies, and tactics to each public, because what will work for one may not work for another.

In their book, *Cutlip and Center's Effective Public Relations*, authors Glen M. Broom and Bey-Ling Sha have identified an excellent list to help with defining target publics from different stakeholder groups. If this book is not in your professional library, consider adding it. I have included an abbreviated list of their nine "Approaches to Defining Publics" below, but for a thorough understanding, please refer to chapter twelve in their book:

1. Geographics—identify people who live in proximity to the university.
2. Demographics—including gender, income, age, marital status, and education.
3. Psychographics—psychological and lifestyle characteristics.
4. Covert power—behind-the-scenes political or economic power (a powerful benefactor?).

5. Position—people of influence or key players (the university coach or professor emeritus?).
6. Reputation—people perceived as "knowledgeable" or "influentials."
7. Membership—affiliation with a group, such as student and alumni associations.
8. Role in the decision process—who are the decision makers?
9. Communication behavior—documenting how participants seek and share information; what media or channels do they use?

STEP 3: COMMUNICATION

So you've identified your goal; it's been endorsed by the president, board, and decision makers; and you've defined the publics. *Now* you can implement the public relations program by communicating to those audiences. It's time to craft and frame your messaging and to identify any barriers to your campaign. This should be a coordinated execution of your strategies and defined tactics.

But first, write down your objectives!

You've identified your key publics, so now it's time to write the objectives for each group, what outcome you hope to achieve, and in what time frame. How will you measure success? As noted in *Effective Public Relations*, "There are only three categories of outcomes: what people are aware of, know, or understand (knowledge outcomes); how people feel (predispositional outcomes); and what people do (behavioral outcomes)." Or, as the authors more succinctly put it, "Learn, feel, do."

Tactics: Now We're Getting to the Fun Part!

Simply put, tactics are the tools public relations strategists use to implement the strategy they've identified. In your case, these tactics can be the social media plan you've chosen for reaching students, or an event featuring a noted speaker who will galvanize your target audience. As the late John Beardsley, APR—a past president of PRSA and a respected leader in public relations—said, "Strategy is a ladder leading to a goal. Tactics are the steps on that ladder."

By the way, PRSA is an excellent organization worthy of your consideration. I encourage you to join and become active in your local chapter. I have benefited from the networking, resources, and commitment to professionalism that PRSA embodies. The Accreditation in Public Relations (APR) credential through the PRSA is an extremely worthwhile goal and a career distinction for you to consider. And the PRSA online library is an outstanding resource of all things public relations. By referencing the PRSA Silver Anvil winners, you will find the very best ideas in PR planning, strategy, and execution that will inspire your program planning (PRSA.org).

And for a worldwide perspective, the International Association of Business Communicators (IABC) is the only global communication association that strives to "advocate for the profession, represent best practices, define the global standard and live by a code of ethics." It's a very worthwhile organization to belong to, and their Gold Quill Awards of Excellence recognize the diversity of communications professionals from around the globe.

Ethics and Acting Responsibly

As the public relations strategist for your college or university, it's important to remember that you must help the leadership of your organization to become the ethical voice of the institution. If there is a problem that needs to be corrected, this must happen before you initiate the public relations campaign. For example, if a college has been criticized for its handling of an issue, the issue itself must be addressed and resolved or mitigated—or a plan put into place to do so—prior to the launch of any communications campaign. Merely communicating that the college knows there is a problem is not enough. Actions do speak louder than words.

Moreover, as Jim Lukaszewski points out, "Our job as PR strategists is to help our bosses become the ethical voice of the organization. We must empower the people who have the power to be ethical and help senior leaders to find the right path. Then our job is to help them to stay on it."

Understanding What the News Media Wants

Because traditional news media and media gatekeepers are some of your most important publics, you need to craft your messages with an eye toward what they are interested in covering. What is the news value to them and to their audience? Consider these six criteria as suggested in *Effective Public Relations* (p. 317) when assessing how to pitch a story to the media:

1. Audience impact—How many people are affected and how serious is the issue?
2. Proximity—Does the story impact your local community, or a broader audience?
3. Timeliness—Broadcast media will respond to breaking news faster than print, but print media can expand on your story.
4. Prominence—Does the story involve a highly recognizable person?
5. Novelty or oddity—Is your news unique or unexpected?
6. Conflict, drama, or excitement.

The 7 Cs of Communications

Effective communications require thoughtful consideration of the media to be used and the tactics you will employ. To be successful, remember to design your communications messages to meet the situation, where it is taking place, the time, and (of course) your audience.

We can all agree that to be effective and reach the desired outcome, a message must be motivating. Consider reviewing the seven Cs of public relations communications and test your strategy by comparing it against each one: Credibility, Context, Content, Clarity, Continuity and Consistency, Channels, and Capability of the audience.

STEP 4: EVALUATION

The final step in the process of public relations management, and arguably the most important, is Evaluation. When you are asked how successful your public relations plan was, what was the return on investment, or ROI, you would need to be ready to justify the effort and point to measurable results. The research that you did in Step 1 will help to define the measurable results. Also, your written strategy and program objectives for each targeted public should be worded in measurable terms, so that when you reach Step 4, you will have the information you need to create the evaluation of the public relations plan. A survey will not always give you the most definitive evaluation of how successful your program was. Consider doing a case study and look for "bottom line" results. Has admissions enrollment in the targeted demographic group increased, and by what percentage? Many university communications departments have created representative groups of students, faculty, staff, alumni, and other publics to test their communications strategies and to gain acceptance and understanding prior to launching the public relations plan. This can also help in Evaluation.

As part of her rebranding campaign for Ohio University, Renea Morris, MEd, APR, Fellow PRSA, vice chancellor, Division of Marketing and Communications at the University of Denver, and the former chief marketing officer at Ohio University, conducted nine surveys and focus groups over a three-year period. Renea noted that the studies gave key audiences and stakeholders the opportunity to offer feedback and helped to inform her campaign planning and development. She created the "Ohio Insiders Group," comprising faculty, staff, students, and alumni, which served as a built-in focus group that enabled her to review strategy with them at each concept stage.

"After the launch of the new branding campaign," Renea explained, "many of our Ohio Insiders Group members commented to me that they felt the process was great and very transparent. As public relations people, many times we find we are fueling the plane by flying it, so we get very myopic. The interviews we conducted with this group and the opportunity to review and test strategy with them, together with the Brand Perception Study we conducted, led to a very successful rebranding for the University and earned us a Silver Anvil Award of Excellence from the Public Relations Society of America." I have reprinted Renae's excellent "Ohio University's 'It's You': Launching a New Brand at a Public University" herein to demonstrate the effectiveness of Research, Analysis, Communication, and Evaluation in developing winning public relations plans.

OHIO UNIVERSITY'S 'it's you': LAUNCHING A NEW BRAND AT A PUBLIC UNIVERSITY

Melamed Riley and Ohio University, Jan 1,2014 - SO16 Silver Anvil Award of Excellence

Summary: 2014 Silver Anvil Award of Excellence Winner — Reputation Management / Brand Management — Government

Programs designed to enhance, promote or improve the reputation of an organization with its publics or key elements of its publics, either proactively or in response to an issue, event or market occurrence.

Ohio University's "it's you" is the culmination of a three-year effort to revitalize the brand at Ohio's first institution of public higher education. The effort was in response to the need for a research-based, collaborative strategy to deliver a distinguishable experience to elevate the brand. The new brand was launched in fall 2013 after a process in which prospective and current students, parents, faculty, staff, and alumni were involved and informed. They were invaluable during planning and development. Because of strong buy-in from such a diverse array of stakeholders, the new brand was well received and recognized, achieving all of its objectives with internal and external audiences.

Full Text: SITUATION ANALYSIS

Though Ohio University, established in 1804, was the first institution of public higher education in the Northwest Territory with a national and international sphere of influence, many of its most positive aspects were not well known and it was often confused with the somewhat younger and larger Ohio State University. The pressures of increasing competition, decreasing numbers of high school graduates in the state, and a struggling economy shifted the idea of marketing as a nicety to a necessity in order to meet student enrollment goals. With only one marketing campaign in the institution's 200 plus year history, there was little awareness of the university beyond the state. Even within Ohio, the university had not distinguished itself in any substantive way from other institutions. Additionally, key findings from a benchmark brand perception study revealed that though the most important attributes sought by high school students lined up with the main points of a newly developed message platform, there was an opportunity to break away from similarly sized universities in the state by owning a single attribute that only Ohio University could deliver. Achieving brand focus would help ensure more verbal cohesion and visual consistency, underscoring the reason why a three year strategy to revitalize the brand was undertaken.

RESEARCH

Over the three year initiative, nine surveys and focus groups gave our key audiences and stakeholders — including prospective and current students, parents, faculty, and staff — opportunities to provide feedback during various phases of the initiative, which helped to inform the planning and development process.

Primary

Fall 2010 – A benchmark "brand perception" study assessed the equity of the Ohio University brand.

Spring 2011 – Melamed Riley, an Ohio based agency, facilitated a "brand essence" workshop attended by the Marketing Advisory Council (MAC). This workshop focused on forming a university value proposition and other key brand elements.

Spring 2011 – Two "personality" surveys to the MAC and a group of new students revealed our culture.

Spring 2012 – Two "creative concept" surveys to test two concepts with prospective students and the university body enabled the communications and marketing team to work on refining the overall creative direction. Ultimately, Ohio University's communications and marketing team came up with the idea of "it's you" as the featured concept.

Fall 2012 – A comparative "brand perception" study showed that the university gained 10 percentage points in unaided brand awareness since the benchmark established two years prior.

Spring 2013 – Two "design and message" surveys conducted to test the design and marketing messages helped the communications and marketing team refine and reshape the creative design.

Secondary

Ohio H.S. graduate projections through 2027 – Western Interstate Commission for Higher Education.

PLANNING

The target audience for the brand initiative was prospective students and their families; senior leadership; current students; staff; faculty; alumni; and the news media. The three year budget was $160,000.

Objectives

The major goal was to implement a three-year brand revitalization strategy to elevate awareness of the Ohio University vision to become the nation's best transformative student-centered learning community and highlight the uniqueness of the Ohio University experience. At the end of the three years, the success of the strategy would culminate with new recruitment marketing materials and a tagline presented to the university community and measured by the following objectives:

1. Increases year over year (2010–2013) on Facebook, Twitter, and YouTube.
2. Increases year over year (2010–2013) in overall news coverage and among faculty research experts.

3. Increases year over year (2010–2013) in applications.
4. Increase in Web traffic to the admissions microsite www.ohio.edu /you during fall recruitment over prior year (Aug.–Nov. 2012 vs. same period in 2013) when new brand look was added.
5. Written proof of the university's acceptance of the new brand look and messages.

Strategies

- Use a collaborative approach to embrace the shared governance model at the university, to consider input, encourage participation, and solicit feedback throughout the process.
- This approach is consistent with the PRSA code of ethics, to foster informed decision-making through open communication.
- Develop a multi-tiered approach to delivering regularly scheduled updates with key internal stakeholder groups to ensure they have multiple ways to give feedback and stay informed.
- Host a launch event hosted by the university president that includes the entire university community in celebration of the new brand.

EXECUTION

The iterative, collaborative nature of the strategy was a key reason for the success of its execution. One unexpected problem, however, was honing in on a creative direction. Four initial concepts were developed, but none were accepted fully. The top two were tested with students and the university body, yielding a clear frontrunner. This helped give Ohio University's communications and marketing team direction and 17 months to prepare for a fall 2013 launch.

Internal Initiatives

- A six member team formed to ensure that 35 brand launch projects were executed on time and on budget. The group met weekly for nine months, then biweekly for eight months until the launch.

- A monthly byline column "Branding OHIO" was created to raise awareness of and build a case for branding at the institution. A total of 25 articles were published between Fall 2010 and Fall 2013.
- A 15 member Marketing Advisory Council (MAC) was formed to help guide the rebranding effort.
- A password protected website was developed to keep certain internal stakeholders informed as the creative process unfolded. The "OHIO Insiders" group received regular updates directing them to review and offer feedback. Six updates were posted during the year before the launch.
- The university president introduced the new brand during an event that was filled to capacity at the main campus and streamed live for its five regional campuses to view.

Additional Tactics

- **Media Relations: Fall 2011** – Launched online faculty experts directory for the media (www.ohio.edu/ucm/media/experts).
- **Web: Fall 2013** – Launched new admissions microsite in time for fall recruiting (www.ohio.edu/you).
- **Social Media: Spring 2013 – Fall 2013** – Launched "Your OHIO Film Festival" and "You in a T-Shirt" social media contests using Facebook, YouTube, and Twitter.

EVALUATION

Success was measured by increases in prospective student interest in the university by the number of applications received, as well as evidence of increased audience awareness and engagement through year over year social media and news media gains. Three surveys after the launch event to the university community, MAC, and 40 member Campus Communicator Network were positive and in support of the new brand. As Ohio University has been known for its Halloween celebrations, it was seen as a compliment to the new brand when two students were seen at the most recent fall celebration wearing "brackets," which are a signature part of the new brand design. Total spent on the initiative over three years was $159250.

SOCIAL MEDIA ENGAGEMENT

	2010	2011	2012	2013
Facebook	22000 (est)	30740	38015	42719
Twitter	10000 (est)	16306	24231	32982
YouTube	69470	96590	111977	134678

ADMISSIONS MICROSITE TRAFFIC

	2012	2013	Change
August	183	2832	1547.5%
September	1221	3521	289.1%
October	1842	6104	331.3%
November	1101	3433	311.8%

www.ohio.edu/you replaced www.ohio.edu/promise on August 7, 2013.

NUMBER OF APPLICATIONS RECEIVED

2010	2011	2012	2013
13366	14983	17466	20771

Total applications received in 2013 represented an institutional record

EARNED MEDIA

	2010	2011	2012	2013
Total	8714	10951	11335	11986
Faculty	104	109	1151	1605

Public Relations Society of America © 2014

The Goal of Research Is to Improve Program Effectiveness!

As noted in *Effective Public Relations,* "Research should be seen as central to the management of public relations, not simply as the means by which practitioners are held accountable and the worth of their programs assessed . . . Evaluation research can tell practitioners both where they started and where they want to end, as well as give insights on how best to get there. And because it is data driven, the research pays off in getting public relations to the management table. But of course, that is not the real goal of evaluation research. Rather the goal is to improve program effectiveness" (p. 358).

PUBLIC RELATIONS AND ADVANCEMENT: TELLING THE STORY TO DONORS

As the public relations officer at your college or university, you will be called upon to help promote the philanthropic efforts of the Advancement or Development Department. The target audience is, of course, current and potential benefactors of the institution. Creating a communications plan to reach these donors requires thoughtful consideration, research, transparency, and creative thinking to establish the connection between your university and the benefactors' shared values. In creating the public relations plan, be sure to foster donor trust, tell the organization's story by way of the students, demonstrate how your mission aligns with their values, and show why your university is worthy of their support.

Great donor communications plans that will attract and retain donors have a few things in common:

- They promote a unified message over all channels, consistent with university branding.
- They inspire people to "give" with a clear call to action.
- They advance the organization's mission.
- They help to create trust in the institution through transparency, communicating both good and bad news.
- They demonstrate how a benefactor's gift has created a difference in a student's life or in the institution.
- They keep donors informed about the organization's educational initiatives, goals, administration, students, alumni, and faculty.

Fostering a collegial, working partnership with the Advancement Officer, Major Gifts team, and staff will help promote your organization to benefactors, inspire trust, and generate support. As in any communications effort, the goal should be to craft a plan that will resonate with the donor in a timely, meaningful way. And the more personalized the message, the better.

For example, a generous donor has just made a multimillion-dollar endowed gift to provide annual scholarships to the university. In addition to the traditional donor stewardship process that the Advancement department will handle, the right message in this case might include a media release to announce the gift, followed by feature story placement in targeted media outlets, a social media campaign, a story in the university magazine, the development of a thank-you video from the students to the donor, and a printed stewardship brochure listing each of the students who received the scholarship with thank-you messages from them. Remember to outline your plan to the donor in advance to be certain they are comfortable with going "public" with the gift.

One of the best resources for those of us in educational communications and advancement is the Council for Advancement and Support of Education (CASE .org), "a global non-profit association dedicated to educational advancement— alumni relations, communications, development, marketing, and advancement services—who share the goal of championing education to transform lives and society." Consider becoming a member of CASE for their excellent research, information, conferences, and the opportunity to network with colleagues worldwide who face many of the same challenges you do.

CASE has developed a Fundraising Fundamentals resource on their website that succinctly outlines the various channels to consider in your communication plan for reaching current and prospective donors. I have included it below as a "Channel Checklist" for not only fundraising communications, but also admissions, alumni affairs, and more. (Reprinted with permission; CASE Fundraising Fundamentals, Part 2, Section 11; © CASE.)

WHAT CHANNELS ARE THERE?

Technology is moving quickly, and new channels of communication are being developed all the time. This section lists some of the main channels and their characteristics.

Direct Channels

Printed material through the post:

- Can reach the addressee directly.
- Great for communicating complicated information or images.
- Often preferred by older readers who are less comfortable reading on screen.
- Harder to ignore or delete than electronic documents.
- Can be shared easily with friends and family.
- Hard to know if it's being read, so measuring impact is difficult.
- Expensive, especially for international distribution.
- Impersonal unless tailored to the individual, which requires a great deal of time.
- High levels of wastage unless the address data are good.

Personalized letters through the post:

- Often perceived as very personal and an indication that the writer has taken some trouble to get in touch.
- Handwritten letters of thanks are particularly valued.
- Often preferred by older readers who are less comfortable reading on screen.
- No way of knowing they are being read and therefore measuring impact is difficult.
- Expensive.
- Time intensive.

Email:

- Inexpensive.
- Mass email can reach large audiences very quickly.
- Great for keeping in touch with prospects once a relationship has been established.
- Can get basic data to measure impact.
- Can be perceived negatively as "spam."
- Can trigger a huge response and overwhelm the office.
- Easily deleted and ignored, especially if not personalized.
- Some people find it intrusive, especially if a work email address is used.
- Informal language may creep in and detract from the message of the email.

E-newsletter:
- Cheap and easy to do.
- Gets news to alumni and prospects in a timely fashion.
- Can get basic data to measure impact.
- Can be viewed as "spam."
- Easily deleted and ignored.

Telephone calls:
- Face to face.
- Extremely personal and effective in building long-term relationships with prospects.
- Typical part of major gift cultivation.
- Can be one on one or a small group.
- Can engage other representatives of the institution.
- Often the best way to relay information because audience can respond, ask questions, etc.
- Can be expensive and time-consuming.
- Can be difficult to organize.
- Can be viewed with suspicion by some people.

Events:
- Effective way of building relationships and introducing new prospects to your institution or specific project.
- Can be expensive if not self-funding.
- Can be time-consuming to organize.

Indirect Channels:

Press releases/PR:
- Good way to build up a general profile and encourage cultural change toward supporting philanthropy.
- Needs strong content to ensure coverage.
- No way of measuring its effectiveness (who reads it).

Website:
- Great for communicating large volumes of unchanging information (policies, etc.) as well as current events.

- Great for news flashes.
- Allows people to interact rather than receive information passively.
- If well organized, can be a useful resource for both external and internal audiences.
- Can measure some data.
- Time-consuming to maintain.
- Difficult to know who is reading it.
- Needs to be able to meet the technical challenge of being read in many browsers, including those on mobile phones.
- Highly visual with capability of displaying photograph and video control, as well as text.

Twitter:
- Great for short bursts of information.
- Good for directing attention to other forms of communication, such as a website.
- Real time tweets can make people off campus feel involved in campus-based events.
- Good for generating a campaign following.
- Quick, easy, and cheap to do.
- Tends to be used by younger audiences.
- Message has to be brief.

Facebook and other social networks:
- Easy and cheap to do.
- Good way of directing readers' attention to other forms of communication, such as the website.
- Good for gathering information about individuals.
- Good way to build a general profile.
- Allows people to interact rather than receive information passively.
- Can be time-consuming to moderate.

LinkedIn and other professional networks:
- Easy and cheap to do.
- Good way of directing readers' attention to other forms of communication, such as the website.
- Good for gathering information about individuals.

- Good for providing additional benefits to prospects through peer-to-peer networking and posting career opportunities.
- Can be time-consuming to moderate.
- Word of mouth.
- Very powerful.
- Free and quick.
- Difficult to stimulate.
- Impossible to control, and people can be talking about your institution both positively and negatively.
- Difficult to measure.

How Do I Choose?

You should choose which channel of communication to use based on these considerations:

- Who is the intended audience?
- How complex is the information? Can it be expressed in a few words (text or Twitter), or does it need a whole webpage?
- Are images required?
- Do you want a response?
- Do you want to be able to find out who has seen or read the message to measure your impact?
- Can you afford it (financially or the time commitment)?
- If it is a fundraising communication, then which channel will have the best return on investment?

Additional Takeaways

Think about your audience. What are you hoping to communicate? To whom? This will help you identify which channels to include within your overall strategy. I am a great proponent of the seven touches of donor cultivation. Aim to "touch" your benefactor seven times during the cultivation process. This could include an initial "get to know you" dinner with the president or dean, followed by a tour of the campus and the opportunity to meet a few students, a personal phone call or handwritten note after the meeting, and mailing a copy of the law school magazine and an invitation to hear a campus speaker. Find out what resonates with your audience and keep refining until you have found the best channels, remembering to stay nimble and ready to change course if necessary.

PUBLIC RELATIONS AND THE ADMISSIONS OFFICE

As the public relations officer for your institution, you can have a tremendous impact on the recruitment and retention of students. Together with the Admissions team, you will need to craft a plan that will strategically communicate with prospective students and get them to apply (your call to action) and enroll. Remember our discussion on the four elements of every communications plan—Research, Analysis, Communication, and Evaluation? Research here might be to enlist a focus group with newly enrolled students to determine how they heard about the college, what made them want to apply and enroll, what they recall about the strategic messaging, and what did and did not resonate. They can also serve as your test group for your communication tactics.

Personalized communications are the key to making an impact with prospective students. Every email, text, web visit, video, letter, postcard, and piece of direct mail should address the prospective student. For even greater impact, assign a personal contact to them. Personalize your communications and watch your clickthrough-to-open rate—and your response rate—soar!

PUBLIC RELATIONS AND THE ALUMNI OFFICE

Alumni are one of the most important publics in your organization. They are your (hopefully) satisfied customers, and they can become some of your most loyal donors and ardent supporters. Alumni are also excellent people to profile in college recruitment campaigns and donor communications: they are your "product" and can demonstrate how successful your organization has been in educating students to succeed.

Communicating with alumni effectively requires the same communications planning and collegial cooperation with Alumni Affairs as you did with reaching out to donors in the Advancement department. Collaborating with the Alumni Affairs team to craft an effective public relations effort will greatly benefit the organization. So, begin, as always, with research. Poll a representative sample of each class year, ask them what they love about their alma mater, what they hope to see in the future, what can be improved, and if they might consider being an Admissions representative for the college. Mine LinkedIn to find out more information about your alumni. Knowledge is power, and the more information you can glean from your research, the more effective you will be in your communications efforts.

Again, personalized communication is imperative; it makes your alumni feel connected and valued. Give them the opportunity to share what they love about your organization, especially during your Day of Giving campaigns and alumni events.

FINAL THOUGHTS

There is much more to be said about the practice of public relations in higher education. Building a solid crisis communications plan, earned media strategies, creating better "town and gown" relationships, and managing the institution's branding are just a few of the valuable subjects of discussion in any analysis of public relations in higher education. The secret to success? Retired four-star general and former US secretary of state Colin Powell said it best: "There are no secrets to success. It is the result of preparation, hard work, and learning from failure." This is true in many professions, and especially for communicators. Effective public relations requires one to prepare, to work hard and work smart, to fail fast, learn from it, and bounce back better.

Serving in this profession has been one of my life's greatest joys and continues to be a profound honor. It is incredibly rewarding to work with devoted professionals who are committed to our vocation and code of ethics.

In closing, I thank my parents for inspiring me to spend my life dedicated to a vocation that allows me to help others with my skills and abilities. I learned early on the value of hard work, preparation, and yes, learning from failure. My mother and father, Samuel and Theresa Caprari, taught me that success was possible, through dedication and commitment to goals. As successful entrepreneurs, often against many odds, they established several businesses and achieved their American dream. I could not ask for better role models to emulate!

CHAPTER 17

Communicating in Europe

Valerio De Molli
Managing Partner and CEO,
The European House—Ambrosetti

The European nations would become a vast common market in which none of the members would find restrictions on individual development, without, however, creating difficulties for the development of others.

It is specifically for the purpose of peace that the League was founded: not for that simulacrum of peace which exists at present, but for a peace based on law and secured by justice, a peace which will allow the peculiarities of national character to develop freely; so that the convenient exchange of the world's goods may become possible; that every man may be given ease to work in the field in which energies can be employed in the service of the community; for a constant exchange of ideas and knowledge for the benefit of all countries; and for that freedom of trade, that unrestricted exchange of natural and industrial products which, alone, can supply the material needs of nations.

—Giuseppe Mazzini

Before discussing communication and how it is done in Europe, I feel we should dedicate a few lines to some geographical and cultural aspects of Europe, reaching back to its origins, that still affect the socioeconomic structure of the modern age. As everybody knows, Europe is not a single country. Indeed, it is a modest western peninsula of the vast Eurasian continent. The total area is about 10.4 million square kilometers, comprising 6.7 percent of the earth's land surface. Although quite small geographically, it is a dense patchwork of many different countries. After a long process, today the European territory counts 50 different states containing more than 740 million inhabitants, 10 percent of the world's population, and around 225 languages. As the southwestern extremity of Eurasia, Europe experiences the biggest variety of climates and terrains on the continent. The result is a diversity that manifests in numerous realms: culture, customs, religion, food, and cuisine. This variety, while keeping Europe from becoming a uniform state, is truly its most valuable trait.

Approaches to communication, therefore, must account for this degree of complexity and heterogeneity to reach its entire target audience. First, however, we need to understand what communication is. Etymology helps us in this regard: the word "communication" derives from the Latin *communis agere*, meaning "to put in common." What do we have to put in common? The purpose—the reason to exist—of a company, organization, government. Purpose is defined through a process of listening and dialogue with internal and external stakeholders: colleagues, suppliers, citizens, associations, social partners, institutions, the media, or shareholders. It means sharing with those interested in a company, and investing in it, why it exists and what kind of influence it wants to have on the world. For companies, therefore, developing effective communication approaches becomes increasingly strategic as they create value that improves their chance of establishing relationships, growing market share, and being recognized globally.

Testifying to the importance of communication for companies, in Europe total advertising spending exceeded €105 billion in 2019, an increase of around 20 percent over 2009, when ad spending dipped to €84 billion. From a global perspective, Europe is the third-largest advertising market in the world, with 20.9 percent of total spending, behind the Asia Pacific region with 34.0 percent and the United States with 36.1 percent. The US remains the largest global advertising market, with around $500 billion invested in advertising in 2019 and growth exceeding the global average of spending increases.

Within Europe, per capita ad spending varies between countries. Austria, Switzerland, and Sweden were the top spenders in 2018 (€501, €392, and €339 per capita, respectively), while Italy was only thirteenth at €130. Spending in the United Kingdom exceeded the global average between 2013 and 2018, while Germany and France were growing at rates below the global average in the same period.

From our vantage as the number-one think tank in Italy, number four in the European Union, and among the most respected and independent out of 11,175 think tanks globally (according to the 2020 edition of the University of Pennsylvania's "Global Go To Think Tank Index Report"), and as a leading strategic management consulting firm, we can observe unprecedented changes in the fields of business and communication, driven by a few megatrends. Beyond increased advertising spending, other exogenous macro-trends in progress might be identified as elements affecting how communicators, including public relations professionals, should approach communication in Europe.

First, technology is one of today's most relevant drivers of change, affecting the daily lives of businesses and individuals. Technologies particularly disruptive to the communications field include artificial intelligence, robotics, virtual reality and augmented reality, the Internet of Things, and blockchain; all have the potential to open new opportunities in the company–consumer relationship. The collective effect of these innovations is to shorten response times in every field of business, including communications. In fact, digitization has changed the communication relationship between a company and a client, especially in business-to-consumer areas.

Before digitization, the basic equation of communication was based on cycle times that were measured in months along a linear structure: the transmitter used to identify a message that was transmitted to the receiver, who returned feedback to the transmitter months later at the soonest. In this paradigm, communication was mainly based on unidirectional media (print media, radio, and television), with characteristics conventional to mass communication. Today, digitization has changed the rules of engagement, and the cycle has shortened in some cases to microseconds. Moreover, communication is conducted predominantly online and must be designed and created ad hoc for digital channels. The content and the container of the message are no longer two different entities.

Second, since the 2000s, social media has changed the world. As Esteban Ortiz-Ospina wrote in "The Rise of Social Media" for the World Economic Forum's

Our World in Data project in September 2019, "The rapid and vast adoption of these technologies is changing how we find partners, how we access information from the news, and how we organize to demand political change . . . The increase in social media use over the last decade has come together with a large increase in the amount of time that people spend online." For instance, in Europe people spend an average of more than four hours per day online, with some countries reaching six hours per day. This rise has had obvious repercussions on companies' communication approaches.

Observing the dynamics of communication expenditure by channel over the last few years, we can see a progressive shift from traditional channels to online ones. It is interesting to highlight how, starting from 2003, European investments in internet communication have sustained the overall performance of the advertising sector, growing by fifteen-fold and rising from 2 percent of total investment in 2003 to 38 percent in 2019. At the same time, spending on traditional channels such as TV and newspapers has contracted, reducing their percentage of total investment by 7 and 20 percentage points, respectively, between 2003 and 2019. Meanwhile, the share dedicated to radio is stable at around 6 percent of total investment.

Examining growth in the 2016–2018 period shows the online channel to be the only one experiencing a steady increase in communication investments, by 8 percent, 7.5 percent, and 7.8 percent, respectively. A recent analysis by the European Communication Monitor in 2020 reinforces this change in paradigm. Indeed, when asked about their perception of the importance of different communication channels and instruments for addressing stakeholders, gatekeepers, and audiences in 2020 (and comparing them with future expectations for 2023), communication practitioners put social media and social networks at the top (87.6%), followed by online communication via websites, email, and intranets (82.1%), spreading news via online mass media (80.0%), and mobile communication (phone/tablet apps, mobile websites; 75.3%). The biggest winner in the 2020–2023 period will be mobile communication (85.7% of communication experts believe they will be highly important), while the biggest loser will be media relations with print newspapers/magazines (with a drop in importance of 23.7% by 2023).

Third, companies' communication approaches are also evolving in accord with changes in sociodemographic structure and with people's preferences and lifestyles. The increase in communication through social media allows companies to reach a younger public, one characterized by specific values, habits, and communication styles. In particular, younger generations such as millennials (born 1981–1996) and Generation Z (born 1997–2012) tend to privilege sharing over possession. They are interested in sharing their purchasing and consumption experiences through social networks, and exert considerable effort in collecting information before making a consumption choice. Eighty percent of millennials in Europe, before buying a product, want to receive detailed information about it (vs. 63% of baby boomers), and 85 percent of them (vs. 67% of baby boomers) show interest in its production process. In addition, consumers are less interested in price and brand when assessing a product, and more interested in the values a company conveys. According to an analysis conducted by the media investment company GroupM on European citizens, only 6.4 percent of consumers consider brand communication activities to be superfluous.

On this topic, the year of the pandemic has been a game changer, disrupting companies' communication approaches as they have tried to anticipate people's needs by communicating values such as empathy, being together, courage, and resilience. COVID-19 has brought to the fore the need to bring the human-to-human approach back into focus. Still, during the pandemic, we have seen communication genuinely rooted in emotion, capable of bringing us together in times of great difficulty.

As a fourth element of disruption, the public debate is increasingly focusing on the need to adopt models for sustainable development adhering to the United Nations' Sustainable Development Goals, further strengthened by the targets of the European Green Deal, as well as showing commitment to Environmental, Social, and Governance criteria, which growing numbers of investors and stakeholders deem essential. For companies and communicators, conveying and translating the idea of sustainability has become one of the most challenging goals. Practitioners should ask themselves: Is it possible to model and measure communication itself along principles of sustainability? How—and how much—can communication reach its own set of sustainable goals? For years, most of its energy has been dedicated to establishing codes of conduct, transparency, and compliance. However, companies do not always monitor compliance to these codes, so they might not be enough. Communication today has a social role, as it influences the public debate and delivers ideas that can shape societal consensus. Hence, European companies have started to discuss a new model that would allow communicators to set goals and key performance indicators to measure the sustainability of communication. Such standards would establish a common language that promotes diversity and inclusion while publicizing its ability to inspire a collective sensibility toward the creation of a more sustainable future.

The extensive use of social media, the integration between channels, the evolution toward two-way communication, the personalization and speed of the messages conveyed, the analysis of the data, the adoption of new technology, and the availability of extremely heterogeneous sources of information have contributed to make information more easily and quickly accessible to everybody. Moreover, in this scenario, information is subject to continuous fact-checking by an increasing number of users, which protects and guarantees the social role of communication in supporting democracy.

The phenomenon of "fake news" has existed since humans started to communicate. However, the internet revolution has amplified it, leading to the emergence of a new digital ecosystem in which misinformation has found fertile ground—and companies, via their external communications, are overexposed to this threat. This is a very delicate issue that might compromise not only companies' reputations, but also the quality of the information ecosystem. For example, according to a 2018 study in Italy, 8.8 million people have been victims of fake news during the last year, and 3.5 million parents have come across incorrect medical information. Therefore, the issue of misinformation must be addressed and managed by individual companies and national institutions, but above all at the European level. Indeed, since 2015, the European Union has started to understand how important challenging fake news will be to the survival of Western democracies and for the advancement of European integration. For this reason, the European Commission created a specific task force against disinformation (East StratCom) with a dedicated website (https://euvsdisinfo.eu/).

Looking at this phenomenon from the side of companies and communicators reveals that fighting or supporting conspiracy theories and fake news might be the cause of severe ethical challenges to companies and communication professionals. As stated by the 2020 edition of the European Communication Monitor,

> "almost half of communication practitioners (46.5%) has experienced several ethical challenges in their day-to-day work during the last 12 months. A smaller portion reports about one issue (18.3%), while 35.1% have not had any issues during that period. The frequency of moral hazards and the overall share of affected communicators has grown within the last years. Ethical challenges differ significantly across Europe: the highest portion of practitioners

without any ethical issue can be found in the Nordic countries, Belgium, and Germany, whereas several ethical challenges were most often reported from Croatia, Portugal, and Poland."

According to the report, the use of digital technologies—social bots, big data analytics, sponsored content, and social media influencers—is rarely regulated by codes of conduct compared to traditional media relations or advertising while it offers many opportunities for communications. For this reason,

"most communication practitioners are challenged by those practices: two out of three (67.6%) state that using bots to generate feedback and followers on social media is extremely or very challenging in terms of ethics. The majority thinks the same for other practices like exploiting audiences' data by applying big data analyses, paying social media influencers to communicate favorably, motivating employees to spread organizational messages on their private social media accounts. Less problems are identified when it comes to profiling and targeting audiences and editing entries in public wikis like Wikipedia."
(2020 edition of the European Communication Monitor)

When thinking about the new paradigm of communication, another potential threat is related to cyber-attacks, which are becoming more and more frequent especially during 2020, the year of the outbreak of the pandemic emergency. Cyber security is indeed a trending topic in communications across Europe: "nearly two thirds of experts (63.2%) have given attention to the debate about cyber security, and 59% of them see cyber security as relevant for their daily work and more than half (54%) of communication practitioners in Europe have already experienced cyber-attacks on their own organizations" (2020 edition of the European Communication Monitor). With regard to cyber security, hacks of website and/or social media accounts by cyber criminals, damages to the digital infrastructure, and stealing of data or sensitive information about stakeholders are the major causes of threats according to the communication practitioners in Europe, especially for the governmental and public sectors. Despite the strong awareness related to cyber security in the field of communication, in Europe a small amount of investment is oriented to the construction of a resilient communication structure. Indeed,

"nearly half of communication professionals (45.5%) are often involved in handling cyber security crises and a third of them (31.1%) address cyber

security in internal communications. But only a quarter of them are involved in employee cyber security education (26.0%) and even less in developing cyber security guidelines and in implementing cyber security technologies (17.7%)." (2020 edition of the European Communication Monitor)

In order to deal with current and upcoming challenges, strong competencies—both communication-specific and general—are considered a key driver of success for outstanding communication within companies:

"Most practitioners (80.9%) believe in the need for constant improvement. Specifically, 68.5% of practitioners thinks that technological competences are crucial, but only 50.6% of them has a highly developed competence in this area. Despite data handling being an important skill for all communicators, a lack of data competencies is particularly striking across all levels, with 50.6% of communicators in Europe under-skilled in this key area. Educational and training efforts to reduce the competence gaps in handling data and technology come mostly from the younger generations of communicators." (2020 edition of the European Communication Monitor)

At The European House—Ambrosetti, we believe that every company has huge challenges in communication today, which gave rise to our mantra, "Every company is a media company." Indeed, we are strongly convinced that companies, in their communication approaches, should fulfill an ethical and social duty toward the public as they ensure easy and quick access to information for everybody sustaining the development of democracy.

Given the numerous challenges and opportunities just described, I believe the three most important strategic issues for the development of communication in Europe in the next few years will be:

- building and maintaining trust toward audiences;
- addressing sustainable development and social responsibility; and
- dealing with the speed and volume of information flow.

To conclude, I would like to underline the extreme importance of the communications capability that each European company must develop. Corporate communication approaches indeed contribute to the image of their country of residence and, consequently, of Europe overall. The ability to effectively communicate the strengths and core values of companies and countries in Europe can therefore represent a key element for future growth strategies by strengthening the geopolitical role of Europe within the global milieu. For this reason, I would like to take the opportunity—in this chapter, dedicated to Europe—to address a thought-provoking consideration to all practitioners and communication experts in every European country. The European House—Ambrosetti recommends the creation of a European Steering Committee on Communication, staffed by institutional representatives of the European countries and a multidisciplinary technical task force, with the aim of defining and dealing with a common communication strategy. In this scenario, the Committee would act as a tool to enable global companies to become more aware about the relevance of communication as a tool to improve their perception across Europe. Specifically, this Committee would be responsible for:

- analyzing how individual European countries are perceived at the global level;
- designing and promoting a uniform European image by identifying common values and attributes among European states and cultures;
- enhancing best communication practices of each country within the wider European context; and
- defining common rules and codes of conduct at the European level, especially regarding communication through social networks and internet-related channels.

In sum, a European Steering Committee on Communication would represent a further step toward a more integrated Europe from a communication point of view.

I thank my assistant, Giulia Tomaselli, for having joined me in writing this chapter.

TAKEAWAYS

1. Europe is a patchwork of several countries with different cultures and traditions that affect the communication approaches they have developed.

2. Communication approaches and content need to be multichannel, consistent, and driven by a unified governance.

3. Some global macro-trends are changing the dynamics of communication in Europe, leading to a radical shift in the hierarchy of communication channels in favor of internet and social networks.

4. Millennials and Generation Z in Europe have a growing need for speedier communications and access to information, but also for ethical consumption and concern regarding the values of the companies they patronize.

5. The extensive use of social media, the integration between channels, the evolution toward two-way communication, the personalization and speed of the messages conveyed, the use of technology, and the availability of heterogeneous sources of information have combined to make information more easily and quickly accessible to everybody.

6. Fake news, misinformation, cyber-attacks, and ethical issues are some of the potential threats arising from the new digital paradigm of communication.

7. In the next few years, the development of communication in Europe will be strictly related to the project of building and maintaining trust toward citizens, addressing sustainable development and social responsibility, and dealing with the speed and volume of information flow.

8. Every company is a media company. We need to be aware of this and behave accordingly.

ACKNOWLEDGMENTS

This book would not have been possible without the efforts of an incredible group of professionals who joined in creating this useful, broad-ranging, up-to-date, and authoritative book. These experts provided me with countless valuable recommendations, and their insights were particularly important in making this handbook reflective of the global nature of modern public relations. The world has changed dramatically since the previous edition was published. It is not only trade that is globalized now, but also communications—and thanks to these contributors, the text reflects that.

I have also tapped into the expertise and knowledge of many of my colleagues and consultants at The Dilenschneider Group, to whom I am indebted. To all, I am very grateful for your sage advice. I would particularly like to thank Robert Laird and Susan Black for their assistance in editing, and Anthony Quiles-Roche and Joan Avagliano for the many hours they spent working with me on the project.

Throughout my career, my wife, Jan, has shown unwavering support and patience. She has stood beside me at every turn and provides me with inspiration in all my endeavors. In this particular volume, my sons, Geoffrey and Peter, helped guide my understanding of the constantly evolving digital revolution that is at the core of the handbook, and I am very grateful to both of them.

INDEX

A

ABC News, 47
Abe, Shinzo, 206
Aboriginal people, 224–225
Accreditation in Public Relations
  (APR), 240
acquisitions, 16
Admissions team, 255
Advancement Officer, 249–250
advertising, 81, 134
advocates, 59, 132
Agnes, Melissa, 129
Airbnb, 121
Air France, 162
alcohol smuggling, 217
algorithms, 166
Alinsky, Saul D., 76, 79, 80
Altimeter Group, 127
Alumni office, 255–256
AMA ("Ask Me Anything")
  discussions, 118
*AMA Handbook of Public
  Relations*, 31
Amazon, 120
ambassadors, on social media,
  132
American Bar Association, 82
American Occupation, 205
Analysis (step 2 of RACE),
  236–239
Angie's List, 119
anti-vaccination movement,
  129–130
Apodaca, Nathan, 117
APR (Accreditation in Public
  Relations), 240
argument, 23–33
articles, editorial, 65
artificial intelligence, 129, 200
"Ask Me Anything" (AMA)
  discussions, 118
audiences
  identifying your, 238
  impact to, 241
  knowing your, 56
  in SO SMArTT, 56–60
augmented reality, 133
Austria, 259
authenticity
  in presentations, 29–30
  with private families, 182
  on social media, 124–125
Avis, 98
Avro Arrow aircraft, 229

B

"background," defined, 109
Baidu, 200
Bancroft family, 177
Bank of America, 106
banks, 73
Baquet, Dean, 120
Bare Knuckles and Back Rooms
  (Rollins), 81
Barron's, 90, 177
Bay of Fundy, 223
Beardsley, John, 239
Benioff, Marc, 94
Ben & Jerry's, 169
bias, confirmation, 99–100
Biden, Joseph, 47
Big Nickel, 224
Bill and Melinda Gates
  Foundation, 175
Bill of Rights (Canada), 218
BingeBooks, 121
Black Lives Matter, 78–79
Black Rock, 94
"black swan" event, 14
Blogger, 120
blogs, 115, 120
Bloomberg, Michael R., 10
BlueJeans, 148
BNA Act, 219
Boeing, 74
Bombas, 75
bookmarking networks, 118–119
boycotts, corporate, 159
brand journalism, 130, 132–133
Brand Perception Study, 242
brand voice, on social media,
  123–124
bridging, 104
briefing management, 103–104
British Columbia, 226
Brogan, Chris, 132
brokerage-run conferences,
  88–89
Brooks, David, 99
Broom, Glen M., 238
Brown, Michael, 79
Brunswick Group, 134
business intelligence, 14
business meetings, with Chinese
  people, 190–193
business partners, 15–16
Business Roundtable, 106
BusinessWire, 101
BuzzFeed, 108

C

ByteDance, 186, 200

calls, 87, 252
Canada, and Canadian culture,
  215–232
  about, 216–219
  American differences from,
    229–230
  differences in, 224–225
  education and professional
    development, 230–231
  landscapes and landmarks in,
    223–224
  media landscapes in, 227–229
  Peace, Order, and Good
    Government Clause,
    219–221
  Québec, 226–229
  regional perspectives in,
    225–226
  trust and distrust in, 221–223
Canada Day, 219
Canadian Broadcasting Company
  (CBC), 228
Canadian Investor Relations
  Institute, 88
capital, 102, 174
Caprari, Samuel, 256
Caprari, Theresa, 256
Carney, Jay, 120
Carter, Jimmy, 75
Cartier, Jacques, 227
CASE (Council for Advancement
  and Support of Education),
  250
Cassidy, Kathy, 141
Caterpillar, 159
CBC (Canadian Broadcasting
  Company), 228
CBS, 167
CCTV, 200
Center for Automotive Research,
  99
Centers of Excellence
  competencies, 127
CEOs. *see also* leadership
  in Canada, 222
  in media, 103
  role of, on investor calls, 87
  on social media, 135
CFOs, on investor calls, 87
Challenger, Gray & Christmas,
  102

Charter of Rights and Freedoms, 218
Chávez, César, 159
Chick-fil-A, 159
China, and Chinese culture, 185–201
  about, 186–188
  business meetings in, 190–193
  making connections in, 188–190
  meals in, 193–199
  media and PR in, 199–200
Chipotle, 80
Churchill, Winston, 11, 37
Cisco Systems, 118
citizen journalism, 128
Citizen United v. Federal Election Commission, 81
City News Service, 99
Clash of Civilization (Huntington), 207
"cleaner, safer, healthier," 44
Cleveland Clinic, 99
clichés, 30
clocks, in Chinese culture, 190
CNN, 98
coalition building, 77–78
Coalition for Action On Innovation, 229
codes of conduct, 263
Cold War, 207
collaboration tools, 148
college education, for government relations, 82
Collins, Lynne, 140
commentary, expert, 61–62
Communicating (Dentsu Public Relations), 212
communications
  in Chinese cultures, 191
  crisis (*see* crisis communications)
  defined, 258
  designing a program for (*see* communications program)
  digital, 6
  donor, 249–250
  for government relations, 79–80
  internal (*see* internal communications)
  during IPO, 91
  with media, 98–99
  personalized, 255
  private family, 178–179
  in RACE (step 3), 239–241
  7 Cs of, 241
  visual, 125
communications program, 49–68
  importance of, 49–50
  and in-person presentations, 67

  internal (*see* internal communications)
  measurement, 66–67
  preparing your, 50–51
  SP SMArTT principles, 51–66
community engagement, 5–12
company website, 102–103, 160
conference calls, with investors, 87
conferences, 63–64, 88–89
confirmation bias, 99–100
Congress, 72
Congressional Research Service, 82
conspiracy theories, 262
Constitution (Canada), 218, 224
consumer review networks, 119–120
content, 126, 134
content-curation networks, 118–119
content marketing, 132–133
Content Marketing Institute, 132
contrarian advice, in presentations, 28–29
corporate boycotts, 159
corporate investor relations (IR), 85–95
  about, 85–86
  brokerage-run conferences, 88–89
  disclosures in, 89–90
  and ESG investing, 93–95
  and Investor Days, 87–88
  during IPOs, 91–92
  media coverage for, 90–91
  schedule of, 86–87
  and social media, 92–93
  and SPAC, 92
corporate social responsibility (CSR), 149–150
corruption, in China, 187
costs, of social media, 115–116
Council for Advancement and Support of Education (CASE), 250
Council for Inclusive Capitalism, 94–95
covert power, 238
Covey, Stephen, 233–234
COVID-19 pandemic
  and community engagement, 1, 7–8
  and crisis communications, 167, 168
  in Europe, 261
  and government relations, 77–78
  and intelligence gathering, 13–14, 20–21
  internal communications during, 153–154
  Investor Days during, 88
  in Japan, 206

language during, 39–42
  media use during, 99
  messaging during, 23–24
Cowessess First Nation, 225
credibility, 61, 99, 105–106
crisis communications, 157–171
  during crisis, 161–164
  and fake news/ disinformation, 165–166
  and outside investigations, 167
  preparation for, 158–161
  and science, 168
  and social media, 127–129
  through internet and social media, 164
  through third parties, 166–167
crisis leadership, 11–12
crisis management, 20–22
critics, messaging for, 56
Cross, James, 220
CSR (corporate social responsibility), 149–150
CTV National News, 228
Cullors, Patrisse, 79
Cuomo, Andrew, 8
Cutie, James, 152
Cutlip and Center's Effective Public Relations (Broom and Sha), 234, 238–239
cyber security, 263

D
Dartmouth College, 120
debate, 36
decision makers, 50, 239
"deep background," 109
deepfakes, 129
Deepwater Horizon spill, 8–9
Dell, 118
Deloitte, 106
Democratic Party, 36–37, 40
demographics, 238
Deng Xiaoping, 185
Dentsu Public Relations, 210–212
DeSantis, Rick, 8
Diermeier, Daniel, 107–108, 166
Dietrich, Arment, 115
digital communication, 6
digitization, 208, 259
Dilenschneider, Robert, 50, 234
Dimon, Jamie, 94
direct channels, for fundraising, 251–252
disclosures, 89–90, 109, 210–211
discussion forums, 117–118
Disney, Abigail, 180
Disney, Roy, 180
diversity, 44
Dogster, 121
Domino's Pizza, 122, 164
donor communications, 249–250
Donozo, Sho, 11–12

Douglas, Tommy, 219
Dower, John W., 205
drinking, in Chinese culture, 195–197
Drucker, Peter, 158
due diligence, "know your partner," 15–16
Dunne, Finley Peter, 80

E

earned media, 5
Easterbrook, Steve, 167
Ebola, 129
economic risks, 17–19
Economics Daily, 200
Edelman Trust Barometer, 221
editorial articles, 65
Edmunds.com, 99
education, for government relations, 82
effect frequency, of messaging, 54
effective messages, 54–55
Effective Public Relations, 239–241, 248–249
8-K Form, 86–87
elections, 80–82
elevator speech, 99
Elizabeth II, Queen, 219
emails, 251
Emanuel, Rahm, 157, 168
Emory University, 129
empathy, 27, 55
Encyclopedia Britannica, 130
endorsements, third-party, 62–63
e-newsletters, 252
Engadget, 108
engagement, 5–12, 124
environmental advocates, 59
environmental stewardship, 106
ESG (environmental, social, and governance) investing, 93–95, 105–106, 222, 261
ethics
    in China, 186
    in higher education, 240
Europe, and European culture, 257–266
European Communication Monitor, 260, 262–263
European Green Deal, 261
European House—Ambrosetti, 264–265
European Steering Committee on Communication, 265
European Union, 262
Evaluation (step 4 of RACE), 242–243, 247–248
events, 252
executives, on social media, 134–135
expert commentary, 61–62
exposing wrongdoings, 20
Exxon Valdez tanker, 159
EY, 106

F

face, defined, 188
Facebook, 108, 116, 121, 129, 165–166, 253
"The Face Plan," 155
"fact-based," 45
fake news, 165–166, 262. *see also* misinformation
Fallon, Jimmy, 117
family offices, 176–179
fatalism, 205
Faulkner, William, 183
federal government, role of, 70
financial capital, 174
Fink, Larry, 94
First Amendment, 81
flagging, 104
Flipboard, 118–119
Floyd, George, 9, 79
focus groups, 74
Forbes, 90, 93
Ford, Henry, 178
Forester de Rothschild, Lynn, 95
Fox, Terry, 230
FOX News, 100
France, 259
Francis, Pope, 94–95
Frates, Pete, 29
French Canadian Nationalism, 227
Friedman, Milton, 94
"A Friedman Doctrine" (Friedman), 94
Front de libération du Québec, 220
fundraising, 250–254
Fundraising Fundamentals, 250–254

G

GAAP (Generally Accepted Accounting Principles), 86
Gallup, 6
Gander, Newfoundland, 230
Garner, Eric, 79
Garrison, John L., Jr., 144, 151
Garza, Alicia, 79
GE Capital, 149, 151, 154–156
General Electric, 119, 141
Generally Accepted Accounting Principles (GAAP), 86
Generation Z, 261
Genie, 149, 154–155
geographics, 238
George, Amy, 146, 148–150, 153
Germany, 259
Getty Museum, 118
gift giving, in Chinese culture, 197–198
Giuliani, Rudy, 11, 187
Glassdoor, 119
Globe and Mail, 228
goals, setting, 236

Gold Quill Awards of Excellence, 240
Goodyear, 121–122
Google, 38
Gorsky, Alex, 106
governance, 106. *see also* ESG investing
government relations, 69–83
    careers in, 82–83
    components of, 70–71
    identifying objectives for, 74
    messaging in, 75
    monitoring for, 73–74
    politics and elections, 80–82
    research for, 71–73
    strategy for, 75
    tactics for, 76–80
Grant, Ulysses S., 77
grassroots, 78–79
green caps, 190
GroupM, 261
Guangming Daily, 200
guanxi, 188–189
guidance, 89
Gulf War, 216

H

Hadfield, Chris, 223
Hakuhodo, 210
Hamilton, Alexander, 36, 69
Harris, Mark, 142
Harrison, Anthony, 147
Harvard Business School, 131
Heinz, H. J., 174–175
Heinz, John, 175
Hersh, Seymour, 99
higher education, 233–256
    and admissions office, 255
    and Alumni office, 255–256
    listening in, 233–234
    Ohio University, 243–249
    promoting philanthropic efforts in, 249–250
    RACE (*see* RACE [Research, Analysis, Communication, Evaluation])
The Hill, 108
hockey, 218
Holmes, Mike, 223
hosting meals, in Chinese culture, 195
HR, alliance with, 146
Huffington Post, 108
human capital, 174
humility, in presentations, 29–30
Huntington Samuel, 207
Hyatt Hotels, 50

I

IABC (International Association of Business Communicators), 240
Ice Bucket Challenge, 29
imagine, as phrase, 44

impressions, measuring, 135–136
inclusion, as phrase, 44
income inequality, in China, 187
indirect channels, for fundraising, 252–253
industry leaders, 58
industry trade associations, 77–78
inequality, income, 187
influencers, 130, 131–132
initial public offerings (IPOs), 91–92
in-person presentations, 67
Instagram, 116–117
Instant Pot, 121
intellectual capital, 102
intelligence
  artificial, 129, 200
  business, 14
intelligence-collection programs, 13–22
  and crisis management, 20–22
  exposing wrongdoing with, 20
  importance of, 13–14
  for "know your partner" due diligence, 15–16
  in media campaigns, 19
  for political, economic, and security risks, 17–19
  strategic, 16–17
intergenerational relationships, 177
internal communications, 139–156
  about, 139–140
  channels of, 147–150
  implementation of, 145–147
  from leadership, 150–152, 156
  mission, vision, and values in, 140–142
  with private families, 179
  strategy for, 142–145
International Association of Business Communicators (IABC), 240
international relations, 206–207
interviews, media, 101
intranet, for internal communications, 147–148
introductions, in Chinese culture, 188–189
investigations, outside, 167
Investopedia, 89
investor calls, 87
Investor Days, 87–88, 101
IPOs (initial public offerings), 91–92
IR. see corporate investor relations
issues analysis, in government relations, 71
Italy, 259

J
Janki, Dan, 151
Japan, and Japanese culture, 203–213
  global multinationals in, 211–212
  history, 203–206
  international relations with, 206–207
  language and Japanese-ness, 207–209
  as a mirror, 212
  Olympic games in, 206
  PR in, 209–211
Jefferson, Thomas, 69
Jenner, Kylie, 131
Johnson & Johnson, 168–169
journalism, citizen, 128
JPMorgan Chase, 94

K
Kaboodle, 121
Kaepernick, Colin, 169
Kaiser Family Foundation, 99
kanji, 208
Kardashian, Kim, 131
Kaufman, Michael T., 219
Keidanren, 211
Kennedy, David, 99–100
Kennedy, John, 38
Kimmel, Jimmy, 27–28
Knight Foundation, 108
"know your partner" due diligence, 15–16
Koch, Charles, 175
Koch, David, 175
KPMG, 106

L
Labrador, 226
Lafley, A. G., 144
language, 35–48
  Japanese, 207–209
  most impactful words and phrases, 43–45
  in Québec, 226–227
Laporte, Pierre, 220
La Presse, 228
Last.fm, 121
law school, 82
leadership. see also CEOs
  crisis, 11–12
  industry, 58
  internal communications from, 150–152, 156
  on social media, 134–135
Leadership PACs, 81
Lean In (Sandberg), 31
Lee, Robert E., 180
legal counsel, for crisis management, 159
length, of presentations, 25, 54
Lévesque, René, 227
Lightner, Candace, 77
LinkedIn, 116, 253–254, 256

listening
  with private families, 182
  for PR professionals, 233–234
  value of, 234
listeria, 220
lobbying, 76–77
logistics plan, for crisis communication, 160
Lukaszewski, James, 237–238, 240
LVMH, 188
Lyft, 74

M
Machiavelli, Niccolò, 157
macro influencers, 132
MADD (Mothers Against Drunk Driving), 77
magazines, print, 228
Major Gifts team, 249–250
Mansbridge, Peter, 223
Maple Leaf Foods, 220–221
marketing, 114, 132–133
MarketWatch, 108
Martin, Trayvon, 79
Mascheroni, Eleanor, 149–150, 154
Mazzini, Giuseppe, 257
McArthur, Douglas, 205
McCain, Michael, 220
McDonald, Laquan, 79
McDonald's, 71, 167
McIntyre, Tim, 122, 164, 166
McKinsey, 102
meals, in Chinese culture, 193–199
media, 97–110
  bridging and flagging with, 104–105
  briefing management for, 103–104
  in Canada, 221, 227–229
  in China, 199–200
  communication with, 98–101
  and company website, 102–103
  and corporate investor relations, 90
  crafting messages for, 240–241
  credibility and trust with, 105–106
  earned, 5
  fragmentation of, and confirmation bias, 99–100
  and intellectual capital, 102
  intelligence for, 19
  negative, 106–108
  new, 108–109
  outreach to, 61–62
  and polling, 47–48
  for public opinion, 74
  relations with, and social media, 130–131

media (*continued*)
  role of, 97–98
  and spokespersonship, 103
  tactics for, 101
  third parties for
    communicating with,
    99
  Washington, DC rules for,
    109
media-sharing networks, 116–117
Medium, 120
meetings, with Chinese people,
  190–193
mega influencers, 131–132
Melamed Riley, 244
membership, 239
memorable messages, 54–55, 75
Mercer, Rick, 223
mergers, 16
messaging
  arguments in (*see* argument)
  during crisis communication,
    161–162
  effective, 54–55
  in government relations, 75
  memorable, 54–55, 75
  positive, 55
  in SO SMArTT, 53–56
  two-way, 124
metrics, for program objectives, 52
metric system, 216–217
mianzi, 188
micro influencers, 132
Microsoft Teams, 148
Midyear Calibration, 143
millennials, 261
Miller, Chris, 169
"Miracle on the Hudson," 128
mirroring, in presentations, 31
misconduct, sexual, 167
misinformation, 129–130,
  165–166, 262
mission, 140–142
mission statement, 141
modesty, 199
money, and campaigns, 81
monitoring, for government
  relations, 73–74
Monsanto, 168
Montgomery, Alabama boycott,
  159
Moonves, Leslie, 167
morals, in China, 186
Morgan, John, 234
Morris, Renea, 242
Mothers Against Drunken
  Driving (MADD), 77
Moutai, 193, 195–197
MSNBC, 100
Murdoch, Rupert, 177
multifamily offices, 177
multimedia, on social media, 125
Munoz, Oscar, 28
Musk, Elon, 30
"mutual respect," 45

N
name cards, 198
The National (tv show), 228
National Investor Relations
  Institute, 92
National Opinion Research
  Center, 74
National Rifle Association, 74
National Sports Act of Canada,
  217
native advertising, 134
negative ads, 81
negative media, 106–108
Netflix, 134
networks
  blogging, 120
  bookmarking, 118–119
  consumer review, 119–120
  content-curation, 118–119
  media-sharing, 116–117
  niche, 120–121
  professional, 253–254
  publishing, 120
  social, 116, 253
Newfoundland, 226
new media, 108–109
newsgroups, 117–118
newsletters, 148, 252
news media, 57
Newsom, Gavin, 8
newspapers, 108
newsrooms, social media, 131
New York Jets, 10
New York Times, 7, 61, 94, 97,
  109, 120, 134, 206, 209
NHK, 208
Niagara Falls, 223
niche networks, 120–121
Nike, 169
Nixon, Richard, 38
"no comment," 105
"no exceptions, no excuses," 45
Nogales, Luis, 152
"not for attribution," 109
Nova Scotia, 226
novelty, 241
Nowlan, Mark, 147, 153
NYC & Company, 11

O
Obama, Barack, 9, 78, 157
objectives
  for government relations, 74
  identifying your, 239
  intelligence-collection efforts
    in, 14
  in SO SMArTT, 52–53
Occupy Wall Street movement,
  179–180
Ocean Spray, 117
October Crisis, 220
Official Languages Act (1988),
  226
"off the record," 109
Ohio University, 242–249

oil spills, 159
One campaign, 45
online collaboration tools, 148
"op-eds," 65
openness, with private families,
  182
opinion pieces, 80
Orange Is the New Black (tv show),
  134
Ortiz-Ospina, Esteban, 259–260
Orwell, George, 35
outside investigations, 167

P
PACs (political action
  committees), 81–82
Paine, Katie, 114
Parc national des Pingualuit, 223
Parizeau, Jacques, 227
Parks, Rosa, 159
Pastaríso, 119
Patel, Neil, 133
patience, with private families,
  182–183
Patterson, John, 152
Peace, Order, and Good
  Government Clause,
  219–221
"Peace of Mind," 45
People's Daily newspaper,
  185–186, 199–200
People's Republic, 185
Perrier's, 159–160
personalized communications,
  255
personalized letters, 251
PESO model of communication,
  115
Pew Research Center, 74, 100,
  108
pharmaceutical industry, 77–78,
  129–130
Pharmaceutical Research
  Manufacturers of America,
  77–78
philanthropic efforts, 249–250
Pickens, Boone, 10
Pinterest, 118–119
Pocket, 118–119
political action committees
  (PACs), 81–82
political science, 82
politics, 17–19, 80–82
polling, 46–48, 73–74
populism, 79
portfolio managers, 57–58
position, 239
Positioning (Ries and Trout), 98
positive messages, 55
posters, for internal
  communications, 148
Powell, Colin, 256
power, covert, 238
pregaming, 193
presentations

contrarian advice in your, 28–29
defining, 24–26
entertaining during, 31–32
fresh thinking in, 29
humility and authenticity in, 29–30
in-person, 67
knowing your audience for, 27–28
mirroring in, 31
simplicity of, 30–31
press conferences, 101
press releases, 101
in Canada, 227
for fundraising, 252
social media, 131
printed materials, 251
print magazines, 228
Pritzker, Jay, 50, 56
private families, 173–184
about, 173–174
communication challenges with, 178–179
disputes in, 180–181
and family office roles, 176–178
market of, 175–176
visibility of, 174–175, 179–180
working with, 181–183
PR News Service, 101
PR Newswire, 151
"a problem solver," 45
professional networks, 253–254
Progressive, 123
project skills, for social media, 126
prominence, 241
protests, 79
proximity, 241
proxy statement, 86
PRSA, 239–240
psychographics, 238
public affairs, 70. *see also* government relations
Public Affairs Council, 70
public opinion, measuring, 73–74
public relations, need for, 1–3
Public Relations Society of Japan, 210
public sector professionals, in Chinese culture, 191
publishing networks, 120
punctuality, in Chinese culture, 192
purpose, defined, 258
PwC, 106

Q
QAnon, 165
quarterly reports, 87
Quartz, 108
Québec, 226–229

Quinnipiac University, 234
Quora, 118

R
RACE (Research, Analysis, Communication, Evaluation), 235–243
Analysis (step 2), 236–239
Communication (step 3), 239–241
Evaluation (step 4), 242–243
Research (step 1), 235–236
Reader's Digest, 141, 143–144, 155, 223
Reagan, Ronald, 75
Reddit, 118
Reg FD (Regulation Fair Disclosure), 101
registration statement (S-1), 91
Regulation Fair Disclosure (Reg FD), 101
related tactics (in SO SMArTT), 60–65
relevancy, of messaging, 55–56
Remembrance Day, 229
renewable energy (case example), 57–58
reporters, 61–62
Republican Party, 36–37, 40, 73
reputation, 239
Reputation Rules (Diermeier), 108
research
analysts of, 57–58
for government relations, 71–73
in RACE (step 1), 235–236, 244–245
respect, 190
return on investment (ROI), 242
"revolving door," 76
Rich, Marc, 187
Ries, Al, 98
"The Rise of Social Media" (Ortiz-Ospina), 259–260
road shows, 91
Rockefeller, John D., 174–177
Rockefeller, Nelson, 175
Rock & Roll Hall of Fame, 116
ROI (return on investment), 242
Rollins, Ed, 81–82
Roundup, 168
Royko, Mike, 99
Rule 10b-5, 89–90
Russ, Susan Fraysse, 150
Ryder, Thomas O., 143–144

S
S-1 (registration statement), 91
safety, 21
Salesforce, 94
Sandberg, Sheryl, 31
Santelli, Rick, 78
Saskatchewan, 225
Sasse, Ben, 38–39
Schwab, Klaus, 12

science, 168
Scott & Whale, 128
SEC. *see* US Securities and Exchange Commission
secretaries, in Chinese culture, 192
security risks, 17–19
Senate, 72, 81
September 11, 2001 attacks, 11–12
The 7 Habits of Highly Effective People (Covey), 233
sexual misconduct, 167
Sha, Bey-Ling, 238
shared values, and government relations, 80
Sherin, Keith, 154
Sign Post Forest, 224
simplicity, of presentations, 30–31
single-family offices, 177
situation (in SO SMArTT), 51–52
Snapchat, 133
social capital, 174
social courtesies, in Chinese culture, 198–199
social listening, 136
social media, 113–138
about, 115–116
and brand journalism/content marketing, 132–133
competencies for management of, 125–127
and corporate investor relations, 92–93
and crisis communication, 164
dehumanization through, 37
in Europe, 259–260
executives on, 134–135
fake news and disinformation on, 165–166
and fragmentation of media, 100
and government relations, 80
growth of, 6
guidelines for use of, 123–125
importance of, 113–114
influencers and ambassadors on, 131–132
lack of control on, 121–122
and media relations, 130–131
monitoring and measuring, 135–136
as paid media, 134
PR activities and, 127–130
Stories on, 133
thought leadership on, 135
types of, 116–121
social media newsroom, 131
social media press release, 131
social networks, 116, 253
social responsibility, 94

social-specific competencies, 126
social values, 106. *see also* ESG
    investing
SOEs (state-owned enterprises),
    186–187
SO SMArTT principles, 51–66
    Audiences, 56–60
    Messages, 53–56
    Objectives, 52–53
    related Tactics, 60–65
    Situation, 51–52
    Strategies, 53
    Timeline, 65–66
SPAC (Special Purpose
    Acquisition Company), 92
speakers' programs, 65
speaking opportunities, 63–64
"speechwriter's rule," 27
"spin," 105, 107, 163
spokespersonship, 61, 103, 163
sponsored content, 134
Sports Illustrated, 29
STAT, 108
state-owned enterprises (SOEs),
    186–187
Stories, 133
storytelling, 31
strategic advisors, 237
strategic intelligence, 16–17
strategies
    for government relations, 75
    for internal communications,
        142–145
    in SO SMArTT, 53
Sullenberger, Chesley "Sully," 128
Summer Games in Tokyo (1964),
    205
Super PACs, 81
Supreme Court, 72
SurveyMonkey, 236
Sutton, Jennifer, 149, 154–155
Suzuki, David, 223
Sweden, 259
Swinimer, Hope, 230
Switzerland, 259

T
tactics
    for communication, 239–240
    for government relations,
        76–80
    strategies vs., 53
Taylor, Breonna, 79
teams
    for crisis communications,
        158–159
    for internal communication,
        146–147
Tea Party, 78–79
TechCrunch, 108
technology, 259

telephone calls, 252
Tencent, 186, 200
10-K Form, 86
Terex Corporation, 141–144,
    153–154
Thanksgiving, 229
thirdAGE, 121
third-party endorsements, 62–63
TikTok, 80, 117
timeline (in SO SMArTT),
    65–66
timeliness, 241
Tk'emlups te Secwepemc First
    Nation, 225
toasting, in Chinese culture,
    195–197
Today show, 119
"together, we can," 45
Tomaselli, Giulia, 265
Tometi, Opal, 79
tone, of social media, 123–124
Toutiao, 200
trade shows, 101
traditional media, 97
transparency, 7
Treaty of Mutual Cooperation
    and Security, 205
TripAdvisor, 119
Trout, Jack, 98
Trudeau, Pierre, 220
Trump, Donald, 46–47, 78, 100,
    121–122, 165
trust
    in Canada and Canadian
        culture, 221–223
    and COVID-19, 40–41
    decline in, 166
    in media, 6
    with media, 105–106
Trusted Media Brands, 141
truth, in messaging, 56
Tumblr, 120
Twitter, 116, 129, 130, 165–166,
    253
two-way messaging, 124
Tyagarajan, Tiger, 24
Tylenol, 168–169

U
Uber, 74
United Airlines, 28–29
United Kingdom, 259
United Nations' Sustainable
    Development Goals, 261
University of Chicago, 74
University of North Carolina, 108
USA Today, 61
Usenet, 115
US Securities and Exchange
    Commission (SEC), 86,
    91, 101

V
values
    defined, 140
    in internal communications,
        140–142
    of private families, 181
Vatican, 94
Versailles, 204
virtual team meetings, 148
vision, 140–142
visual communication, 125
Vox, 108

W
Wall Street Journal, 61, 90, 97
Wang Qishan, 187
Warby Parker, 117
War Measure Act, 220
Warters, Tom, 151, 152, 155–156
Washington Post, 47
wealthy families. *see* private
    families
web presence, 64
websites
    for crisis communication, 160
    fundraising on, 252–253
    as information source for
        journalists, 102–103
WeChat, 188–189, 191
Wendy's, 123–124
Whitmer, Gretchen, 8
"Who Cares Wins" Study, 93
Why Should the Boss Listen to You?
    (Lukaszewski), 237
Wickenden, David, 145
Williams, John, 151–152
Williams, Serena, 30
Winfrey, Oprah, 29
winter sports, 217
WordPress, 120
World Economic Forum, 106
World War I, 216

X
Xi Jinping, 187
Xinhua News Agency, 185–186,
    199–200

Y
Yelp, 119–120
YouTube, 116–117, 166
Yukon University, 225

Z
Zhang Yiming, 200
Zimmerman, George, 79
Zuckerberg, Mark, 37

ABOUT THE AUTHORS

William Kemmis Adler is a communications strategist and counselor who serves as Director of Corporate Communications at Terex Corporation. He previously held senior communications posts at GE Capital, The New York Times Company, Reader's Digest Association, and PR Newswire. He began his career as a journalist with United Press International. He and his team have been recognized with IABC Gold and Silver Quill Awards, Telly Awards, and a PRSA Big Apple Award.

Stephen M. Coan, PhD, is President of Sea Research Foundation and served as President of the Jason Foundation for Education. He serves on the boards of several family foundations, including the Feinstein Family Foundation and the Cal Ripken Sr. Foundation. He has been a national philanthropic advisor to wealthy families and fundraising professional for over thirty years.

Jonathan Dedmon is a Principal of The Dilenschneider Group with more than forty-five years' experience in the media and agency public relations and marketing communications, including twenty-eight years with The Dilenschneider Group in Chicago. During his public relations and marketing communications career, Mr. Dedmon has worked across a variety of industries, including real estate, architecture and construction, legal affairs, financial services, education, energy, manufacturing, transportation, environmental services, healthcare, food and agriculture, and consumer products. He also has worked with e-commerce clients and with a number of trade associations and in education and the arts.

Valerio De Molli has been Managing Partner and Chief Executive Officer of The European House—Ambrosetti since 2000. In 2008, he led the management buyout of The European House—Ambrosetti along with other partners, thereby settling with the founder. He is also Director of London's Ambrosetti Group Limited, Chairman of The European House—Ambrosetti Middle East, Senior Advisor of the venture capital fund United Ventures, and Mentor of the Kairos Society, an association of young American entrepreneurs. He is a member of the boards of directors of numerous companies. He is the author of *Towards Excellence, Boards of Directors: A Tool for an Effective System of Corporate Governance, Proposals and Recommendations* (Sperling & Kupfer, May 2005), and *The Fundamentals of Strategic Management—Paradigms of the Corporate System* (IPSOA, January 2009). He founded and continues to chair important think tanks, including Observatory on Europe in Brussels, Observatory on the Excellence of Corporate Governance in Italy, Meridiano Sanità, and Cashless Society, among others. Since 1992, he has been responsible for The European House—Ambrosetti's Forum "Intelligence on the World, Europe, and Italy," which is held every September at Villa d'Este in Cernobbio, Italy.

Jack Devine is a Founding Partner and President of The Arkin Group LLC, which specializes in international crisis management, strategic intelligence, investigative research, and business problem solving. He is a thirty-two-year veteran of the Central Intelligence Agency. Mr. Devine served as both Acting Director and Associate Director of the CIA's operations outside the United States from 1993–1995, where he had supervisory authority over thousands of CIA employees involved in sensitive missions worldwide. In addition, he served as Chief of the Latin American Division from 1992–1993 and was the principal manager of the CIA's sensitive projects in Latin America.

Robert L. Dilenschneider formed The Dilenschneider Group in October 1991. Headquartered in New York and Chicago, the firm provides strategic advice and counsel to Fortune 500 companies and leading families and individuals around the world, with experience in fields ranging from mergers and acquisitions and crisis communications to marketing, government affairs, and international media. Prior to forming his own firm, Mr. Dilenschneider served as president and chief executive officer of Hill & Knowlton, Inc., from 1986 to 1991, tripling that firm's revenues to nearly $200 million and delivering more than $30 million in profit. Mr. Dilenschneider was with that organization for nearly twenty-five years. Mr. Dilenschneider started in public relations in 1967 in New York, shortly after receiving a BA from the University of Notre Dame and an MA in journalism from Ohio State University. Mr. Dilenschneider has been called the "Dean of American Public Relations Executives" and is widely published. He has lectured before scores of professional organizations and colleges, including the University of Notre Dame, Ohio State University, New York University, and the Harvard Business School.

Art Gormley, a Principal with The Dilenschneider Group, joined the firm in 1992, shortly after it was founded. He oversees the firm's financial relations practice and has worked with the Wall Street and international investment communities for more than twenty-five years. Mr. Gormley has counseled the chief executives, chief financial officers, and boards of directors of countless clients, including some of the world's largest publicly held corporations. In addition, Mr. Gormley is a highly experienced crisis communicator who has guided clients in their dealings with financial restatements, shareholder litigation, activist investors, and management changes, as well as investigations involving the Securities and Exchange Commission, Internal Revenue Service, and the US Department of Justice, among other government agencies.

Donna Caprari Heiser, APR, CFRE is Chief Advancement and External Affairs Officer and former Chief Communications Officer at Ave Maria School of Law. She has more than 40 years of experience as a philanthropic, communications and marketing strategist across a broad range of industries and non-profits. Prior to joining Ave Maria School of Law, she founded and managed her own advertising and public relations firm , providing strategic counseling and advice to Fortune 500 clients in business, technology, health care, education, banking, legal, and the nonprofit sector. As a communications, event management and philanthropic strategist and counselor, she has raised over $100 million in support of education and charitable causes and created highly successful events featuring some of the most respected thought leaders in America today. A graduate of Rosemont College, she is a Certified Fund Raising Executive (CFRE) by CFRE International, recognized by the Public Relations Society of America (PRSA) as an Accredited Public Relations Counselor (APR) and has received dozens of Addy Awards for successful communications campaigns and initiatives throughout her career. She greatly enjoys building relationships and helping clients to execute their strategic vision.

Shel Holtz, SCMP, is Director of Internal Communications at Webcor, a San Francisco–based commercial contractor. He is responsible for employee and executive communications, as well as social media. He also supports Webcor's corporate public relations efforts. Before joining Webcor in October 2017, Mr. Holtz spent twenty-one years as Principal of Holtz Communication + Technology, where he brought more than forty years of organizational communications experience in both corporate and consulting environments to his long list of clients. He is experienced in employee communications, corporate public relations, crisis communications, media relations, financial communications, investor relations, marketing communications, and compensation and benefits communications. In addition to integrating technology into communications strategies, his expertise includes strategic communications planning, change management, organizational culture, business initiative, and communications research.

Michael N. Kamsky is currently an MBA student at the Tsinghua School of Economics & Management in Beijing. Michael spent a large part of his childhood growing up in Beijing. He graduated high school from The Dalton School in New York City, and graduated from Princeton University with a BA in East Asian Studies. He spent his junior year of college at Tsinghua University, where all his courses were taught in Chinese at the Tsinghua School of Economics & Management and at the Tsinghua Law School. While at Princeton, Michael interned for Skybridge Capital, followed by a two-year period as an analyst for Acacia Partners, a hedge fund founded by Warren Buffett. Michael is fluent in Chinese.

Virginia A. Kamsky is the Founder, Chairman, and Chief Executive Officer of Kamsky Associates, Inc. (KAI), a strategic advisory firm with offices in Beijing and New York City. Following Ms. Kamsky's arrival in China in 1978, KAI was one of the first approved foreign advisory firms in China. KAI has been responsible for advising on deals in excess of USD $15 billion for its client base, which includes preeminent companies worldwide.

Robert W. Laird joined The Dilenschneider Group in March 2005 after a career of more than thirty years as an award-winning newspaperman and more than ten years as a senior press officer in New York City and state governments. He came to Dilenschneider directly from the *New York Daily News*, where he served, over the course of more than twenty-five years, as an editorial writer, deputy editorial page editor, Op-Ed Page columnist, and, for the final ten years, Op-Ed Page editor. Mr. Laird won several awards for his editorials, most notably for a series on New York's affordable housing crisis. Several of the columnists he oversaw as Op-Ed Page editor also won major awards, including one Pulitzer Prize for Commentary.

George Lence, Cofounder and President of Nicholas & Lence Communications, a full-service public relations and government/community affairs firm, has over thirty-five years of legal and government affairs experience. Chosen as one of New York's Responsible 100 outstanding corporate citizens by *City & State New York*, Mr. Lence directs full-service lobbying efforts on behalf of clients such as Hornblower Cruises & Events, Clean Energy Fuels, Gray Line CitySightseeing, The Times Square Advertising Coalition, BUS4NYC, The Broadway Association, and the New York Coalition of Code Consultants. Before forming Nicholas & Lence in 2007, Mr. Lence served for six years as Chief Operating Officer & General Counsel at NYC & Company, New York City's official tourism marketing and promotion organization.

Frank Luntz has written, supervised, and conducted more than 2,500 surveys, focus groups, ad tests, and dial sessions in more than two dozen countries and six continents over the past twenty years. His political knowledge and skills are recognized globally, and he has served as an election consultant and commentator in Canada, Britain, Ireland, Germany, Austria, the Netherlands, Australia, Venezuela, and Ukraine.

Amanda Mattingly is a managing director at The Arkin Group LLC, an international risk consulting firm specializing in strategic business intelligence and political economic risk analysis. Previously, Ms. Mattingly worked in the Bureau of Western Hemisphere Affairs at the US Department of State and the Office of Inter-American Affairs at the US National Security Council. Ms. Mattingly is a security fellow with the Truman National Security Project and a former Watson Fellow.

Cristyne Nicholas founded Nicholas & Lence Communications, an award-winning, multi-platform firm that specializes in strategic public and government relations efforts to increase visibility and ROI for a diverse roster of clients, including CEOs, major corporations, media companies, destinations, healthcare, cultural attractions, and transportation companies. NLC has been recognized multiple times in the *Observer*'s "Most Powerful Public Relations Firms in America." In 2017, Ms. Nicholas was awarded the "Above & Beyond" award by *City & State New York*. Cristyne is a public relations veteran well known for her dedication and commitment as CEO and President of NYC & Company, rebuilding NYC's $27 billion tourism industry following the tragic events of September 11. Her achievements there include increasing membership from 890 businesses to 2,000, increasing annual budget revenues from $10 million to $35 million, and launching New York City's first consumer TV advertising campaign, resulting in a 40 percent increase in visitations.

Ned Raynolds is a veteran corporate communications executive and strategic advisor with more than thirty years' experience, versed in all phases of external and internal communications. His focus is on positioning companies that are facing serious challenges with the news media, employees, customers, and the investment community, often working in a team approach with senior management, legal counsel, and outside advisors. Mr. Raynolds previously managed corporate communications for American Airlines for the East Coast, including New York, Boston, and Washington, DC. At American, he enlisted specialty media to reach nearly half a million high-value consumers in Greater New York.

Sarah L. Manley Robertson, ABC. Sarah has a passion for communicating with purpose. She has a strong track record of not just establishing and leading teams, but also delivering results. When the stakes are high and the environment complex,

Sarah excels at bringing team members together to share diverse perspectives to generate insight-driven solutions and engage stakeholders. Sarah is a trusted adviser who can be counted on to communicate a company's vision whether in a press landscape dominated by critics, across social media in a crisis, or by engaging colleagues during organizational transformation. Sarah has navigated major U.S. and Canadian public health crises, class action & litigation, U.S. bankruptcy proceedings, mergers & acquisitions and she has overseen social responsibility mandates for large organizations. Sarah knows that words matter and she guides organizations and leaders to choose them carefully. She is committed to both learning and continuing to leverage her skills to work on the toughest challenges. She is proudly Canadian, now living in Prospect, Nova Scotia, with her husband, teenage son, and their rescued black & tan, Beau.

Edward Rollins is a veteran political analyst and campaign manager. His successes in the political arena began as far back as his victory run for student body president at California State University. His forty-year career as a political strategist serves as an inspiration to the students of CSU. Mr. Rollins has served four United States presidents. He was in charge of the White House Office of Political Affairs and the White House Office of Intergovernmental Affairs, as well as serving as the deputy chief of staff during the Reagan administration. In 1984, he managed President Reagan's landslide reelection campaign, winning forty-nine of fifty states. He has had managerial roles in nine other presidential campaigns and was inducted into the Political Consultants Hall of Fame in 2011.

Joshua W. Walker, PhD, President and CEO of Japan Society, is a perpetual bridge-builder, citizen diplomat, trained academic, and global enthusiast, with more than two decades of experience in international business and diplomacy. Dr. Walker's private-sector experience includes serving as Global Head of Strategic Initiatives and Japan in the office of the President of Eurasia Group; CEO and president of the USA Pavilion at the 2017 World Expo in Astana, Kazakhstan; founding dean of the APCO Institute; and senior vice president of global programs at APCO Worldwide, a leading global strategic communications firm. He has worked in numerous roles at US government agencies, including the State Department and the Defense Department. He is a Senior Fellow at the Center for the Study of the Presidency and Congress, and teaches at Columbia University's School of International and Public Affairs. A Fulbright Scholar, Presidential Leadership Scholar, and Rockefeller Fellow of the Trilateral Commission, Dr. Walker earned a bachelor's degree from the University of Richmond, a master's degree from Yale University, and a doctorate from Princeton University.